ANALYTICAL
READING &
REASONING

DR. ARTHUR
WHIMBEY

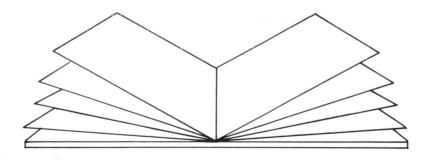

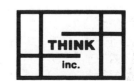

INNOVATIVE SCIENCES, INC.

To Colonel C. Mike Gilrod for his warm friendship and his support of educational research over many years.

Edited by: John J. Glade

First Edition

ISBN 0-913804-99-1

Library of Congress Catalog Card Number: 82-82630

COPYRIGHT NOTICES AND ACKNOWLEDGMENTS

The author is deeply indebted to John Glade of Innovative Sciences, Inc. for his fine editorial assistance in shaping a set of laboratory exercises to improve analytical reading and reasoning skills into a formal, comprehensive instructional text.

Research for this book was partially supported by grant #G008005201 from the Fund for the Improvement of Post-Secondary Education.

Grateful acknowledgment is made for permission to reprint the following copyright material:

The phonetic system of word pronunciation used in this book is provided by *The American Heritage School Dictionary*, copyright ©1972, 1977 by Houghton Mifflin Company. Used with the permission of Houghton Mifflin Company, Boston, Massachusetts.

From Russel L. Adams, *Great Negroes, Past & Present*, copyright ©1964 by Afro-Am Publishing Co., Inc. Reprinted with permission of Afro-Am Publishing Co., Inc., Chicago, Illinois.

From "Airport 1980: Atlanta's Hartsfield," *TIME*, September 29, 1980. Reprinted with permission.

From Solomon F. Bloom, *Europe and America*, copyright 1961. Published by Harcourt Brace Jovanovich, Inc. Reprinted by permission of Harcourt Brace Jovanovich, Inc., New York, New York.

From Brinton/Christopher/Wolff, *A History of Civilization: Vol. Two: 1715 to the Present*, 2nd edition, ©1960, pp. 13-14, 145, 189. Reprinted by permission of Prentice-Hall, Inc., Englewood Cliffs, New Jersey.

From "Can a Union Strangle Nation's Largest City," *U.S. News & World Report*, April 14, 1980, copyright ©1980. Reprinted by permission.

From "Disease," *Encyclopedia Americana*, 1977 edition, Volume D. Reprinted with permission of the *Encyclopedia Americana*, copyright 1981, Grolier Inc.

From "Dog," *Encyclopedia Americana*, 1977 edition, Volume D. Reprinted with permission of the *Encyclopedia Americana*, copyright 1981, Grolier Inc.

From "Electricity," *Encyclopaedia Britannica*, 14th edition, (1971), 8:142. Reprinted with permission of Encyclopaedia Britannica, Chicago, Illinois.

From *Elements of Biology*, third edition, by Paul Weisz. Copyright ©1969 by McGraw-Hill Book Company. Used with the permission of McGraw-Hill Book Company.

From "Energy-Wise Buying," *The FAMILY HANDYMAN Magazine*, February 1980, copyright ©1980, The Webb Co., 1999 Shepard Road, St. Paul, Minnesota 55116. Reprinted with permission.

From "Eocene and Paleocene," *Encyclopaedia Britannica*, 14th edition, (1971), 8:622. Reprinted with permission of Encyclopaedia Britannica, Chicago, Illinois.

From John Edwin Fogg, *Latin America: A General History*, copyright ©1969 by Macmillan Publishing Co., Inc. Reprinted with permission of Macmillan Publishing Co., Inc., New York, New York.

From *Grzimek's Animal Life Encyclopedia*, Volume 10, by Bernhard Grzimek. Copyright ©1972 by Van Nostrand Reinhold Company. Reprinted by permission of the publisher.

From Jon Halter, "1980 Christmas Stamps," *Boy's Life*, December 1980. Reprinted by permission of Boy Scouts of America, Magazine Division, Dallas, Texas.

From "International Law," *Encyclopedia International*, 1981 Edition, Volume 9. Reprinted with permission of *Encyclopedia International*, copyright 1981, Lexicon Publications, Inc.

From Jean Joslin, "Canine Heartworm Disease," *Boy's Life*, December 1980. Reprinted with permission of Jean Joslin.

From Gerrit P. Judd, *A History of Civilization*, copyright ©1966 by Gerrit P. Judd. Reprinted with permission of Macmillan Publishing Co., Inc., New York, New York.

From "Juliana Quits Her Throne," *Newsweek*, February 1980. Copyright ©1980 by Newsweek, Inc. All rights reserved. Reprinted by permission.

From "Latest in Health," *U.S. News & World Report*, April 14, 1980, copyright ©1980. Reprinted by permission.

From Nick Lyons, "Shedding Fifty," *Family Health*, May 1980, copyright ©1980 by Family Health. Reprinted with permission.

From "Made in The Shade," *The FAMILY HANDYMAN Magazine*, May/June 1980, published by The Webb Co., 1999 Shepard Road, St. Paul, Minnesota 55116. Originally published by Chevron Chemical Co., San Francisco, California. All efforts to contact the copyright holder of this material have proved unsuccessful. An appropriate fee for this use will be reserved by the publisher.

From *Men of Space*, Volume 1, by Shirley Thomas. Copyright ©1960 by Shirley Thomas. Reprinted with permission of the publisher Chilton Book Company, Radnor, Pennsylvania.

From *The Negro Almanac: A Reference Work On The Afro-American*, compiled and edited by Harry A. Ploski and Warren Marr II, New York: The Bellwether Co. Copyright ©1976. All efforts to contact the copyright holder of this material have proved unsuccessful. An appropriate fee for this use will be reserved by the publisher.

From Nettles, Curtis P., *The Roots of American Civilization*, copyright ©1981 by Irvington Publishers, Inc. Reprinted with permission.

From "Nevada," *The New Book of Knowledge*, 1971 edition, Volume N. Reprinted with permission of *The New Book of Knowledge*, copyright 1981, Grolier Inc.

From Deanna Sclar, "The Fabulous Fordmobile and the Model A," *Boy's Life*, November 1980. Reprinted with permission of Deanna Sclar.

From Vincent M. Scramuzza and Paul L. MacKendrick, *The Ancient World*, copyright ©1958 by Holt, Rinehart and Winston. Reprinted with permission of the publisher Holt, Rinehart and Winston, New York, New York.

From Daniel Seligman, "A Bad Day in Sioux Falls," *Fortune*, January 12, 1981. Reprinted by permission.

From Dr. Seuss, "But for Grown-Ups Laughing . . .," *The New York Times*, November 16, 1952. Copyright ©1952 by The New York Times Company. Reprinted by permission.

From *Systems of Society*, third edition, by Manuel Medoza and Vince Napoli, Lexington, Massachusetts: D.C. Heath and Company, 1982. Reprinted by permission of the publisher.

From "That's All I Hope" by J. P. McEvoy, *Reader's Digest*, January 1947. Reprinted by permission.

From James Thurber, "My Own 10 Rules for a Happy Marriage." From *Thurber Country*, published by Simon and Schuster. Copyright ©1953 James Thurber. Copyright ©1971 Helen W. Thurber and Rosemary T. Sauers. Reprinted by permission.

From "The Truth About Saving Water," *The FAMILY HANDYMAN Magazine*, May/June 1980, copyright ©1980, The Webb Co., 1999 Shepard Road, St. Paul, Minnesota 55116. Reprinted with permission.

From Walter Wallbank, Alastair Taylor, Nels Bailkey and George Jewsbury, *Civilization Past & Present*, fifth edition, copyright ©1978 by Scott, Foresman and Company. Reprinted with permission.

From "Where Was the Cradle of Civilization" by Ronald Schiller, *Reader's Digest*, August 1980. Reprinted by permission.

From Rob Wilder, "Family Health," *Parents'*, April 1980. Reprinted by permission.

From *The World's History* by Frederic Lane, Eric Goldman, and Earling Hunt, copyright ©1947, 1950, 1954, 1959 by Harcourt Brace Jovanovich, Inc., and reprinted with their permission.

ABOUT THE AUTHOR

If I have succeeded in my inquiries more than others,
I owe it less to any superior strength of mind, than
to a habit of patient thinking.

—Sir Isaac Newton

If any one phrase best sums up Dr. Arthur Whimbey's philosophy of instruction, it may be: "The key to academic and professional success lies in mastering the habit of patient thinking." For over 15 years, Dr. Whimbey has researched and developed teaching materials and study programs for training individuals in the skill of patient, systematic, accurate thinking.

In 1975, Dr. Whimbey (with Linda Shaw Whimbey) published *Intelligence Can Be Taught*, which introduced his philosophy for improving thinking and reasoning ability, popularly referred to as "cognitive therapy." He has also published articles in numerous magazines and journals, including *Educational Leadership, Educational Psychology, Phi Delta Kappan, Saturday Review/ World, Psychology Today,* and *Journal of Reading.* His research on improving intellectual performance has been successfully applied in high schools and colleges across the country, and has twice been reviewed in *The New York Times.*

Dr. Whimbey received his Ph.D. from Purdue University. Among the positions he has held are: NIMH Senior Postdoctoral Fellow, Institute of Human Learning, University of California at Berkeley; Coordinator of Communication Labs, Developmental Education Program, Bowling Green State University; Resident Scholar in the Center for Academic Skills, City College of New York; Visiting Professor, Reading Department, Xavier University; Resident Scholar, Department of Reading, Clark College. He has also served on the Editorial Boards of the *Problem Solving Newsletter* and the *Human Intelligence International Newsletter.*

PREFACE

Educators willing to gaze ahead into the twenty-first century can conjure up many different scenarios and a few useful suggestions. Across all levels of education (elementary, secondary, college, adult continuing and professional), perhaps the most frequent analysis made is that traditional methods of education—heavy reliance on the teaching of subject matter knowledge—are inadequate for preparing individuals for the "future shock" world in which they will live. Schools and businesses cannot possibly keep up with the ever-expanding pool of knowledge individuals will need to master; there is simply not enough time in the educational day. As a result, more and more of the responsibility for academic, professional and life learning will fall upon the individual him/herself.

This poses a crucial challenge to the educational system, and to individuals. All individuals must be trained in the reading, thinking and reasoning skills that will enable them to effectively process, analyze and learn information on their own as supplement to, or in the absence of, direct instruction. Individuals must become competent in comprehending information they encounter, incorporating that information into their existing knowledge, and using that information to make decisions and solve problems. Dr. Whimbey has created in ANALYTICAL READING & REASONING an excellent tool for helping educators and learners meet this challenge.

ANALYTICAL READING & REASONING presents a formal approach to developing in individuals the cognitive skills that are the keys to much of learning, especially learning from written material. Reading is, and will increasingly be, a primary mode of learning. In school, individuals learn from essays, encyclopedias and, of course, textbooks. In work, individuals learn from manuals, reports, memos, journals and computer printouts. In homelife, newspapers, magazines, cookbooks, etc. provide much of the information needed to be mastered on a daily basis. From the adolescent years on, most of the information we must learn or otherwise deal with stems from or is supported by written material. Unfortunately, recent research reveals that many of today's learners are unable to fully comprehend or apply much of what they read. A case in point are the findings of the National Assessment of Educational Progress (NAEP), a federally-sponsored effort to assess educational programs. The NAEP reports test and now retest data showing that although in general our nation's students competently comprehend the literal information in written material, a large percentage of students exhibit weaknesses in higher-level comprehension and thinking skills. Students are found to be weak in applying thinking and reasoning skills to analyzing arguments and relationships, using inferential comprehension abilities to go "beyond the information given," and in solving problems based upon written information and data (National Assessment of Mathematics, 1979; National Assessment of Reading and Literature, 1981). The exercises in this book provide an excellent methodology for improving these crucial thinking, inferential comprehension and problem solving abilities.

In this book, Dr. Whimbey has effectively accumulated much of what we know about how to teach individuals to learn from what they read—to comprehend and use powerful vocabulary, to understand what they read, to better sense the author's full meaning, to see inferences and implications, and to draw conclusions from a series of points only some of which contribute to a key idea. On a broader scale, this book builds individuals' abilities to process information in a logical way and to make judgments and decisions based upon data.

The careful sequence of exercises presented in the units is the culmination of 15 years of research by Dr. Whimbey on methods for improving cognitive and academic skills. The rationale underlying the success of these exercises was first summarized by Dr. Whimbey in the now-classic article entitled "Teaching Sequential Thought: The Cognitive Skills Approach," which appeared in the December, 1977 issue of *Phi Delta Kappan*. More recently, Fred Hechinger, Education Editor of *The New York Times*, wrote that John Monro, formerly dean at Harvard, "says the Whimbey method greatly improved his . . . students' ability to perform mental tasks that are ordinarily associated with the idea of intelligence." And Professor Bill Sadler, director of the freshman core program at Bloomfield College, explained to Hechinger that the Whimbey approach was successfully used in subject areas ranging from english and history through chemistry, with the emphasis being on the systematic analysis and logical examination of written passages and problems. A further indicator of the success of Dr. Whimbey's methodology was cited in the October, 1980 issue of the *Journal of Reading*. Here it was reported that the Whimbey method used for just five weeks in Project SOAR brought about gains of approximately two years on the Nelson-Denny Reading Test and 100 points on the Scholastic Aptitude Test (SAT). The instructional design of this book is clearly well proven; its applications span regular coursework, college preparation, study skills improvement, cognitive skills development, and PSAT, SAT and GRE (Graduate Record Examination) preparation.

If we are to better equip individuals for a complex life in a future-shock world, they must be trained to think analytically and logically and to apply these cognitive skills to the information they must master, the judgments and decisions they must make, and the problems they must solve. These skills are surely important enough to compel direct instruction; schools and businesses must make it known that they are serious about doing it since they are better equipped to provide this instruction than any other social institution.

ANALYTICAL READING & REASONING is an excellent device for fostering the conscious development of individuals' cognitive learning skills. The need for such materials is great. The need for individuals to use such materials is even greater. The twenty-first century beckons not from afar, but from just around the corner.

Dr. Gordon Cawelti
Executive Director
Association for Supervision
 and Curriculum Development
Alexandria, VA
October, 1982

INTRODUCTION

Every year in our society there are fewer unskilled jobs, but an increasing number of positions requiring strong analytical reading and reasoning ability. Computer programmer, architect, airline pilot, doctor, salesperson, accountant, and other well-paying occupations involve comprehending and digesting technical and complicated information.

Most good jobs demand at least two years of college or technical school, for which the ability to read and think analytically is a prerequisite. Moreover, on entering college, graduate school, law school or medical school, a standardized test covering reading and reasoning skills must be taken. In fact, a respectable score on a standardized test of vocabulary, reading and math skills is required to join most police forces or enlist in the armed forces. In the modern world, a person who cannot read and think analytically well is like a race horse with a broken leg or a lion that has lost its teeth.

This book will strengthen your ability to read and think analytically—to understand precisely what you read and mentally organize the information so you see the relationships between ideas and can apply them effectively. The first unit shows you how to build your vocabulary in all your reading by getting the meaning of words from context. An extensive vocabulary is invaluable not only in reading, but also in speaking and writing. It can help you sell yourself to an employer or client, as well as allow you to communicate articulately. This skill is so important that each of the remaining units of this book opens and closes with two sets of vocabulary exercises.

Units 2, 5, 7 and 11 fortify your ability to get the main idea and important facts from sources like newsmagazines, encyclopedias, journals, reports and textbooks. Unit 3 will help you to visualize spatial and geometrical descriptions, so important in scientific and technical reading and reasoning. Units 4 and 9 strengthen your skill in understanding the order of events or quantities, which is the basis of comprehending time data, procedures and many types of comparisons. In Unit 6, your skill in analyzing cause-effect and premise-conclusion relationships will be expanded. Unit 8 provides training in organizing data through classifying information into general-specific hierarchies, and Unit 10 builds your abilities to comprehend complex language expressions such as proverbs and the use of the double negative.

With the successful completion of Unit 11, you will have become quite a sophisticated reader and thinker, capable of reading and comprehending the full scope of textual material.

STUDY HINTS

It is of primary importance as you work the exercises in this book that you <u>place your major emphasis on accuracy</u>. Do not try to read the selections or answer the exercises quickly. Instead, try to be 100% correct in your answers. Research has shown that learners who are academically and professionally most successful and score highest on standardized tests are able to complete all the exercises in this book with total accuracy.

For all the exercises in this book *except the WORD POWER exercises*, use a dictionary to look up any unfamiliar words you encounter. Therefore, keep a dictionary handy as you work through each unit. Expanding your vocabulary is a sure way to improve your communication skills, your academic aptitude and your standardized test scores.

The *Expanded Solution Key* provides detailed explanations of the answers to the exercises. If you are working as part of a group, follow your leader's instructions concerning the checking of answers. If you are working individually, check your answers after each exercise. This way you will have immediate feedback on your progress through each unit.

Pace your work so that you can devote full concentration to every exercise. Do not work so steadily that you become mentally fatigued. If possible, take periodic breaks.

Reading analytically for full comprehension is like playing chess—it requires strong concentration and is hard mental work. It is so hard that some good readers, such as college professors, report they need a 10 minute break every hour when reading analytically. But the effort you make in accurately working the exercises in this book will be well rewarded by giving you a better understanding of textbooks, research reports, journals, memos and other technical materials. Also, you will find yourself achieving higher school grades, greater on-the-job effectiveness, and improved scores on tests like the SAT, ACT, GRE, LSAT, Armed Services Entrance Exam, employment tests and other such gatekeepers of desired positions in life. Therefore, whether you work through this book individually or with a class, give the exercises the time and effort they require so that you may derive the maximum benefit from them. They will arm you with a life-long advantage in all your academic, intellectual and occupational pursuits.

Arthur Whimbey
Atlanta, Georgia

October, 1982

CONTENTS

UNIT

1

READING FOR CONTEXT CLUES AND VOCABULARY GROWTH

OBJECTIVES: When you have completed this unit you should

- be able to determine a word's meaning from four types of context clues;
- know the meanings of the following POWER WORDS.

POWER WORDS

acrid	vagabond	lucrative	anthology
pinnacle	metamorphosis	masticate	enigma
hyperbole	veracity	mandatory	laudable
anticlimactic	labyrinth	polysyllabic	avert
axiomatic	appellation	capitulate	mirage
bravado	superfluous	pristine	satire
allude	zenith	rapport	affluent
acquiesced	terrestrial	abridged	altruistic
aesthetic	terse	contiguous	anachronism
advent	precedent	aberrant	tantamount

INTRODUCTION

Perhaps the most basic skill in comprehending reading material is understanding what the individual words mean: knowing the definitions of words and the ways in which words are used. Much of the time this skill does not seem to be a "skill" at all. Through previous learning and experience you already know the meanings of most of the words you read. But sometimes you will come across words you are not familiar with —you don't know what they mean. Often, these "stumbling block" words can prevent you from comprehending the full meaning of an entire passage. This is when the "skill" of understanding the meaning of a word becomes an essential reading tool.

Certainly, when you encounter a word you do not understand you should always think of looking up that word in a dictionary. But many times, by careful analysis, you can figure out the word's meaning from the rest of the sentence in which it is used; from the *sentence context* in which it is used. This is the skill of understanding word meaning—being able to analyze the context in which a word is used so that the word's meaning becomes clear to you.

Being able to determine a word's meaning by analyzing the sentence context in which it is used not only speeds your reading, but also provides you with the exact meaning of a word as it is used by a writer in a particular sentence. How often have you gone to the dictionary to look up the meaning of a word, only to find that there may be over 10 definitions listed. For example, the word "mark" has over 30 definitions. By themselves, the assortment of definitions may not be all that helpful. But if you have analyzed the *context* of the sentence in which the word is used, you should be able to identify the definition that fits the particular sentence you are reading with little difficulty.

This unit will develop your skill in identifying a word's meaning from the sentence context in which it is used. Specifically, this unit will teach you to recognize, and then analyze for word meaning, four general "cases" wherein a word's meaning can be determined from context. These four cases are:

CASE I: Meaning Stated With Punctuation
CASE II: Meaning Stated Without Punctuation
CASE III: Meaning Given By Contrast
CASE IV: Meaning Inferred From Ideas in the Sentence.

Each of the four cases is covered in turn on the following pages of this unit. Starting with the next page, begin your study of how to figure out a word's meaning from the context of the sentence in which it is used.

CASE I: Meaning Stated With Punctuation

Read the following sentence and try to determine the meaning of "banter."

John's banter, his lively teasing and joking, made the time pass quickly.

The definition of "banter"—lively teasing and joking—is clearly included within the sentence itself. It is simply set off by commas from the rest of the sentence.

Through the punctuation, the writer has defined this key word within the sentence itself and thus made sure that the meaning of the sentence is clear. You are able, by analyzing the context of the sentence (identifying the phrase set off by commas), to easily determine the meaning of "banter." There is no need for you to interrupt your reading and refer to a dictionary.

A great deal of reading material makes use of this technique—setting off the meaning of a word with punctuation from the rest of the sentence—to help the reader's comprehension. The above example used commas to set off the definition of "banter." There are also other forms of punctuation which do the same thing. Study the following two sentences and try to figure out the meaning of the underlined word in each sentence.

Liza tries to visit all of her relatives' homes during <u>Hanukkah</u> (an 8-day Jewish holiday).

His will to live was <u>indomitable</u>—strong, forceful, undefeatable—and eventually his health began to improve.

In each sentence, the punctuation of the sentence sets off the meaning of a key word from the rest of the sentence. The definition of "Hanukkah" is set off by parenthesis; the meaning of "indomitable" is set off by dashes.

Try now the WORD POWER: CASE I exercise set. This set will build your skill in analyzing sentence contexts for word "meaning stated with punctuation."

INSTRUCTIONS FOR THE EXERCISES

On the next three pages you will find a set of exercises labelled WORD POWER: CASE I. These exercises will develop your skill in analyzing sentence contexts for word "meaning stated with punctuation." They will also add 10 Power Words to your everyday language vocabulary.

Read the directions for each section of the exercise set carefully. Work slowly. Aim for 100% accuracy.

Word Power: Case I

Directions: Study each of the Power Words below. Note how each word is pronounced. In each of the sentences, the meaning of the Power Word is set off from the rest of the sentence by punctuation such as commas, parentheses, or dashes. Read each of the sentences to figure out what the Power Word means. In the left-hand margin next to each Power Word, <u>write a word or phrase from the sentence which defines that Power Word.</u>

| Power Words | acrid | hyperbole | axiomatic | allude | aesthetic |
| | pinnacle | anticlimactic | bravado | acquiesced | advent |

1. **acrid** | ăk′ rĭd |
   - The medicine was acrid—sharp and unpleasant.

2. **pinnacle** | pĭn′ ə kəl |
   - When Napoleon was at the pinnacle, the peak, of his power, he governed most of western Europe.

3. **hyperbole** | hī **pûr′** bə lē |
   - Hyperbole (exaggeration) is used in literature to emphasize a point or create humor.

4. **anticlimactic** | ăn′ tē klī **măk′** tĭk |
   - After the excitement and thrill of seeing the Rocky Mountains, seeing the Catskill Mountains is anticlimactic—less exciting or spectacular.

5. **axiomatic** | ăk′ sē ə **măt′** ĭk |
   - It was axiomatic—self-evident—that studying the 200-page text for just two hours was inadequate preparation for the comprehensive test.

6. **bravado** | brə **vă′** dō |
   - The young woman's bravado, her boastful claim of fearlessness, was challenged when her friend asked her to go skydiving.

7. **allude** | ə **lōōd′** |
   - She will occasionally allude (refer indirectly) to her husband's waist size in the hope that he will take the hint and begin dieting.

8. **acquiesced** | ăk′ wē **ĕsd′** |
   - Roberto was not happy his parents withdrew him from college but he acquiesced, quietly accepting their decision.

9. **aesthetic** | ĕs **thĕt′** ĭk |
   - Aesthetic judgment—judgment about beauty—becomes keener with experience.

10. **advent** | ăd′ vĕnt′ |
    - The advent of spring—the arrival of that warm season—was cause for celebration after the particularly long, harsh winter.

ă pat / ā pay / â care / ä father / ĕ pet / ē be / ĭ pit / ī pie / î fierce / ŏ pot / ō go / ô paw, for / oi oil / ŏŏ book /
ōō boot / ou out / ŭ cut / ü fur / *th* the / th thin / hw which / zh vision / ə ago, item, pencil, atom, circus

Meaning Comprehension: Case I

Directions: Use what you have learned from the context sentences to identify the correct definition of each Power Word. In the blank next to each Power Word, write the letter of its correct definition.

Power Words	Definitions
_____ acrid	a. refer to indirectly, hint at
_____ pinnacle	b. less significant or striking than what came before
_____ hyperbole	c. pretended courage, claimed fearlessness
_____ anticlimactic	d. obvious, self-evident, taken for granted
_____ axiomatic	e. exaggeration, over-statement
_____ bravado	f. extremely sharp and unpleasant to the tongue or nose
_____ allude	g. highest point, summit
_____ acquiesced	h. arrival or coming of something new
_____ aesthetic	i. accepted or agreed to something without protest
_____ advent	j. relating to beauty

Context Application

Directions: Each of the following sentences has a blank where a word is missing. Use what you have learned about the Power Words to determine which Power Word best belongs in each of the blanks. Then write the appropriate Power Word in each blank. Use each Power Word only once.

1. Since Stu didn't do any homework, it was _____ that he would fail the exam.

2. After seeing the championship contest, the minor contests that followed were _____ .

3. Luther's _____ caused the others to dare him to try the dangerous stunt.

4. Please do not directly mention or even _____ to her husband's death.

5. To say "He ate like a horse" is an example of _____ .

6. After working very hard for many years to advance in the company, her death at the _____ of her career was tragic.

7. The homemade wine was a nasty, _____ drink.

8. Although Judy didn't want to go to the movie, she _____ because she didn't want to cause an argument.

9. The _____ of the Christmas season in early December puts many people in a jovial mood.

10. A successful artist needs both technical skill and _____ sensitivity.

Muscle Builder
Analogies

Directions: Each exercise below is an analogy, with one or two terms missing. Choose the Power Word which belongs in each blank of the analogy so that the analogy reads correctly. Write the appropriate Power Word in each blank. Note that some of the Power Words will not be used.

1. DOWN is to UP as BOTTOM is to _____

2. ADVENT is to ARRIVAL as EXAGGERATION is to _____

3. ALLUDE is to HINT as _____ is to SELF-EVIDENT

CASE II: Meaning Stated Without Punctuation

Read the following sentence and try to determine the meaning of "gregarious."

Jocey is such a gregarious person that she always enjoys the company of other people.

The definition of "gregarious"—tending to enjoy the company of other people—is stated within the sentence context. However, in this case it is not set off by punctuation.

Study the sentence below and attempt to figure out the meaning of the underlined word.

When Gus was <u>skydiving</u> yesterday he practiced techniques for controlling the parachute during the fall from the plane to the ground.

Again, the definition of "skydiving" is stated within the sentence context—a fall from a plane to the ground using a parachute.

Careful analysis of many sentences will reveal that the meaning of a key word is clearly stated in the other words of the sentence.

INSTRUCTIONS FOR THE EXERCISES

Try now the WORD POWER: CASE II exercise set. This set will build your skill in analyzing sentence contexts for word "meaning stated without punctuation."

Word Power: Case II

Directions: Study each of the Power Words below. Note how each word is pronounced. In each of the sentences, the meaning of the Power Word is stated within the sentence. Read each of the sentences to figure out what the Power Word means. In the left-hand margin next to each Power Word, <u>write the word or phrase which defines that Power Word.</u>

Power Words					
	vagabond	veracity	appellation	zenith	terse
	metamorphosis	labyrinth	superfluous	terrestrial	precedent

1. **vagabond** | **văg′** ə bŏnd′ |
   - A vagabond's wandering from place to place prevents him or her from developing long friendships.

2. **metamorphosis** | mĕt ə **môr′** fə sĭs |
   - The process of a caterpillar changing into a butterfly is called metamorphosis.

3. **veracity** | və **răs′** ĭ tē |
   - Gilda's veracity is so well known that she has acquired a reputation for honesty.

4. **labyrinth** | **lăb′** ə rĭnth′ |
   - The halls in the building formed a labyrinth which made going from one office to another similar to finding one's way through a maze.

5. **appellation** | ăp′ ə **lā′** shən |
   - Her family gave her the appellation "Einstein" because this name befitted her almost straight 'A' record in college.

6. **superfluous** | sŏŏ **pûr′** floo′ əs |
   - The pretzels Fred brought to the party were superfluous, since we already had more than enough food.

7. **zenith** | **zē′** nĭth |
   - When hula hoops were at the zenith of their popularity and selling more than ever before or after, children were seen playing with them everywhere.

8. **terrestrial** |tə **rĕs′** trē əl |
   - An arboreal animal like a monkey lives in a tree, whereas a terrestrial animal like an elephant lives on the ground.

9. **terse** | tûrs |
   - His remarks were terse and yet those few words clearly expressed his strong feelings on the issue.

10. **precedent** | **prĕs′** ĭ dnt |
    - A legal decision which judges refer to in later cases is called a precedent.

ă pat / ā pay / â care / ä father / ĕ pet / ē be / ĭ pit / ī pie / î fierce / ŏ pot / ō go / ô paw, for / oi oil / ŏŏ book /
ōō boot / ou out / ŭ cut / ü fur / th the / th thin / hw which / zh vision / ə ago, item, pencil, atom, circus

Meaning Comprehension: Case II

Directions: Use what you have learned from the context sentences to identify the correct definition of each Power Word. In the blank next to each Power Word, write the letter of its correct definition.

Power Words

_____ metamorphosis
_____ vagabond
_____ veracity
_____ labyrinth
_____ appellation
_____ superfluous
_____ zenith
_____ terrestrial
_____ terse
_____ precedent

Definitions

a. a striking change in form, appearance, or character

b. name

c. truthfulness, honesty

d. one who moves from place to place without a fixed home, irresponsible wanderer

e. a maze with intricate passageways and blind alleys

f. brief and to the point, concise, having few words

g. highest point, peak

h. more than required, excessive, unnecessary

i. living on land; on or relating to the earth

j. something that occurred earlier that may be used as an example to follow later

Context Application

Directions: Each of the following sentences has a blank where a word is missing. Use what you have learned about the Power Words to determine which Power Word best belongs in each blank. Then write the appropriate Power Word in each blank. Use each Power Word only once.

1. Because José changed jobs so often, his father called him an occupational _____.

2. Dr. Jekyll drank a chemical which caused the _____ of this gentleman into the ugly, evil Mr. Hyde.

3. "Sloth" was an appropriate _____ for him because he was lazy like the animal with that name.

4. Since the witness was a proven liar, the jury put little faith in the _____ of his testimony.

5. The swamp was a _____ of waterways and many hunters became permanently lost.

6. The _____ of success for the chemist was winning the Nobel prize.

7. In solving word problems you must use all the necessary information and discard the _____ information.

8. The teacher wouldn't excuse Tom's absence because he was afraid to set a _____ and have other students demand similar treatment.

9. The letter was not lengthy but _____ ; the writer got right down to business.

10. A chicken is a _____ bird since it lives on the ground rather than in trees.

Muscle Builder Analogies

Directions: Each exercise below is an analogy, with one term missing. Choose the Power Word which belongs in each blank of the analogy so that the analogy reads correctly. Write the appropriate Power Word in each blank. Note that some of the Power Words will not be used.

1. TERSE is to NECESSARY as LONG-WINDED is to

    _____

2. APPLE is to FRUIT as STEVEN is to _____

3. TRUTHFULNESS is to VERACITY as WANDERER is to

    _____

CASE III: Meaning Given By Contrast

Try to determine the meaning of "facetious" as you read the following sentence.

Brenda responded to the question with a facetious rather than a serious answer.

From the context of the sentence you can conclude that "facetious" means the opposite of "serious." Thus, "facetious" means humorous or lighthearted or meant to be funny.

In many sentences a word's meaning can be understood by analyzing with what that word is *contrasted* in the sentence. In the above example, "facetious" is contrasted with "serious." Since you know the meaning of the familiar word "serious," you can conclude by contrast what "facetious" must mean.

In this example, the phrase "rather than" presents the contrast—. . . a facetious *rather than* a serious answer. There are many other ways in which contrasts are presented within sentences. Study the sentence below and try to comprehend the meaning of "dictate."

It was clear from the tone of his voice that the statement was not a request but a dictate.

In this sentence, the words "not" and "but" work together to present the contrast—. . . *not* a request *but* a dictate. Since you know what a "request" is—something asked for—you can conclude from the contrast what a "dictate" must be—something ordered or commanded or demanded.

By analyzing the contrasts presented in sentences, you can often find clues to the meaning of key words.

INSTRUCTIONS FOR THE EXERCISES

Try now the WORD POWER: CASE III exercise set. This set will develop your skill in analyzing sentence contexts for word "meaning given by contrast."

Word Power: Case III

Directions: Study each of the Power Words below. Note how each word is pronounced. In each of the sentences, the meaning of the Power Word can be determined from how that word is contrasted with other words or ideas in the sentence. Read each of the sentences to figure out what the Power Word means. In the left-hand margin next to each Power Word, <u>write a word or short definition which defines that Power Word.</u>

Power Words	lucrative	mandatory	capitulate	rapport	contiguous
	masticate	polysyllabic	pristine	abridged	aberrant

1. **lucrative** | **lōo′** krə tĭv |
   - The business was not lucrative and the owners lost a great deal of money.

2. **masticate** | **măs′** tĭ kāt′ |
   - You should masticate properly rather than swallow your food in lumps.

3. **mandatory** | **măn′** də tôr′ ē |
   - Getting up at 6 A.M. is not voluntary but mandatory in the army.

4. **polysyllabic** | pŏl′ ē sĭ **lăb′** ĭk |
   - He used polysyllabic words whenever possible and preferred them to simple one- and two-syllable words.

5. **capitulate** | kə **pĭch′** ə lāt′ |
   - She refused to capitulate but continued to fight for what she knew was right.

6. **pristine** | **prĭs′** tēn′ |
   - The belching smokestacks of the factories in the mountain valley are a sharp contrast to the pristine beauty of the snow-covered peak.

7. **rapport** | ră **pôr′** |
   - The boss did not have a good rapport with her employees but was constantly bickering with them and threatening to fire them.

8. **abridged** | ə **brĭjd′** |
   - The paperback was not abridged but contained the whole story.

9. **contiguous** | kən **tĭg′** yōo′ əs |
   - Canada and the U.S. are contiguous, whereas Canada and Mexico are separated by the U.S.

10. **aberrant** | ăb **ĕr′** ənt |
    - The child's behavior is totally normal and in no way aberrant.

ă pat / ā pay / â care / ä father / ĕ pet / ē be / ĭ pit / ī pie / î fierce / ŏ pot / ō go / ô paw, for / oi oil / ŏŏ book /
ōō boot / ou out / ŭ cut / ü fur / th the / th thin / hw which / zh vision / ə ago, item, pencil, atom, circus

Meaning Comprehension: Case III

Directions: Use what you have learned from the context sentences to identify the correct definition of each Power Word. In the blank next to each Power Word, write the letter of its correct definition.

Power Words

_____ lucrative
_____ masticate
_____ mandatory
_____ polysyllabic
_____ capitulate
_____ pristine
_____ rapport
_____ abridged
_____ contiguous
_____ aberrant

Definitions

a. abnormal, atypical, not the usual, deviant
b. having more than three syllables
c. give in, yield, surrender
d. chew
e. required, demanded by command
f. relationship of mutual understanding and trust
g. original, primitive, pure, uncorrupted by man
h. shortened, condensed
i. touching along boundaries, next to each other
j. profitable, worthwhile, money making

Context Application

Directions: Each of the following sentences has a blank. Use what you have learned about the Power Words to determine which Power Word best belongs in each blank. Then write the appropriate Power Word in each blank. Use each Power Word only once.

1. Small dictionaries are generally _____ and do not contain all the words found in a large dictionary.

2. Florida and Georgia are _____ and have a lengthy common border.

3. Medicine and dentistry can be _____ professions which afford one a comfortable lifestyle.

4. The general said that before he would _____, he would let his entire army fight to the death.

5. "Capitulate" is _____ while its synonym "yield" is monosyllabic.

6. Rain was not normal for that time of year, and the _____ weather caught many people without umbrellas.

7. Since they do not have teeth and therefore cannot _____, newborn infants cannot be fed solid food.

8. Sad to say, the _____ forest will soon fall victim to the lumberjack's chainsaw.

9. The teacher's _____ with students was poor and he could not control the class.

10. A neat, well-groomed appearance is _____ in the armed services.

Muscle Builder Analogies

Directions: Each exercise below is an analogy, with one term missing. Choose the Power Word which belongs in each blank of the analogy so that the analogy reads correctly. Write the appropriate Power Word in each blank. Note that some of the Power Words will not be used.

1. SEE is to EYE as _____ is to MOUTH

2. WHOLE is to PART as COMPLETE is to _____

3. NORMAL is to ABERRANT as VOLUNTARY is to _____

CASE IV: Meaning Inferred From Ideas in the Sentence

Try to determine the meaning of "luminous" from its use in the following sentence.

Bob had a clock with a luminous dial, so it wasn't necessary to turn the light on to see the time at night.

From the sentence you can conclude that "luminous" means shining or glowing or giving off light. This definition is not stated in the sentence, but you can infer this meaning from the situation described in the context of the sentence—if it wasn't necessary to turn the light on to see the time at night, then clearly the "luminous" dial must be a dial that gives off its own light (glows, shines).

Often in your reading it will be possible to figure out the meaning of a new or unfamiliar word by analyzing the ideas presented in the context of the sentence. As in the above example, the ideas of the sentence can provide clear clues to the meaning of key words.

INSTRUCTIONS FOR THE EXERCISES

Try now the WORD POWER: CASE IV exercise set. This set will develop your skill in analyzing sentence contexts for word "meaning inferred from ideas in the sentence."

Word Power: Case IV

Power Words	anthology	laudable	mirage	affluent	anachronism
	enigma	avert	satire	altruistic	tantamount

1. **anthology** | ăn **thŏl'** ə jē |
   - The anthology contained poems written by English poets.

2. **enigma** | ĭ **nĭg'** mə |
   - The enigma seemed unsolvable and continued to puzzle his mind for months.

3. **laudable** | **lô'** də bəl |
   - The book was not laudable and did not deserve the good reviews it received.

4. **avert** | ə **vûrt'** |
   - To avert a collision with the oncoming car, Tara drove off the road.

5. **mirage** | mĭ **räzh'** |
   - A mirage of water in a desert is an illusion caused by the sun thinning the air.

6. **satire** | **săt'** īr' |
   - The comedienne's satire on how the Senate wastes time was so funny that even the Senators laughed.

7. **affluent** | **ăf'** lōo' ənt |
   - Through hard work and good luck the family became affluent and eventually owned over half the real estate in town.

8. **altruistic** | ăl' trōo' **ĭs'** tĭk |
   - George Washington Carver was an altruistic scientist whose research was directed at improving the income of poor southern farmers.

9. **anachronism** | ə **năk'** rə nĭz' əm |
   - A horse-drawn carriage on an interstate highway is an anachronism.

10. **tantamount** | **tăn'** tə mount' |
    - In some people's opinion, the publication of classified military information is tantamount to treason.

Meaning Comprehension: Case IV

Directions: Use what you have learned from the context sentences to identify the correct definition of each Power Word. In the blank next to each Power Word, write the letter of its correct definition.

Power Words

_____ anthology

_____ enigma

_____ laudable

_____ avert

_____ mirage

_____ satire

_____ affluent

_____ altruistic

_____ anachronism

_____ tantamount

Definitions

a. illusion, something falsely believed to exist

b. deserving praise, praiseworthy

c. prevent, turn away to avoid

d. something unexplained, puzzle, mystery

e. having the same meaning or effect, equivalent

f. something happening or existing out of its proper (usually earlier) time period

g. unselfish, concerned about the welfare of others

h. collection of literary works

i. ridicule (making fun) of some human folly or vice; a book, play, etc. which ridicules

j. wealthy, rich

Context Application

Directions: Each of the following sentences has a blank. Use what you have learned about the Power Words to determine which Power Word best belongs in each blank. Then write the appropriate Power Word in each blank. Use each Power Word only once.

1. The actor gave a _____ performance and the audience responded with a standing ovation.

2. The lost traveler thought she saw a pond of water in the desert, but it was a _____ .

3. A little courtesy would help _____ many highway accidents.

4. Where the universe ends is an _____ that has haunted scientists for centuries.

5. Russia's refusal to remove troops from the Chinese border was _____ to a threat against Chinese national security.

6. Wind-powered ships are an _____ in modern commercial shipping.

7. The _____ included works of most 19th-century French novelists.

8. The writer used _____ to poke fun at the corruption of the town's mayor.

9. As some people become _____ , their desire for more wealth increases rather than decreases.

10. Asked to share his candy, the child experienced a conflict between selfish desires and _____ impulses.

Muscle Builder Analogies

Directions: Each exercise below is an analogy, with one term missing. Choose the Power Word which belongs in each blank of the analogy so that the analogy reads correctly. Write the appropriate Power Word in each blank. Note that some of the Power Words will not be used.

1. STINGY is to GENEROUS as SELFISH is to _____

2. POOR is to AFFLUENT as CAUSE is to _____

3. ENIGMA is to MYSTERY as _____ is to ILLUSION

ADDITIONAL ASSIGNMENTS

1. Look up the definitions of the words below in a dictionary. On a piece of notepaper, write these definitions. Refer to these definitions as you complete the following exercises.

   Note: In completing the following exercises, do not use any of these words more than once.

edification	devoid	retract	malign
reverberation	lucid	writhe	chronic

2. Pick one of the above words and write a sentence on the lines below in which the meaning of the word is stated with punctuation (Case I).

   _____   _____

   _____

3. Pick one of the above words and write a sentence on the lines below in which the meaning of the word is stated without punctuation (Case II).

   _____   _____

   _____

4. Pick one of the above words and write a sentence on the lines below in which the meaning of the word is given by contrast (Case III).

   _____

   _____   _____

5. Pick one of the above words and write a sentence on the lines below in which the meaning of the word can be inferred from the rest of the sentence (Case IV).

   _____

   _____

UNIT
2

UNDERSTANDING THE MAIN TOPIC AND ANALYZING THE FACTS

OBJECTIVES: When you have completed this unit you should

- be able to select the best title reflecting the main topic of a passage;
- be able to answer questions about facts presented in a passage;
- know the meanings of the following POWER WORDS.

POWER WORDS

heterogeneous	deviation	heterochromatic	expedient
homogeneous	precocious	regress	acute
succinct	tedious	dilemma	oblivious
archaic	monotheism	heteromorphic	allocate
lucid	vendetta	microcosm	arid
prosaic	scathing	repentant	capital
comprises	reticent	macrocosm	exotic
polyglot	polytheism	premonition	bouyancy

Word Power I

Directions: Study each of the Power Words below. Note how each word is pronounced. Then read the context sentences to figure out what each Power Word means. In the left-hand margin next to each Power Word, try to jot down a synonym or short definition which defines that word.

Power Words	heterogeneous	succinct	lucid	comprises
	homogeneous	archaic	prosaic	polyglot

---

1. **heterogeneous** | hĕt′ ər ə **jē′** nē əs |
   - That football player's skills are so heterogeneous, he can play several positions.
   - I'm not sure what the main theme of that course is; the books on the reading list are very heterogeneous.

2. **homogeneous** | hō′ mə **jē′** nē əs |
   - The students in this school all come from the same neighborhood, so they are quite homogeneous in their social background.

3. **succinct** | sək **sĭngkt′** |
   - An adage like "A stitch in time saves nine" expresses a weighty idea succinctly in a few words.
   - Jacob's speech was long-winded and hard to follow, but Dena's speech was succinct and to the point.

4. **archaic** | är **kā′** ĭk |
   - Annette believes all her father's ways are old-fashioned and his ideas on proper dress are archaic.
   - "Thee" is an archaic form of the pronoun "you."

5. **lucid** |**loo′** sĭd |
   - Although grandmother is old, her letters are lucid and amusing.
   - Paul gave a lucid explanation of the complex argument.

6. **prosaic** | prō **zā′** ĭk |
   - Technical writing may be prosaic, but literary writing must be moving and surprising.
   - Research reports must give prosaic descriptions of even the most exciting experiments and discoveries.

7. **comprises** | kəm **prīz′** ĭz |
   - The bulk of the course's reading list comprises short stories by famous authors.
   - The Union comprises fifty states.

8. **polyglot** | **pŏl′** ē glŏt′ |
   - A job in overseas sales would be easier for a polyglot.
   - For her trip to Europe, the President selected an interpreter who was a polyglot.

ă pat / ā pay / â care / ä father / ĕ pet / ē be / ĭ pit / ī pie / î fierce / ŏ pot / ō go / ô paw, for / oi oil / ŏŏ book /
ōō boot / ou out / ŭ cut / û fur / th the / th thin / hw which / zh vision / ə ago, item, pencil, atom, circus

Meaning Comprehension

Directions: Use what you have learned from the context sentences to identify the correct definition of each Power Word. In the blank next to each Power Word, write the letter of its correct definition.

Power Words	Definitions
_____ heterogeneous	a. consists of, is composed of, includes
_____ homogeneous	b. one who speaks several languages
_____ succinct	c. similar in kind or nature
_____ archaic	d. having main idea expressed well with few words
_____ lucid	e. belonging to an earlier time; primitive
_____ prosaic	f. clear, rational, bright
_____ comprises	g. dull, flat, unimaginative, commonplace
_____ polyglot	h. differing in kind; having dissimilar ingredients

Context Application

Directions: Each of the following sentences has two blanks. Use what you have learned about the Power Words to determine which Power Word best belongs in each of the blanks. Then write the appropriate Power Word in each blank. Use each Power Word only once.

1. In a _____ world, where everyone spoke the same language, a _____ would be unneeded, and perhaps unheard of.

2. Good writing is _____ rather than confused or ambiguous, and _____ rather than wordy.

3. A successful writer avoids _____ or outdated terms and dull, _____ expressions.

4. A _____ population _____ people of different origins.

Muscle Builder Analogies

Directions: Each exercise below is an analogy, with one or two terms missing. Choose the Power Word which belongs in each blank of the analogy so that the analogy reads correctly. Write the appropriate Power Word in each blank. Note that some of the Power Words will not be used.

1. NEW is to OLD as MODERN is to _____

2. CLEAR is to LUCID as UNIMAGINATIVE is to _____

3. SIMILAR is to _____ as DIFFERENT is to
   _____

Word Power II

Directions: Study each of the Power Words below. Note how each word is pronounced. Then read the context sentences to figure out what each Power Word means. In the left-hand margin next to each Power Word, try to jot down a synonym or short definition which defines that word.

Power Words	deviation	tedious	vendetta	reticent
	precocious	monotheism	scathing	polytheism

1. **deviation** | dē′ vē ā′ shən |
   - Any deviation from these treatment instructions will result in illness.
   - Theft is a deviation from accepted social behavior.

2. **precocious** | prĭ **kō′** shəs |
   - Many outstanding people did not appear precocious in childhood.
   - That child genius is precocious in all areas of math.

3. **tedious** | tē′ dē əs |
   - The ceremony was tedious and put the audience to sleep.
   - Copying paragraphs out of books is a tedious task.

4. **monotheism** | **mŏn′** ō thē ĭz′ əm |
   - Christianity is a monotheistic religion.
   - The ancient Greeks did not practice monotheism, they worshipped many gods.

5. **vendetta** | vĕn **dĕt′** ə |
   - The vice president's vendetta and continual battle with the president disrupted the company.

6. **scathing** | **skā′** thĭng |
   - Her harsh, scathing remarks revealed her intense anger.
   - Julio says he quit his job because of his boss' continued scathing criticism of his work.

7. **reticent** | **rĕt′** ĭ sənt |
   - He does not constantly talk about his accomplishments but tends to be reticent about them.
   - It is very hard to carry on a conversation with someone who is reticent.

8. **polytheism** | **pŏl′** ē thē ĭz′ əm |
   - The ancient Greeks were polytheistic, believing in gods such as Zeus, Mercury, Apollo, Venus, and others.
   - A Christian does not believe in polytheism, but solely in one God.

ă pat / ā pay / â care / ä father / ĕ pet / ē be / ĭ pit / ī pie / î fierce / ŏ pot / ō go / ô paw, for / oi oil / ŏŏ book /
ōō boot / ou out / ŭ cut / û fur / *th* the / th thin / hw which / zh vision / ə ago, item, pencil, atom, circus

Meaning Comprehension

Directions: Use what you have learned from the context sentences to identify the correct definition of each Power Word. In the blank next to each Power Word, write the letter of its correct definition.

Power Words

_____ deviation
_____ precocious
_____ tedious
_____ monotheism
_____ vendetta
_____ scathing
_____ reticent
_____ polytheism

Definitions

a. belief in one God
b. belief in a plurality of gods
c. tiresome, boring because slow or repeated
d. severe, bitter, cutting
e. departure from the established or normal
f. inclined to remain silent, quiet
g. intense feud, long-lasting hostility
h. mentally advanced, developed ahead of time

Context Application

Directions: Each of the following sentences has two blanks. Use what you have learned about the Power Words to determine which Power Word best belongs in each of the blanks. Then write the appropriate Power Word in each blank. Use each Power Word only once.

1. In the army, any _____ from the rules resulted in a _____ tongue-lashing by the sergeant.

2. The child is _____ in schoolwork, but she is shy and _____ socially.

3. He had talked about their long-standing _____ and his desire to have revenge for so long, it was no longer exciting but just _____ .

4. Since "mono" means "one", "poly" means "many," and "theism" refers to god, it follows that _____ is belief in a single God and _____ is belief in multiple gods.

Muscle Builder Analogies

Directions: Each exercise below is an analogy, with one or two terms missing. Choose the Power Word which belongs in each blank of the analogy so that the analogy reads correctly. Write the appropriate Power Word in each blank. Note that some of the Power Words will not be used.

1. BOLD is to SHY as OUTGOING is to _____

2. MENTALLY ADVANCED is to _____ as DULL is to TEDIOUS

3. SINGLE is to MULTIPLE as _____ is to _____

(HINT: Be sure to write the two Power Words in their correct order so that the analogy is precise.)

INTRODUCTION

In this unit you will add to the analytical reading skills you developed in Unit 1. Here, you will build your abilities in analyzing the MAIN TOPIC of a reading passage and in identifying and analyzing facts presented in reading passages.

The exercises in this unit all consist of short reading passages, chosen from a variety of text materials (textbooks, newspapers, news magazines, reports, encyclopedias) and selected to represent a range of subject areas (history, current events, business, science, human relations). Following each reading passage is a small set of questions—in the familiar form of reading comprehension questions—designed to improve your skills in analyzing and comprehending text passages.

The questions are of three types:

1. Questions that ask you to evaluate possible titles for the passage (to identify the MAIN TOPIC of the passage);

2. Questions that ask about facts (details) mentioned in the passage;

3. Questions that ask you to interpret the meaning of a word as it is used in the context of a passage.

Through your study of this unit, you will become comfortable and competent in analyzing reading passages for topic and for factual meaning. The skills you develop here will be invaluable aids to your work in the later units of this book.

INSTRUCTIONS FOR THE EXERCISES

It is recommended that you read each passage slowly and carefully. Make sure that you understand each idea presented in the passage before moving on in your reading to the next idea. If you come across any unfamiliar words, try to figure out their meanings by analyzing the sentence contexts in which those words are used (as you learned to do in Unit 1).

In answering the questions about facts presented in the passage, again work carefully. Do not work too quickly or thoughtlessly. Be certain of each answer before moving on to the next question. Most people find that they must reread sections of the passage to pin down the *best* answer to each question. YOUR GOAL IS 100% ACCURACY! Some of the questions will ask you for the line numbers of the lines where you found an answer. This will help you learn to pinpoint your search for information in a passage.

The first question after each passage will ask you to evaluate possible titles for the passage. This will help you develop a solid "feel" for the MAIN TOPIC of a reading passage. To illustrate the procedure for answering this "title" question, study the example below.

EXAMPLE—Read this passage.

> Ever since the 1930s, archaeologists have believed that the Tigris and Euphrates valley in ancient Mesopotamia (now Iraq) was the "cradle of civilization," where, around 8000 B.C., people first settled in villages to cultivate wild grain and domesticate animals. By 6000 B.C. they had begun hammering crude objects of copper, and by about 3000 B.C. they had acquired the know-how to alloy copper with tin to create durable metal tools and weapons, thus ushering in the Bronze Age.

Now try to answer the question below. The three lettered phrases (A), (B), and (C) are descriptions of the three possible titles listed. One of the titles is *too broad*—it covers a broader, bigger topic than the passage is really about. One title is *too narrow*—it covers only a small part of what the passage is about. And, one title is a *comprehensive title*—it covers what the entire passage is about, and only what the passage is about; it is neither too broad nor too narrow. The comprehensive title best states the MAIN TOPIC of the passage. Can you match the three descriptions to the three possible titles for the example passage?

Below are three possible titles for this passage. In each blank, write the letter of the phrase (A, B, or C) which best describes that title.

_____ **The History of the Human Race**
_____ **The First Cultivation of Grain by Humans**
_____ **The Beginning of Civilization**

    (A) too narrow
    (B) too broad
    (C) comprehensive title

Check your work with the answer on the next page.

ANSWER:

___B___   The History of the Human Race

___A___   The First Cultivation of Grain by Humans

___C___   The Beginning of Civilization

The title "The History of the Human Race" is too broad. The passage does not cover the entire history of human beings.

The title "The First Cultivation of Grain by Humans" is too narrow. Cultivation of grain is only one specific detail presented in the passage. It is not the main topic of the passage.

The title "The Beginning of Civilization" does reflect the MAIN TOPIC of the passage. The entire passage deals with a theory of how and where civilization began. Therefore, "The Beginning of Civilization" is a comprehensive title.

Begin working now on the exercises that follow. Remember, work carefully. Your goal is 100% accuracy.

PASSAGE A

1 A strike by 33,000 bus and subway drivers in
2 early April plunged this financially troubled me-
3 tropolis into another wrenching crisis.
4 Frustration gripped New York City during
5 the transit shutdown as more than 3 million
6 commuters scrambled for other ways of getting
7 around town. Confusion was compounded by a
8 one-day strike against a railroad serving 95,000
9 rush-hour commuters from Long Island. Motor-
10 ists encountered massive traffic jams. Other
11 commuters used helicopters, boats, bicycles—
12 even roller skates. One man died walking across
13 the Brooklyn Bridge.

1. Below are three possible titles for this passage. In
   each blank, write the letter of the phrase (A, B or
   C) which best describes that title.

   _____ Problems of Large Urban Centers
   _____ Transit Strike Hits New York
   _____ Man Dies Walking Across Brooklyn
             Bridge

   (A) comprehensive title
   (B) too broad
   (C) too narrow

2. Approximately how many people were affected
   by the bus and subway strike?

   ☐ (A) 33,000
   ☐ (B) 3,000,000
   ☐ (C) 95,000

3. On which line(s) did you find the answer to the
   preceding question?

   LINE NUMBER(S): _____

4. According to the passage,

   ☐ (A) New York City has the world's worst
             transportation problems
   ☐ (B) New York City has economic
             problems
   ☐ (C) New York City has 33,000 buses and
             subways

PASSAGE B

1 Like a lot of conscientious men and women
2 who work and worry too severely and grow
3 unconscious of their bodies, I woke up one morn-
4 ing in my mid-40s to find myself transformed (in
5 the night, it seemed) into a blimp.
6 It was no joke.
7 My cheeks looked like apples, my thighs
8 were lumpy stumps and my belly—don't ask! My
9 four children mocked me when I mentioned my
10 early days of glory on the basketball courts and,
11 when our bed collapsed, my wife threatened the
12 worst.

1. Below are three possible titles for this passage. In
   each blank, write the letter of the phrase (A, B or
   C) which best describes that title.

   _____ Health Hazards and Social Problems of
             Being Overweight
   _____ Experiences in Realizing I was Over-
             weight at Mid-40
   _____ The Night the Bed Collapsed

   (A) too narrow
   (B) too broad
   (C) comprehensive title

2. The writer's children ridiculed him

   ☐ (A) because his cheeks looked like apples
             and his thighs like lumpy stumps
   ☐ (B) when he claimed he was once athletic
   ☐ (C) when the bed collapsed
   ☐ (D) Both (B) and (C)

3. The word "transformed" in the first paragraph
   immediately precedes

   ☐ (A) a parenthesis
   ☐ (B) the letter "i"
   ☐ (C) the letter "f"
   ☐ (D) the word "myself"

4. The word "transformed," according to the context, means

   ☐ (A) electrified
   ☐ (B) changed form
   ☐ (C) changed place
   ☐ (D) changed language

PASSAGE C

1   Queen Juliana of the Netherlands has never
2 been a very predictable monarch, and last week
3 she sprang yet another surprise on her 14 million
4 subjects. Speaking from Soestdijk Palace outside
5 Amsterdam, the Queen announced that she
6 would abdicate on April 30, her 71st birthday.
7 With tears in her eyes, she said she would hand
8 the throne over to her oldest daughter, Crown
9 Princess Beatrix. Juliana was not the least bit coy
10 in explaining her decision: she was getting too old
11 for the job. "There comes a time," she said in a
12 four-minute television address, "when your
13 strength fades and you can no longer fulfill your
14 tasks as before."

1. Below are three possible titles for this passage. In each blank, write the letter of the phrase (A, B, or C) which best describes that title.

    _____ The Netherlands' Royal and Political Scene
    _____ Juliana Abdicates the Netherlands' Throne
    _____ Princess Beatrix Becomes Queen of the Netherlands

    (A) too narrow
    (B) comprehensive title
    (C) too broad

2. The word "abdicate," according to the context, means

    ☐ (A) hate, loathe
    ☐ (B) resign a throne or high office
    ☐ (C) to carry off by force

3. According to the passage, the Netherlands' people

    ☐ (A) expected Queen Juliana to resign because she was 71 years old
    ☐ (B) did not expect Queen Juliana's resignation
    ☐ (C) cried during the resignation speech

4. Queen Juliana announced her abdication

    ☐ (A) in the Netherlands' newspapers
    ☐ (B) in a long television address lasting several hours
    ☐ (C) in a short television speech

PASSAGE D

1   In sheer size no other airport in the world can
2 match it. With its twin terminals and 138 boarding
3 gates, the new passenger complex at the William
4 B. Hartsfield Atlanta International Airport, which
5 opened last week, sprawls over an area equiva-
6 lent to 45 football fields. The $500 million jetport is
7 far bigger than its closest rival: the terminal at Dallas/
8 Fort Worth Airport covers a mere 29 football
9 fields.

1. Below are three possible titles for this passage. In each blank, write the letter of the phrase (A, B or C) which best describes that title.

    _____ The Dallas/Fort Worth Airport
    _____ The Atlanta Airport: World's Largest
    _____ The World's Major Airports

    (A) too broad
    (B) too narrow
    (C) comprehensive title

2. How many terminals does the Atlanta Airport have?

    ☐ (A) 138
    ☐ (B) 2
    ☐ (C) 29
    ☐ (D) 45

3. According to the passage,

    ☐ (A) the Dallas/Fort Worth Airport cost $500 million
    ☐ (B) the Dallas/Fort Worth Airport is the second largest in Texas
    ☐ (C) the Dallas/Fort Worth Airport is the second largest on earth
    ☐ (D) the Dallas/Fort Worth Airport is the world's largest

4. On which line(s) did you find the answer to the preceding question?

LINE NUMBER(S): _____

PASSAGE E

1 Saving water has been overlooked as a prac-
2 tical way to cut down on a homeowner's "cost of
3 living." But the multiplying effect of water conser-
4 vation can actually cut down on a half dozen
5 other bills you faithfully pay every year.
6 Using less water in your home can not only
7 shrink your water bills, it can also reduce your hot
8 water heating bills, your sewer bills, minimize
9 pumping equipment costs, plus cut down on your
10 sewer problems.

1. Below are three possible titles for this passage. In
each blank, write the letter of the phrase (A, B,
or C) which best describes that title.

_____ How to Earn and Save More Money
_____ Saving on Water Bills
_____ Saving Water to Save Money

    (A) too narrow
    (B) too broad
    (C) comprehensive title

2. In the first paragraph, how many bills does the
writer suggest you can reduce?

☐ (A) just your water bill
☐ (B) your water bill plus six others
☐ (C) a dozen bills
☐ (D) a half dozen bills

3. Assuming sewer problems can be costly, how
many expenses does the writer say in the second
paragraph you can shrink?

☐ (A) 1
☐ (B) 3
☐ (C) 4
☐ (D) 5

PASSAGE F

1 Within months you can start looking for new
2 yellow-and-black "Energy Guide" labels on seven
3 types of household appliances because of new
4 federal regulations. The labels will show the
5 energy-efficiency rates of comparable appliances
6 and estimates of annual energy costs for the
7 appliance.
8 The new labels are the result of a federal
9 appliance label program required under the 1975
10 Energy Policy and Conservation Act. It is jointly
11 managed by the Dept. of Energy and the Federal
12 Trade Commission. The new rule supersedes all
13 state and local rules and places the responsibility
14 for labeling on the appliance manufacturers.

1. Below are three possible titles for this passage. In
each blank, write the letter of the phrase (A, B or
C) which best describes that title.

_____ Energy-Efficiency Rates for Some Appli-
         ances
_____ New Energy Labels on Appliances
_____ New Ideas to Help Cut Energy Costs

    (A) too broad
    (B) too narrow
    (C) comprehensive title

2. The "Energy Guide" labels will provide information on

☐ (A) the energy-efficiency of similar devices
☐ (B) the yearly estimated energy cost for an
     appliance
☐ (C) the monthly estimated energy cost for
     an appliance
☐ (D) Both (A) and (C), but not (B)
☐ (E) Both (A) and (B), but not (C)

3. On which line(s) did you find the answer to the
preceding question?

LINE NUMBER(S): _____

4. The word "supersedes" in the last sentence,
according to the context, means

☐ (A) law
☐ (B) overrides
☐ (C) abundance
☐ (D) maximizes

PASSAGE G

¹   Most of us who grew up in the fifties and
² sixties did so in neighborhoods characterized by
³ familiar faces, friendly merchants, a sense of
⁴ safety, and stability. But since that time society
⁵ has been in considerable flux, and, in many cases,
⁶ the traditional residential neighborhood has
⁷ changed. For one thing, people today are much
⁸ more geographically mobile. Also, they switch
⁹ careers more frequently, divorce more often, and
¹⁰ now labor statistics indicate that just as many
¹¹ women are working as men (although many in
¹² part-time jobs).

1. Below are three possible titles for this passage. In each blank, write the letter of the phrase (A, B, or C) which best describes that title.

    _____ Neighborhoods in the Fifties
    _____ Historical Changes in American Society
    _____ Neighborhoods in the Fifties and Sixties
    Compared to Neighborhoods Today

    (A) too broad
    (B) too narrow
    (C) comprehensive title

2. The main idea of the passage is that

    ☐ (A) people are more geographically mobile today
    ☐ (B) there is more divorce today
    ☐ (C) neighborhoods are much less stable today

3. In the context of this passage, the word "flux" means

    ☐ (A) change
    ☐ (B) thread
    ☐ (C) cotton
    ☐ (D) power

4. The phrase "geographically mobile," according to the context, means

    ☐ (A) moving to different places
    ☐ (B) interested in geography
    ☐ (C) a portable piece of sod
    ☐ (D) hesitant to move

PASSAGE H

¹   With the possible exception of the most arid
² deserts, the high, frozen mountain peaks, and the
³ perpetually icebound, sterile polar regions, prob-
⁴ ably no place on earth is devoid of life. The two
⁵ main types of habitat are the *aquatic* and the
⁶ *terrestrial*. Both range from equator to pole and
⁷ from a few thousand feet below to a few thousand
⁸ feet above sea level. *Ocean* and *fresh water* are
⁹ the main subdivisions of the aquatic habitat, and
¹⁰ *air* and *soil* of the terrestrial.

1. Below are three possible titles for this passage. In each blank, write the letter of the phrase (A, B or C) which best describes that title.

    _____ Types of Animals and Their Habitats
    _____ Types of Habitats
    _____ Aquatic Habitats

    (A) too narrow
    (B) comprehensive title
    (C) too broad

2. In the first sentence, the phrase "devoid of," according to the context, means

    ☐ (A) full of
    ☐ (B) without
    ☐ (C) characterized by

3. Which is not a terrestrial animal?

    ☐ (A) eagle
    ☐ (B) shark
    ☐ (C) lion

4. The Mississippi River is an example of

    ☐ (A) a terrestrial habitat
    ☐ (B) an aquatic habitat
    ☐ (C) an arid desert

5. According to this context, a "habitat" is

    ☐ (A) a place inhabited by some type of plant or animal
    ☐ (B) a habit or regular behavior of an animal
    ☐ (C) a type of city

PASSAGE I

1   There are several types of garden structures
2 that can add to your outdoor living enjoyment.
3   They're known loosely under such names as
4 pergolas, arbors, bowers, ramadas, lath houses,
5 overheads, egg-crates, shade shelters and gaze-
6 bos. Whatever you choose to call them, their
7 primary purpose is to break the intensity of the
8 sun for the comfort of the people below.
9   Some auxiliary benefits are to give a feeling
10 of partial enclosure, add a structural element in
11 scale with the garden, and offer support for climb-
12 ing vines and protection for shade-loving plants.

1. Below are three possible titles for this passage. In each blank, write the letter of the phrase (A, B or C) which best describes that title.

    _____ Uses of Garden Structures
    _____ Types and Uses of Garden Structures
    _____ Things and Ways to Improve Your Garden

    (A) too broad
    (B) too narrow
    (C) comprehensive title

2. Pergolas and gazebos are examples of

    ☐ (A) climbing vines
    ☐ (B) shade-loving plants
    ☐ (C) garden structures

3. The major benefit of garden structures is to

    ☐ (A) give a feeling of partial enclosure
    ☐ (B) offer support for climbing vines
    ☐ (C) provide shade for plants
    ☐ (D) provide shade for people

4. The word "benefits," according to the context, means

    ☐ (A) programs
    ☐ (B) dances
    ☐ (C) values
    ☐ (D) requests

PASSAGE J

1   A special group of chemicals—amino acid
2 benzyl esters—has been discovered that shows
3 promise of cutting the toll from sickle-cell anemia,
4 a major health problem in the U.S., especially for
5 blacks. This chemical group can prevent the dis-
6 tortion of red blood cells into sickle-cell shapes, a
7 first step toward developing an effective drug
8 against this disease. The discovery, reported in
9 the *Proceedings of the National Academy of*
10 *Sciences*, was made by teams of researchers at
11 the Massachusetts Institute of Technology and at
12 the Weizmann Institute of Science in Israel.

1. Below are three possible titles for this passage. In each blank, write the letter of the phrase (A, B or C) which best describes that title.

    _____ Chemical Discoveries for Fighting Diseases
    _____ Discovery of Chemicals to Fight Sickle-Cell Anemia
    _____ Chemicals to Fight Sickle-Cell Anemia Discovered at MIT

    (A) comprehensive title
    (B) too broad
    (C) too narrow

2. According to the passage,

    ☐ (A) amino acid benzyl esters are a complete cure for sickle-cell anemia
    ☐ (B) amino acid benzyl esters keep red blood cells from changing shape
    ☐ (C) Both (A) and (B)

3. The discovery announced in this passage was made by

    ☐ (A) a world-famous chemist
    ☐ (B) a single group of scientists
    ☐ (C) two groups of scientists

4. On which line(s) did you find the answer to the preceding question?

    LINE NUMBER(S): _____

PASSAGE K

¹ Carbohydrates are so named because they
² consist of carbon, hydrogen, and oxygen, the last
³ two in a 2:1 ratio, as in water. The general atomic
⁴ composition usually corresponds to the formula
⁵ $C_x(H_2O)_y$, where x and y are whole numbers.
⁶ If x and y are low numbers, from 3 to about 7,
⁷ then the formula describes the composition of the
⁸ most common carbohydrates—the simple sug-
⁹ ars, or monosaccharides. In these, the carbon
¹⁰ atoms form a chain to which H and O atoms are
¹¹ attached. Frequent reference will be made to
¹² *pentose* sugars, which contain 5 carbon atoms
¹³ per molecule, and to *hexose* sugars, each of
¹⁴ which contains 6 carbon atoms per molecule.

1. Below are three possible titles for this passage. In each blank, write the letter of the phrase (A, B or C) which best describes that title.

   _____ Definition and Examples of Carbohydrates
   _____ The Chemistry of Foods
   _____ The Chemical Make-Up of Simple Sugars

   (A) too broad
   (B) too narrow
   (C) comprehensive title

2. In the last sentence, according to the context, the prefixes *pent* and *hex* mean

   ☐ (A) six and five, respectively
   ☐ (B) five and six, respectively
   ☐ (C) three and seven, respectively

3. In the first paragraph, x and y are

   ☐ (A) numbers representing letters
   ☐ (B) letters representing numbers
   ☐ (C) the x and y chromosomes in human genetics

4. According to the passage,

   ☐ (A) carbohydrates are simple sugars
   ☐ (B) simple sugars are carbohydrates

PASSAGE L

¹ The administration issued its first formal
² report on human rights around the world today.
³ The report, prompted by pressure from interna-
⁴ tional human rights organizations, said that the
⁵ situation was worsening in Central America and
⁶ several African nations. In El Salvador, however,
⁷ the Administration reported "there is a down-
⁸ ward trend in political violence."
⁹ In the introduction to the report, the Admini-
¹⁰ stration reiterated what it has in the past de-
¹¹ scribed as its evenhanded approach to the place
¹² of human rights in world affairs, saying that the
¹³ United States "has always, and will always, take
¹⁴ the lead in condemning human rights violations,
¹⁵ regardless of the specific nations involved."

1. Below are three possible titles for this passage. In each blank, write the letter of the phrase (A, B or C) which best describes that title.

   _____ The Role of Human Rights in International Politics
   _____ Human Rights Violations in El Salvador
   _____ The Administration Report on Human Rights

   (A) comprehensive title
   (B) too narrow
   (C) too broad

2. The word "reiterated," according to the context, means

   ☐ (A) repeated
   ☐ (B) condemned
   ☐ (C) criticized

3. According to the passage, the human rights situation in Central America is

   ☐ (A) getting better
   ☐ (B) getting poorer

4. According to the passage, political violence in El Salvador is

   ☐ (A) increasing
   ☐ (B) decreasing
   ☐ (C) neither increasing nor decreasing

PASSAGE M

1   Dr. Charles Drew was not yet 50 when he
2 died in an automobile accident, but, as explained
3 in *Great Negroes Past And Present*, "already his
4 contribution to medicine had saved hundreds of
5 thousands of lives during World War II. Dr. Drew
6 was a pioneer in blood plasma preservation.
7 Before his time there was no efficient way to store
8 large quantities of blood plasma for use during
9 emergencies or for use in wartime where thou-
10 sands of lives depended on the availability of
11 blood for blood transfusions. After Dr. Drew this
12 was no longer a problem, for he discovered ways
13 and means of preserving blood plasma in what are
14 commonly known as blood banks.
15   Beginning his research into the proper use of
16 blood plasma at Columbia University, Dr. Drew
17 became an authority on the subject and was
18 asked by the British to set up a plasma program
19 for them. He later did the same thing for the
20 United States in 1942 and won the Springarn
21 medal in recognition of his contributions to Negro
22 progress. At the time of his death in 1950 Dr.
23 Drew was chief surgeon and chief of staff at
24 Freedmen's Hospital."

1. Below are three possible titles for this passage. In each blank, write the letter of the phrase (A, B or C) which best describes that title.

    _____ British Plasma Program Set Up by Charles Drew
    _____ Major Contributors to Medical Research
    _____ Charles Drew's Work in Preserving Blood for Transfusions

    (A) too broad
    (B) too narrow
    (C) comprehensive title

2. Charles Drew's contribution was in

    ☐ (A) convincing people to donate blood to be used in saving lives
    ☐ (B) developing a method of preventing blood from becoming useless between the time it is donated and the time it is needed
    ☐ (C) founding Columbia University

3. Which of the following statements is correct about Charles Drew?

    ☐ (A) He began his research on blood at Freedmen's Hospital and eventually became chief of staff at Columbia University.
    ☐ (B) He began his research on blood at Columbia University and eventually became chief of staff at Freedmen's Hospital.
    ☐ (C) He began his research on blood at Freedmen's Hospital and eventually became chief of staff there.

4. How many years after setting up the plasma program in the United States did Drew die?

    ☐ (A) 1942
    ☐ (B) 1950
    ☐ (C) 8
    ☐ (D) 50

Word Power III

Directions: Study each of the Power Words below. Note how each word is pronounced. Then read the context sentences to figure out what each Power Word means. In the left-hand margin next to each Power Word, try to jot down a synonym or short definition which defines that word.

Power Words	heterochromatic	dilemma	microcosm	macrocosm
	regress	heteromorphic	repentant	premonition

1. **heterochromatic** | hĕt′ ə rō krə **măt′** ĭk |
   - A bright heterochromatic outfit is inappropriate for a solemn occasion like a funeral.
   - The American flag is heterochromatic.

2. **regress** | rĭ **grĕs′** |
   - Since you know progress means moves forward, you can deduce the meaning of regress.
   - Lucinda found that constant practice was needed or else her judo skills would regress.

3. **dilemma** | dĭ **lĕm′** ə |
   - He hadn't worked much all semester and faced the dilemma of studying math and failing history, or vice versa.

4. **heteromorphic** | hĕt′ ə rō **môr′** fĭk |
   - In contrast to identical twins, fraternal twins are heteromorphic.
   - H_2O is a familiar heteromorphic molecule, existing as either a solid, a liquid, or a gas.

5. **microcosm** | mī′ krə kŏz′ əm |
   - A person who doesn't read the newspaper or watch the TV news lives in his or her own microcosm.

6. **repentant** | rĭ **pĕn′** tnt |
   - When she saw the harm she had done, she was deeply repentant.
   - An apology is an act of a repentant person.

7. **macrocosm** | măk′ rə **kăz′** əm |
   - Beyond our solar system is the rest of the universe, the macrocosm.

8. **premonition** | prē′ mə **nĭsh′** ən |
   - He had a premonition it would snow, so he unpacked the shovels.
   - Joanne felt an unexplainable premonition that trouble was ahead.

ă pat / ā pay / â care / ä father / ĕ pet / ē be / ĭ pit / ī pie / î fierce / ŏ pot / ō go / ô paw, for / oi oil / ŏŏ book /
ōō boot / ou out / ŭ cut / ü fur / th the / th thin / hw which / zh vision / ə ago, item, pencil, atom, circus

Meaning Comprehension

Directions: Use what you have learned from the context sentences to identify the correct definition of each Power Word. In the blank next to each Power Word, write the letter of its correct definition.

Power Words

_____ heterochromatic
_____ regress
_____ dilemma
_____ heteromorphic
_____ microcosm
_____ repentant
_____ macrocosm
_____ premonition

Definitions

a. choice between two unsatisfactory alternatives; problem that appears unsolvable
b. feeling regret for wrongdoing
c. large world, universe, great world
d. little world
e. forewarning, prior knowledge of a forthcoming event
f. move backwards
g. having different colors
h. having different forms

Context Application

Directions: Each of the following sentences has two blanks. Use what you have learned about the Power Words to determine which Power Word best belongs in each of the blanks. Then write the appropriate Power Word in each blank. Use each Power Word only once.

1. Since _____ means "little world" and _____ means "large world," evidently "micro" means "little" and "macro" means "large."

2. Tom was sincerely _____ for neglecting his homework and allowing his quiz grades to _____ from their previous high level.

3. Through a dream Liza had a _____ she would be faced with a _____ , and this helped her prepare mentally for a tough decision.

4. The words _____ , "having different colors," and _____ , "having different forms," both stem from "hetero" which means "different."

Muscle Builder Analogies

Directions: Each exercise below is an analogy, with one or two terms missing. Choose the Power Word which belongs in each blank of the analogy so that the analogy reads correctly. Write the appropriate Power Word in each blank. Note that some of the Power Words will not be used.

1. SMALL is to LARGE as _____ is to _____

2. FORWARD is to BACKWARD as PROGRESS is to _____

3. ONE is to MANY as MONOCHROMATIC is to _____

Word Power IV

Directions: Study each of the Power Words below. Note how each word is pronounced. Then read the context sentences to figure out what each Power Word means. In the left-hand margin next to each Power Word, try to jot down a synonym or short definition which defines that word.

Power Words	expedient	oblivious	arid	exotic
	acute	allocate	capital	buoyancy

1. **expedient** | ĭk **spē′** dē ənt |
   - In the rain an umbrella is expedient.
   - Running away is an expedient reaction to overwhelming fear.

2. **acute** | ə **kyōōt′** |
   - Although the magistrate was old, his judgment was acute.
   - Tara's special training gave her an acute awareness of the difficulties of the task.

3. **oblivious** | ə **blĭv′** ē əs |
   - When Phil studies he is oblivious to the people or noises about him.
   - The pilot was concentrating so hard that he was oblivious to the copilot's request and did not respond.

4. **allocate** | **ăl′** ə kāt′ |
   - The committee allocated $300 for travel and $600 for telephone.
   - The Swansons allocate ten percent of their income for the purchase of savings bonds.

5. **arid** | **ăr′** ĭd |
   - Creatures of the desert live in an arid environment.

6. **capital** | **kăp′** ĭ tl |
   - Capital is necessary for a business to buy equipment, which is then called capital equipment.
   - Companies sell stock as a means of raising capital.

7. **exotic** | ĭg **zŏt′** ĭk |
   - A trip to South America is a treasury of exotic experiences.
   - The San Diego Zoo has an excellent exhibit of exotic birds rarely seen in North America.

8. **buoyancy** | **boi′** ən sē |
   - Phil's happy, buoyant personality is a great social asset.
   - Because of her buoyancy, Rachel was still able to enjoy the party even after her hard day's work.

ă pat / ā pay / â care / ä father / ĕ pet / ē be / ĭ pit / ī pie / î fierce / ŏ pot / ō go / ô paw, for / oi oil / ŏŏ book /
ōō boot / ou out / ŭ cut / ü fur / *th* the / th thin / hw which / zh vision / ə ago, item, pencil, atom, circus

Meaning Comprehension

Directions: Use what you have learned from the context sentences to identify the correct definition of each Power Word. In the blank next to each Power Word, write the letter of its correct definition.

Power Words

_____ expedient
_____ acute
_____ oblivious
_____ allocate
_____ arid
_____ capital
_____ exotic
_____ buoyancy

Definitions

a. distribute resources for specific purposes
b. without moisture, very dry
c. lightheartedness; ability to recover from set-backs; ability to float
d. unaware, unnoticing
e. advantageous, useful, efficient
f. keen, discerning; severe
g. foreign; interestingly different
h. resources such as money for investment; central, most important

Context Application

Directions: Each of the following sentences has two blanks. Use what you have learned about the Power Words to determine which Power Word best belongs in each of the blanks. Then write the appropriate Power Word in each blank. Use each Power Word only once.

1. Management's inability to effectively _____ the company's _____ resources led to bankruptcy.

2. To prevent dehydration on a hike of appreciable distance in an _____ area, it is _____ to carry canteens of a consumable fluid.

3. The _____ spices and foods from various lands were not lost on him, for he had an _____ sense of taste.

4. At breakfast, Mr. Jones is generally half asleep and _____ to the _____ of his good-natured wife.

Muscle Builder Analogies

Directions: Each exercise below is an analogy, with one or two terms missing. Choose the Power Word which belongs in each blank of the analogy so that the analogy reads correctly. Write the appropriate Power Word in each blank. Note that some of the Power Words will not be used.

1. FOREIGN is to EXOTIC as LIGHTHEARTEDNESS is to

   _____

2. ARCTIC REGION is to FROZEN as DESERT REGION is to

   _____

3. USEFUL is to EXPEDIENT as UNAWARE is to _____

ADDITIONAL ASSIGNMENTS

1. Pick a paragraph or short selection from one of your own textbooks, encyclopedias, or other sources. Then write a title which is "too narrow," one which is "too broad," and one which is "comprehensive." Let a peer read the paragraph and decide which title fits each description.

2. Using what you have learned about the meaning of "homogeneous" (page 22), write a sentence on the lines below in which the meaning of "homogeneous" is given by contrast (Case III).

   _____

   _____

3. Using what you have learned about the meaning of "capitulate" (page 12), write a sentence on the lines below in which the meaning of "capitulate" is inferred from the rest of the sentence (Case IV).

   _____

   _____

4. Using what you have learned about the meaning of "rapport" (page 12), write a sentence on the lines below in which the meaning of "rapport" is stated with punctuation (Case I).

   _____

   _____

5. Using what you have learned about the meaning of "acute" (page 38), write a sentence on the lines below in which the meaning of "acute" is stated without punctuation (Case II).

   _____

   _____

UNIT
3
COMPREHENDING SPATIAL DESCRIPTIONS

OBJECTIVES: When you have completed this unit you should

- be able to make a diagram from a written description of a geometrical figure or the path of a moving object;
- be able to answer questions about cities, rivers, and directions on a map;
- know the meanings of the following POWER WORDS.

POWER WORDS

olfactory	compassionate	verbatim	impromptu
bibliophile	meticulous	fortuitous	statute
philanthropist	innovation	marital	skepticism
herbivorous	emancipate	cacophony	adhere
carnivorous	contemporaries	reciprocal	scrutinized
omnivorous	virtually	exorbitant	impenetrable
misanthrope	upheaval	paradox	vigilance
Francophile	fidelity	gourmet	nullified
inaudible			

Word Power I

Directions: Study each of the Power Words below. Note how each word is pronounced. Then read the context sentences to figure out what each Power Word means. In the left-hand margin next to each Power Word, try to jot down a synonym or short definition which defines that word.

Power Words

| olfactory | philanthropist | carnivorous | misanthrope | inaudible |
| bibliophile | herbivorous | omnivorous | Francophile | |

1. **olfactory** | ŏl **făk′** tə rē |
   - Fragrant flowers are an olfactory delight.
   - The skunk is notorious for its assault on a predator's olfactory organ.

2. **bibliophile** | **bĭb′** lē ə fīl′ |
   - Keri is a bibliophile and has an extensive library.
   - To be a book reviewer one must be a devout bibliophile.

3. **philanthropist** | fĭ **lăn′** thrə pĭst |
   - The rich philanthropist gave money to education, libraries and other institutions that benefit mankind.

4. **herbivorous** | hər **bĭv′** ər əs |
   - A sheep is a herbivorous animal.
   - Lions feed on meat and therefore are not herbivorous.

5. **carnivorous** | kär **nĭv′** ər əs |
   - Humans are omnivorous, not carnivorous, since they eat vegetables as well as meat.
   - A carnivorous animal must live in an area where prey is easily found.

6. **omnivorous** | ŏm **nĭv′** ər əs |
   - Wolves are carnivorous, not omnivorous, since their diet is almost exclusively meat.
   - An omnivorous animal usually eats a varied diet although it may prefer one main type of meat or plant.

7. **misanthrope** | **mĭs′** ən thrōp′ |
   - The misanthrope shunned human company and became a hermit.
   - Misanthropes prefer jobs which do not require contact with other people.

8. **Francophile** | **frăng′** kō fīl′ |
   - After a visit to France in her teens, Velma became a Francophile for life.

9. **inaudible** | ĭn **ô′** də bəl |
   - Raul spoke so softly he was almost inaudible.
   - Some dog whistles emit a sound which is inaudible to humans but clearly heard by dogs.

ă pat / ā pay / â care / ä father / ĕ pet / ē be / ĭ pit / ī pie / î fierce / ŏ pot / ō go / ô paw, for / oi oil / ŏŏ book /
ōō boot / ou out / ŭ cut / û fur / th the / th thin / hw which / zh vision / ə ago, item, pencil, atom, circus

Meaning Comprehension

Directions: Use what you have learned from the context sentences to identify the correct definition of each Power Word. In the blank next to each Power Word, write the letter of its correct definition.

Power Words

_____ olfactory
_____ bibliophile
_____ philanthropist
_____ herbivorous
_____ carnivorous
_____ omnivorous
_____ misanthrope
_____ Francophile
_____ inaudible

Definitions

a. related to the sense of smell
b. one who likes France or the French
c. not audible, not hearable
d. eating meat for food
e. one who donates money or performs other acts to benefit mankind
f. hater of mankind
g. lover of books
h. eating plants for food
i. eating both plants and meat for food

Context Application

Directions: Each of the following sentences has two or three blanks. Use what you have learned about the Power Words to determine which Power Word best belongs in each of the blanks. Then write the appropriate Power Word in each blank. Use each Power Word only once.

1. Members of the feline (cat) family eat meat and thus are _____ , while members of the bovine (cow) family are strictly _____ , and members of the primate (human, monkey) family are _____ , although they tend to eat more fruit than flesh.

2. Most dogs have a keener _____ sense than humans, allowing them to follow a faint scent, and a keener auditory sense, allowing them to hear high-pitched whistles that are _____ to humans.

3. Since a _____ is a lover of books and a _____ loves or supports France, you can tell the Greek syllable "phil" must mean "love of."

4. Since a _____ is a helper of mankind (literally, a "lover" of mankind from the fact that "phil" means "love of") and a _____ is a hater of mankind, evidently "anthrop" means "relating to mankind."

Muscle Builder Analogies

Directions: Each exercise below is an analogy, with one or two terms missing. Choose the Power Word which belongs in each blank of the analogy so that the analogy reads correctly. Write the appropriate Power Word in each blank. Note that some of the Power Words will not be used.

1. EAR is to AUDITORY as NOSE is to _____

2. VEGETABLE is to HERBIVOROUS as MEAT is to _____

3. BOOKS is to BIBLIOPHILE as FRANCE is to _____

Word Power II

Directions: Study each of the Power Words below. Note how each word is pronounced. Then read the context sentences to figure out what each Power Word means. In the left-hand margin next to each Power Word, try to jot down a synonym or short definition which defines that word.

Power Words	compassionate	innovation	contemporaries	upheaval
	meticulous	emancipate	virtually	fidelity

---

1. **compassionate** | kəm **păsh′** ə nĭt |
   - A compassionate person offers comfort and solace in times of trouble.

2. **meticulous** | mə **tĭk′** yə ləs |
   - To gain time, the lawyer was meticulous in his cross-examination of the witness.
   - Isaac is so meticulous about his appearance that he spends hours in front of the mirror.

3. **innovation** | ĭn′ ə **vā′** shən |
   - Thomas Edison maintained that progress and innovation came from perspiration.
   - The telephone was a major innovation in communication.

4. **emancipate** | ĭ **măn′** sə pāt′ |
   - Death, he said, would emancipate him from his misery.
   - One major result of the Civil War was that slaves were emancipated.

5. **contemporaries** | kən **tĕm′** pə rĕr′ ēs |
   - An artist's contemporaries, the people of his time, may judge him differently than will posterity.

6. **virtually** | **vûr′** chōō′ ə lē |
   - Beethoven was virtually deaf when he composed his last great symphonies.
   - In many countries, virtually the only decision maker is the president or the dictator.

7. **upheaval** | ŭp **hē′** vəl |
   - The revolution and disruptive upheaval were followed by a new government.
   - When Mrs. Owen's husband died, she experienced a great upheaval in her lifestyle.

8. **fidelity** | fĭ **dĕl′** ĭ tē |
   - Fidelity in a marriage means being faithful to one's spouse, while fidelity in sound equipment means reproducing sounds accurately.

ă pat / ā pay / â care / ä father / ĕ pet / ē be / ĭ pit / ī pie / î fierce / ŏ pot / ō go / ô paw, for / oi oil / ŏŏ book /
ōō boot / ou out / ŭ cut / û fur / *th* the / th thin / hw which / zh vision / ə ago, item, pencil, atom, circus

Meaning Comprehension

Directions: Use what you have learned from the context sentences to identify the correct definition of each Power Word. In the blank next to each Power Word, write the letter of its correct definition.

Power Words	Definitions
_____ compassionate	a. faithfulness; accuracy
_____ meticulous	b. sympathetic, caring
_____ innovation	c. almost, for all practical purposes
_____ emancipate	d. extreme care for details, unduly fussy
_____ contemporaries	e. extreme agitation or disorder
_____ virtually	f. free, release from bondage
_____ upheaval	g. people living at the same time
_____ fidelity	h. a new device or idea; an improvement

Context Application

Directions: Each of the following sentences has two blanks. Use what you have learned about the Power Words to determine which Power Word best belongs in each of the blanks. Then write the appropriate Power Word in each blank. Use each Power Word only once.

1. The Wright brothers' _____ in transportation, the airplane, was ridiculed by many of their _____

2. It took a national _____ , the Civil War of 1861-1865, to _____ the American slaves.

3. In the play *The Odd Couple*, Felix is so neat and _____ , it is _____ impossible to live with him and maintain one's sanity.

4. The honesty and _____ in their marriage stemmed from their both being _____ people.

Muscle Builder Analogies

Directions: Each exercise below is an analogy, with one or two terms missing. Choose the Power Word which belongs in each blank of the analogy so that the analogy reads correctly. Write the appropriate Power Word in each blank. Note that some of the Power Words will not be used.

1. AGITATION is to UPHEAVAL as SYMPATHETIC is to

   _____

2. FUSSY is to METICULOUS as FAITHFULNESS is to

   _____

3. AID is to HARM as _____ is to ENSLAVE

INTRODUCTION

A large amount of reading material—textbooks, instruction manuals, schematic diagrams, maps, charts—present information about geometrical and geographical descriptions which you must be able to follow precisely and comprehend clearly, or the meaning of the entire material can be lost.

This unit will strengthen your sense of direction, your spatial organization skills, and your ability to visualize and draw the ideas presented through written descriptions of spatial relationships.

It will also deepen your understanding of and ability to apply everyday arithmetic and geometry, which are so important in reading maps, graphs, diagrams, charts, instruction sheets, and text material in the social and physical sciences, business, and real-life.

INSTRUCTIONS FOR THE EXERCISES

The exercises in this unit present spatial relationships which you will be asked to interpret and then represent in a diagram. For most of the exercises a grid marked off in squares is provided. You will read a written description of a spatial relationship and then diagram this information on the grid. To illustrate the procedure you will follow for these exercises, here are two examples.

EXAMPLE 1

For the exercise which follows, <u>let the length of one square represent one mile</u>. Also, <u>let the direction of any line be defined by the compass</u>. The diagram below illustrates the distance and direction of different lines starting from point X. Study this diagram. Then try the exercise beneath it.

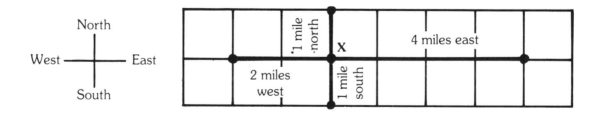

Exercise: *Starting at point A, draw a line extending 3 miles east.*

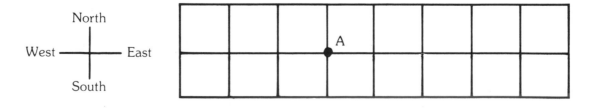

ANSWER: Here is how you should have drawn the line.

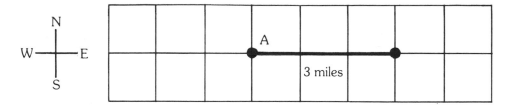

Note that the line extends across three squares because the length of a square in this exercise represents 1 mile. So, 3 squares equal 3 miles. Also, the line extends to the right from point A because the compass shows that <u>east</u> is to the right.

EXAMPLE 2

For this exercise, <u>let the length of one square represent 5 miles,</u> as shown in these illustrations.

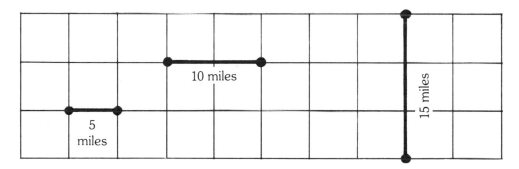

<u>Exercise:</u> *Starting at point P, a car travelled 10 miles south, 15 miles west, 10 miles north, and then back to point P. Draw the path of the car.*

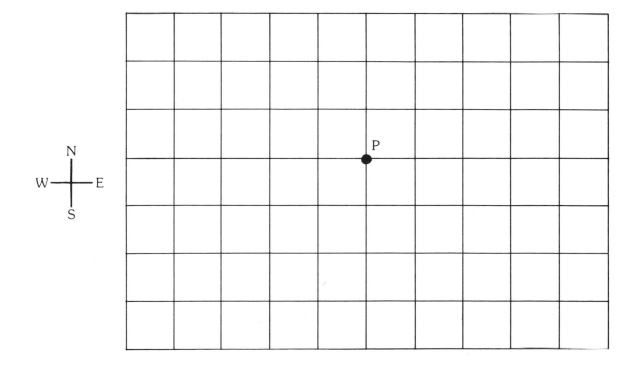

ANSWER: Here is the path of the car.

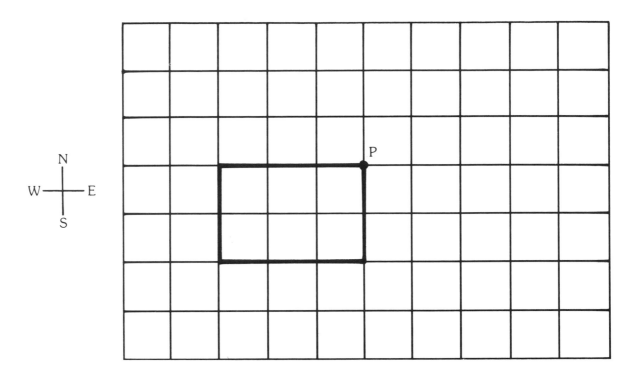

The first line drawn extends two squares to the south because the length of a square in this exercise equals 5 miles. Similarly, the second line extends three squares to the west ("15 miles west"), the third line extends two squares to the north ("10 miles north"), and the final line extends back to point P ("and then back to point P").

Begin now with the exercises commencing on the next page.

EXERCISE 1

For this exercise, let the length of one square represent 2 miles, as shown in these illustrations.

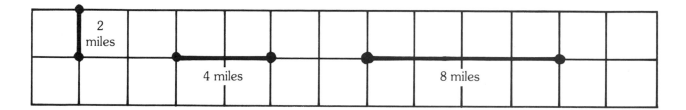

Starting at point A, draw a line extending 6 miles west.

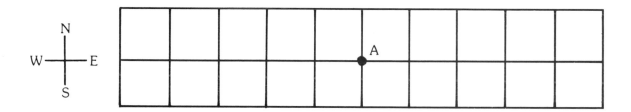

EXERCISE 2

For this exercise, let the length of one square represent 3 miles.

Starting at point P, draw a line extending 12 miles south.

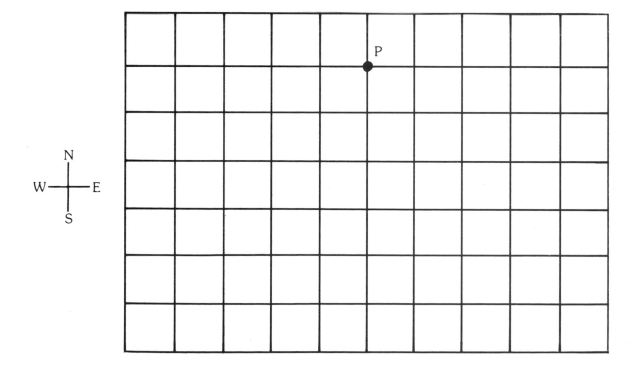

EXERCISE 3

Let the length of one square equal 3 miles.

(A) From the gas station, a car travelled 6 miles west, then 12 miles south. Draw the path of the car.

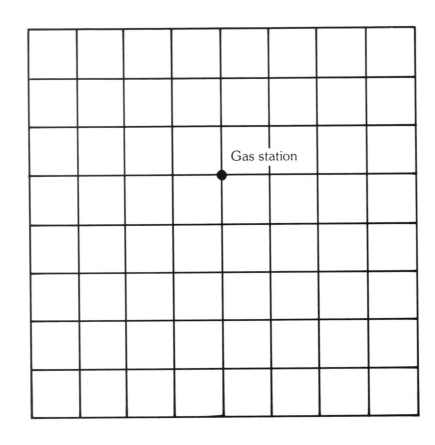

(B) How many total miles did the car travel? _____

EXERCISE 4

Let the length of one square equal 1 inch.

A caterpillar drank from a puddle of spilt alcohol and became intoxicated. The caterpillar staggered 2 inches east, 1 inch south, 2 inches east, 1 inch south, and continued in this pattern until it had staggered a total of 12 inches. Then the caterpillar fell asleep. Draw the entire path the caterpillar staggered.

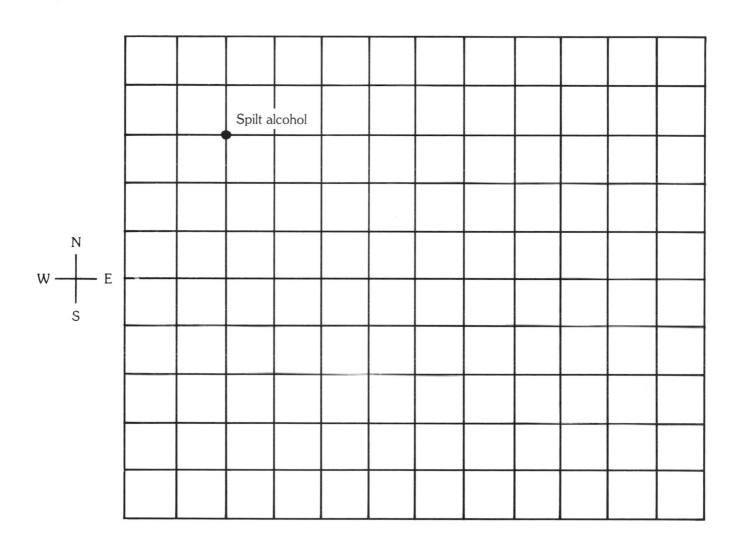

EXERCISE 5

Let the length of one square equal 2 yards.

(A) Starting at point A, the borders of a garden run 10 yards east, 6 yards north, 10 yards west, and then back to point A. Make a diagram of the garden with the lengths written next to each side.

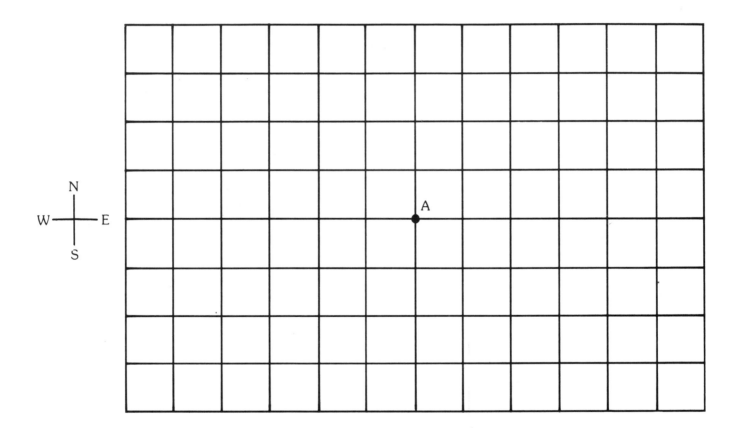

(B) What is the total distance around the garden (the garden's perimeter)? _____

EXERCISE 6

Let the length of one square equal 3 miles.

(A) A ship left the dock, travelled 12 miles south, 3 miles east, 6 miles south, 9 miles east, straight north until it was directly east of the dock, and then straight west back to the dock. Make a diagram of the ship's path with the distances written next to every section of the trip.

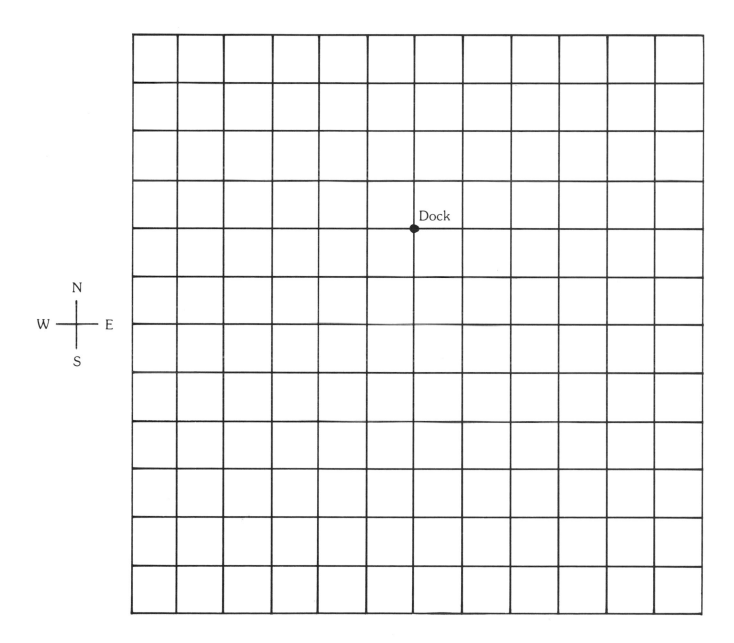

(B) What was the total distance travelled by the ship? _____

EXERCISE 7

Let the length of one square represent 4 miles.

(A) From the northeast corner of Mr. Scrooge's estate, the surrounding brick wall runs 16 miles south, 12 miles west, 8 miles north, 20 miles west, 8 miles south, 12 miles west, north to an oak tree which is directly west of the northeast corner, and then straight east back to the northeast corner. Draw the brick wall around the estate, writing the length for all sides.

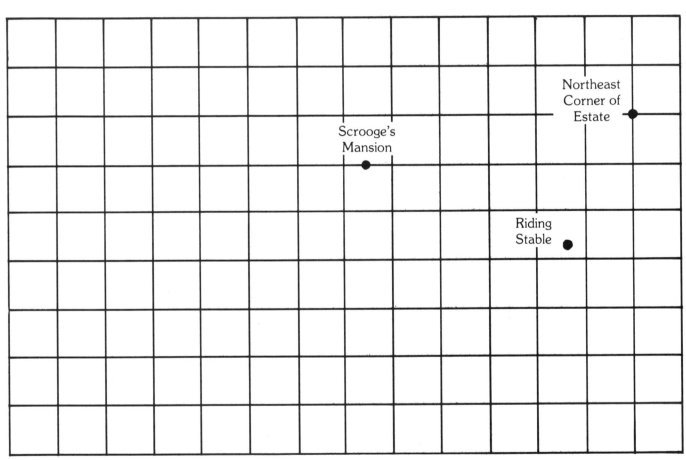

(B) Mr. Scrooge has decided that he wants to string barbed-wire fencing along the top of the entire brick wall. How many miles of barbed-wire fencing will he need? _____

(C) Draw an 'X' on the diagram at the point where the oak tree is located.

EXERCISE 8

Let the length of one square represent 1 mile.

(A) From where a reconnaissance helicopter pilot first sighted what she took to be an enemy nuclear submarine at the edge of her country's territorial waters, she pursued the vessel north 7 miles, east 2 miles, north 1 mile, east 5 miles, south 3 miles, east 2 miles, straight south until she was due east from the point of first sighting, west to that point—and then the vessel abruptly disappeared. Draw the path of the vessel, with the length written for each section. (NOTE: You may find it helpful to cross out each part of the problem after you draw it.)

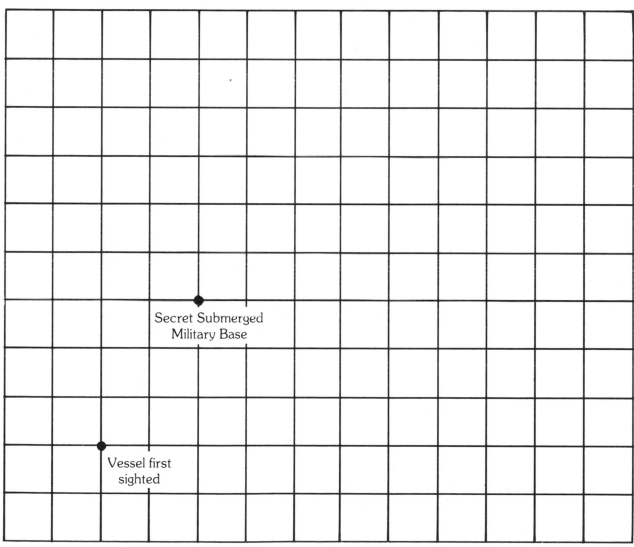

Secret Submerged
Military Base

Vessel first
sighted

(B) What was the total distance travelled by the vessel? _____

EXERCISE 9

Let the length of one square equal 2 feet.

(A) A political prisoner wanted to memorize the shape of a totally dark room in which he was confined, so he walked along the walls counting off the number of steps he took in his stocking feet, knowing that each step was exactly one foot long. Starting at the corner with the sink, he walked 10 ft., turned right and went 6 ft., turned right again for 4 ft., right for 2 ft., left for 4 ft., left for 6 ft., right for 2 ft., and then right again until he found himself back at the sink, although he lost count in measuring the length of the final wall. Draw a diagram of the room with the length written for each wall. (NOTE: The prisoner didn't know in which directions were north, south, east and west, so you can draw the room in any orientation.)

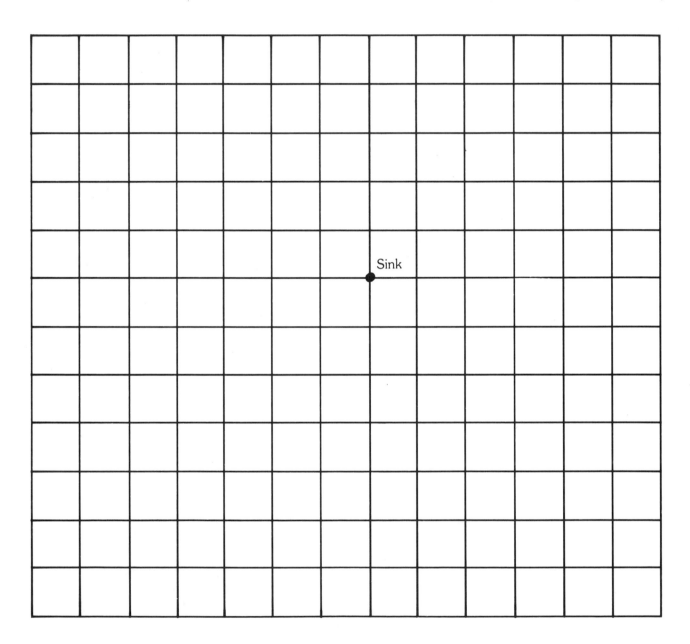

(B) If the captors want to string an electrified wire along the walls around the entire room, how many feet of wire will be needed? _____

EXERCISE 10

Let the length of a <u>square's diagonal</u> equal 2 miles, as shown in these illustrations.

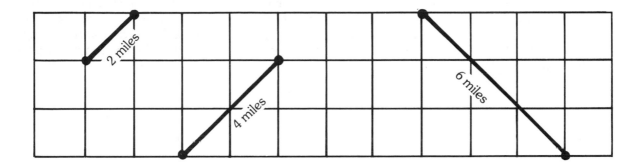

(A) Starting at point A, the borders of a military complex run 6 miles northwest, 8 miles northeast, 4 miles southeast, 6 miles southwest, straight southeast to a position directly northeast of point A, and then southwest straight back to point A. Draw the military complex with the lengths written on each side.

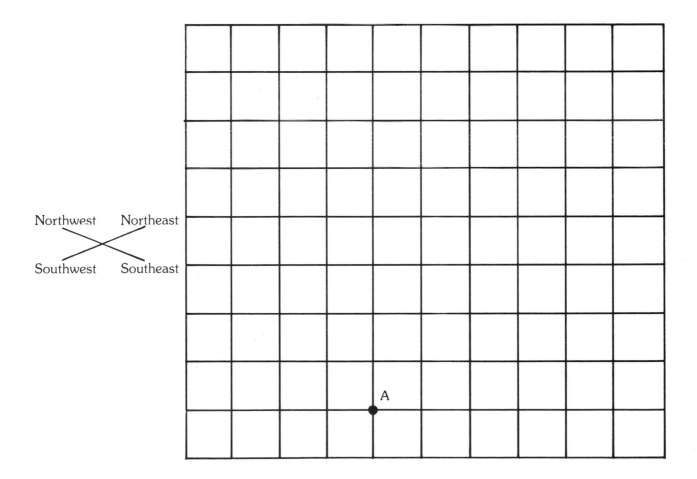

(B) What is the total distance around the military complex (the complex's perimeter)? _____

EXERCISE 11

Let the length of one square's diagonal equal 3 yards.

(A) Starting at point P, the borders of a garden run southeast for 15 yards, southwest for 3 yards, northwest for 6 yards, southwest for 6 yards, northwest for 3 yards, southwest for 3 yards, straight northwest to a position directly southwest of point P, and then straight back to point P. Draw the garden with the length written on each side. (NOTE: You may find it helpful to cross out each part of the written description after you draw that part.)

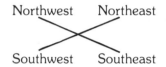

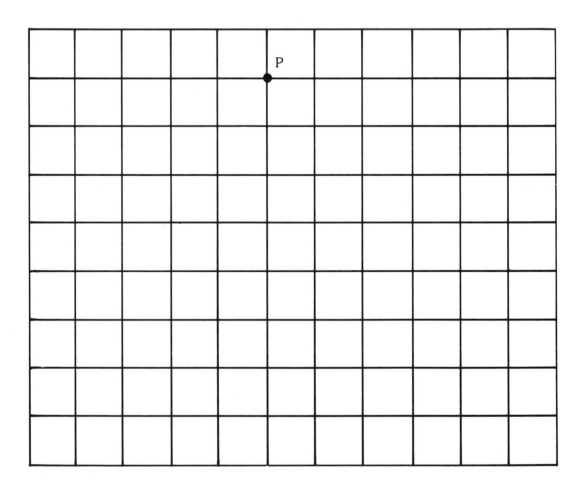

(B) What is the length of the garden's perimeter? _____

EXERCISE 12

Webster's New Collegiate Dictionary defines "cross of Lorraine" as: a cross with two crossbars having the upper one intersecting the upright above its middle and the lower one which is longer than the upper one intersecting the upright below its middle.

From this description, draw a "cross of Lorraine" in the space below.

EXERCISE 13

Draw this situation in the space below: There are four squares and inside each square there are three circles.

EXERCISE 14

Draw this situation in the space below: There are three circles and inside each circle there are two squares and two triangles.

EXERCISE 15

A) Draw this situation in the space below: There are three squares. Inside one square there are two circles and one triangle, inside another square there are two triangles and one circle, and inside the third square there is one triangle.

B) How many triangles are there altogether? _____

EXERCISE 16

A) Draw this situation in the space below: There are two large squares, and inside each large square there are two smaller squares, and inside each of these smaller squares there are three even smaller squares.

B) How many total squares are there? _____

EXERCISE 17

Draw this situation in the space below: There is a large square-shaped office space. This large space has been divided into three equal-sized rooms. In one room there is a rectangular table and a square desk. In the second room there is a circular table and a rectangular desk. In the third room there are three circular tables.

EXERCISE 18

Draw a diagram which shows the following situation in the space below: Camille has created a rectangular-shaped garden that measures 14 feet wide and 28 feet long. She intends to arrange the garden in the following way. First, she will divide the garden into two equal-sized squares. In one of these squares she will plant only corn. She will split the second square into two rectangles. In one of these rectangles she will plant only potatoes. In the second rectangle she will plant tomatoes and green beans. (NOTE: On your diagram, be sure to write the plants Camille intends to grow in each section of her garden. Also, write the length in feet of each side of each section of the garden.)

SPATIAL DESCRIPTIONS AND MAPS

The reading of maps and the comprehension of geographical relationships are heavily dependent on the ability to analyze and interpret the spatial information shown on the map. The following exercises will develop your ability to apply the spatial comprehension skills you have been building throughout this unit to the understanding of the geographical information presented on maps.

To solve each of the following exercises, refer to the map on page 63. NOTE: Use the lines of longitude and latitude on this map to determine directions. Longitude lines run from the bottom of the map (south) to the top (north). Latitude lines run from the left side of the map (west) to the right side (east).

EXERCISE 19

Check (√) the correct statement.

☐ (A) England and France are on the same body of land.
☐ (B) England is on a separate island from the body of land on which France is found.

EXERCISE 20

Check the correct statement.

☐ (A) England and Scotland are on the same island.
☐ (B) England and Scotland are on different islands.

EXERCISE 21

Check the correct statement.

☐ (A) England and Ireland are on the same island.
☐ (B) England and Ireland are on different islands.

EXERCISE 22

Which body of water separates England from France?

☐ (A) North Sea   ☐ (B) English Channel   ☐ (C) Bay of Biscay

---

EXERCISE 23

Which country is approximately one-half the size of Poland?

☐ (A) Spain   ☐ (B) Rumania   ☐ (C) Czechoslovakia

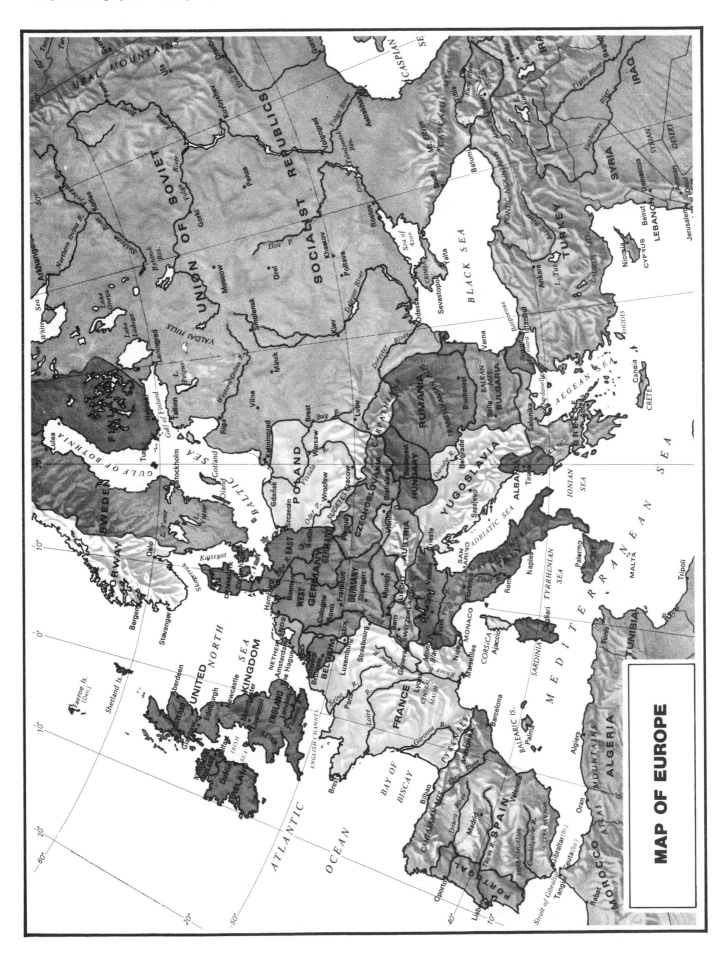

MAP OF EUROPE

EXERCISE 24

Check the correct statement.

☐ (A) Madrid is in Ireland and Dublin is in Spain.
☐ (B) Madrid is in Spain and Dublin is in Ireland.

EXERCISE 25

Merchandise can be shipped from Warsaw to Cracow on which river?

☐ (A) Rhine　　☐ (B) Thames　　☐ (C) Elbe　　☐ (D) Vistula

EXERCISE 26

Merchandise can be shipped from Lyons to Marseilles on which river?

☐ (A) Rhine　　☐ (B) Mississippi　　☐ (C) Saone　　☐ (D) Rhone

EXERCISE 27

Which river runs through London?

☐ (A) Ebro　　☐ (B) Wales　　☐ (C) Thames　　☐ (D) Danube

EXERCISE 28

Check the correct statement.

☐ (A) England is west of Poland.
☐ (B) England is east of Poland.

EXERCISE 29

Check the correct statement.

☐ (A) Italy is south of Sweden.
☐ (B) Italy is north of Sweden.

EXERCISE 30

If you flew from London to Berlin you would have travelled generally

☐ (A) north　　☐ (B) west　　☐ (C) east　　☐ (D) south

EXERCISE 31

If you flew from Paris to Florence and then to Munich you would have travelled generally

- ☐ (A) northwest first, and then north
- ☐ (B) southwest first, and then north
- ☐ (C) southeast first, and then north

EXERCISE 32

If you flew from Belgrade to Moscow and then to Newcastle, your trip would have taken you generally

- ☐ (A) northwest, and then east
- ☐ (B) northeast, and then east
- ☐ (C) northeast, and then west

EXERCISE 33

With respect to Madrid, Naples is

☐ (A) north   ☐ (B) east   ☐ (C) south   ☐ (D) west

EXERCISE 34

With respect to Berlin, Naples is

☐ (A) east   ☐ (B) north   ☐ (C) west   ☐ (D) south

EXERCISE 35

With respect to Minsk, Oslo is

☐ (A) southeast   ☐ (B) southwest   ☐ (C) northeast   ☐ (D) northwest

EXERCISE 36

With respect to Paris, Beirut is

☐ (A) southwest   ☐ (B) northwest   ☐ (C) southeast   ☐ (D) northeast

Word Power III

Directions: Study each of the Power Words below. Note how each word is pronounced. Then read the context sentences to figure out what each Power Word means. In the left-hand margin next to each Power Word, try to jot down a synonym or short definition which defines that word.

Power Words	verbatim	marital	reciprocal	paradox
	fortuitous	cacophony	exorbitant	gourmet

1. **verbatim** | vər **bā′** tĭm |
   - Jack could quote the law verbatim, yet never obeyed it.
   - Elena has used that excuse so often that I know it verbatim.

2. **fortuitous** | fôr **tōo′** ĭ təs |
   - Fortuitously, the test contained questions on exactly the topics he studied.
   - I got the job due to a fortuitous event; the very day I applied someone had quit.

3. **marital** | **măr′** ĭ təl |
   - They took their marital vows in an outdoor wedding.
   - Disagreements between husband and wife about money are the most common cause of marital arguments.

4. **cacophony** | kə **kŏf′** ə nē |
   - The cacophony of a beginner learning the trumpet can produce severe headaches.
   - An alarmed parrot produces quite a cacophony.

5. **reciprocal** | rĭ **sĭp′** rə kəl |
   - Two countries may establish a reciprocal trade agreement to stimulate both their economies.

6. **exorbitant** | ĭg **zôr′** bĭ tənt |
   - The price of gasoline has become exorbitant.
   - Hasn't Ari been absent for an exorbitant length of time?

7. **paradox** | **păr′** ə dŏks′ |
   - It seems paradoxical that Florence desires friends so greatly yet is hostile to everyone.
   - "Everything I say is a lie" is an example of a paradox.

8. **gourmet** | **gŏor′** mā′ |
   - A gourmet enjoys only fine food, while a gourmand likes excessive amounts of fine food.
   - Juanita is such a gourmet that she only enjoys eating at the best restaurants.

ă pat / ā pay / â care / ä father / ĕ pet / ē be / ĭ pit / ī pie / î fierce / ŏ pot / ō go / ô paw, for / oi oil / ŏŏ book /
ōō boot / ou out / ŭ cut / û fur / th the / th thin / hw which / zh vision / ə ago, item, pencil, atom, circus

Meaning Comprehension

Directions: Use what you have learned from the context sentences to identify the correct definition of each Power Word. In the blank next to each Power Word, write the letter of its correct definition.

Power Words

_____ verbatim
_____ fortuitous
_____ marital
_____ cacophony
_____ reciprocal
_____ exorbitant
_____ paradox
_____ gourmet

Definitions

a. a seeming contradiction
b. judge of fine food and drink
c. affecting both parties equally, mutual
d. unpleasant, harsh sound
e. more than appropriate, excessive
f. relating to marriage
g. in the exact words, word for word
h. lucky, fortunate, occurring by chance

Context Application

Directions: Each of the following sentences has two blanks. Use what you have learned about the Power Words to determine which Power Word best belongs in each of the blanks. Then write the appropriate Power Word in each blank. Use each Power Word only once.

1. She quoted _____ the professor's words, "The universe must have had a beginning, but how could anything come from nothing," yet her mind could not resolve the _____ .

2. Mrs. Turner is a _____ , so it is _____ that her husband is the chef at a fine restaurant.

3. For a good _____ relationship, the love between husband and wife should be _____ .

4. A music critic who went to the rock concert claimed he paid an _____ price to sit through three hours of solid _____ .

Muscle Builder Analogies

Directions: Each exercise below is an analogy, with one or two terms missing. Choose the Power Word which belongs in each blank of the analogy so that the analogy reads correctly. Write the appropriate Power Word in each blank. Note that some of the Power Words will not be used.

1. GLARE is to LIGHT as _____ is to SOUND

2. ART is to COLLECTOR as FOOD is to _____

3. SPARSE is to EXORBITANT as UNFORTUNATE is to

_____ .

Word Power IV

Directions: Study each of the Power Words below. Note how each word is pronounced. Then read the context sentences to figure out what each Power Word means. In the left-hand margin next to each Power Word, try to jot down a synonym or short definition which defines that word.

Power Words

impromptu	skepticism	scrutinized	vigilance
statute	adhere	impenetrable	nullified

---

1. **impromptu** | ĭm **prŏmp'** toō' |
   - The comedian had not rehearsed but gave an impromptu performance.
   - Luther sang impromptu for the children.

2. **statute** | **stăch'** ōot |
   - The statutes of the county prohibit the consumption of alcohol.
   - According to the new statute, all eighteen year old males must register for the military draft.

3. **skepticism** | **skĕp'** tĭ sĭz' əm |
   - She listened to the flying saucer tale with a skeptical ear.
   - Mr. Ramirez's skepticism was catchy and soon nobody favored the project.

4. **adhere** | ăd **hîr'** |
   - An athlete must adhere to a rigorous training schedule.
   - Adhere to your beliefs even in the face of great skepticism.

5. **scrutinized** | **skroōt'** n īzd |
   - The detective scrutinized the room for evidence.
   - The teacher scrutinized the papers for grammatical errors.

6. **impenetrable** | ĭm **pĕn'** ĭ trə bəl |
   - Pat had erected impenetrable personality defenses to protect his once-broken heart.
   - A successful fortress must be impenetrable to attackers.

7. **vigilance** | **vĭj'** ə ləns |
   - The Food and Drug Administration maintains a continual vigilance against the spread of disease.
   - Her vigilance enabled her to see the enemy before they saw her.

8. **nullified** | **nŭl'** ə fĭd |
   - An antacid is taken to nullify excessive stomach acid.
   - Because both parties failed to live up to the terms of the contract, the contract was nullified.

ă pat / ā pay / â care / ä father / ĕ pet / ē be / ĭ pit / ī pie / î fierce / ŏ pot / ō go / ô paw, for / oi oil / ŏŏ book /
ōō boot / ou out / ŭ cut / ū fur / *th* the / th thin / hw which / zh vision / ə ago, item, pencil, atom, circus

Meaning Comprehension

Directions: Use what you have learned from the context sentences to identify the correct definition of each Power Word. In the blank next to each Power Word, write the letter of its correct definition.

Power Words

_____ impromptu
_____ statute
_____ skepticism
_____ adhere
_____ scrutinized
_____ impenetrable
_____ vigilance
_____ nullified

Definitions

a. made null, reduced to nothing
b. examined closely
c. on the spur of the moment, without preparation
d. law
e. not capable of being penetrated or pierced
f. an attitude of doubt
g. stick to or by
h. watchfulness against danger

Context Application

Directions: Each of the following sentences has two blanks. Use what you have learned about the Power Words to determine which Power Word best belongs in each of the blanks. Then write the appropriate Power Word in each blank. Use each Power Word only once.

1. An _____ speech should not be _____ as critically as a planned speech.

2. A _____ which no longer serves a purpose in protecting humans or the things they care about may be _____ by a popular vote.

3. Because he had been lied to frequently, his vigilance was constant and his _____ was strong and _____ .

4. Military leaders insist that we must _____ to a policy of _____ against attack, lest we be surprised.

Muscle Builder Analogies

Directions: Each exercise below is an analogy, with one or two terms missing. Choose the Power Word which belongs in each blank of the analogy so that the analogy reads correctly. Write the appropriate Power Word in each blank. Note that some of the Power Words will not be used.

1. CARELESS is to CAREFUL as SKIMMED is to _____

2. RELIGIOUS is to HERETICAL as FAITH is to _____

3. EXPECTED is to SURPRISING as PLANNED is to

_____

ADDITIONAL ASSIGNMENTS

1. Write a problem like number 8 on the lines below. You may use one of the grids which follow on the next pages to help you write the problem. Let a peer use one of the other grids in solving the problem.

_____

_____

_____

_____

2. Write a problem like number 9 on the lines below. Use the grids which follow on the next pages in writing the problem and having a peer solve it.

_____

_____

_____

_____

3. Write a problem like number 11 on the lines below. Use the grids which follow on the next pages in writing the problem and having a peer solve it.

_____

_____

_____

_____

4. Using what you have learned about the meaning of "bibliophile" (page 42), write a sentence on the lines below in which the meaning of "bibliophile" is given by contrast (Case III).

_____

_____

5. Using what you have learned about the meaning of "innovation" (page 44), write a sentence on the lines below in which the meaning of "innovation" is stated without punctuation (Case II).

_____

_____

Use this grid to complete Additional Assignment #1.

Use this grid to complete Additional Assignment #1.

Use this grid to complete Additional Assignment #2.

Use this grid to complete Additional Assignment #2.

Use this grid to complete Additional Assignment #3.

Use this grid to complete Additional Assignment #3.

UNIT
4

WRITTEN DESCRIPTIONS OF ORDER: TIME AND SIZE

OBJECTIVES: When you have completed this unit you should

- be able to comprehend and represent with a diagram written descriptions of serial order;
- know the meanings of the following POWER WORDS.

POWER WORDS

figment	remiss	celibacy	destitute
regicide	pariah	intimidated	panacea
dearth	nefarious	surreptitiously	euphoria
euphemistic	omnipotent	autobiography	indolent
construed	procrastinator	lecherousness	alleviate
genocide	mercenary	amphibious	eulogize
apparition	omniscient	virtuoso	depleted
plagiarism	ostracized	predilection	fiasco

Word Power I

Directions: Study each of the Power Words below. Note how each word is pronounced. Then read the context sentences to figure out what each Power Word means. In the left-hand margin next to each Power Word, try to jot down a synonym or short definition which defines that word.

Power Words

figment	dearth	construed	apparition
regicide	euphemistic	genocide	plagiarism

---

1. **figment** | **fĭg′** mənt |
   - The child's story of thieves was not true but just a figment of her overactive imagination.

2. **regicide** | **rēj′** ə sīd′ |
   - Regicide was one means of becoming king in medieval Europe.
   - A case of regicide, the beheading of King Louis XVI, was one of the outcomes of the French Revolution.

3. **dearth** | dûrth |
   - A dearth of financial support caused the museum to close.
   - A rationing system was begun in response to the dearth of gasoline.

4. **euphemistic** | yōō′ fə **mĭs′** tĭk |
   - Calling the student's term paper "weak" was euphemistic since it was absolutely terrible and looked as if it had been written in fifteen minutes.
   - "Passed away" is a euphemistic phrase for "dead."

5. **construed** | kən **strōōd′** |
   - One football player construed the instructions incorrectly so the team lost its last game.
   - The three students each construed the teacher's question differently, and each gave a different answer.

6. **genocide** | **jĕn′** ə sīd′ |
   - Hitler attempted genocide of Germany's entire Jewish population.

7. **apparition** | ăp′ ə **rĭsh′** ən |
   - An apparition may not hurt you physically, but it can scare you to death.
   - On the dark, foggy night Joanna found it easy to believe that she had just seen an apparition.

8. **plagiarism** | **plā′** jə rĭz′ əm |
   - Copying something someone else wrote without giving them credit is called plagiarism.
   - Plagiarism usually violates the copyright laws.

ă pat / ā pay / â care / ä father / ĕ pet / ē be / ĭ pit / ī pie / î fierce / ŏ pot / ō go / ô paw, for / oi oil / ŏŏ book /
ōō boot / ou out / ŭ cut / û fur / *th* the / th thin / hw which / zh vision / ə ago, item, pencil, atom, circus

Meaning Comprehension

Directions: Use what you have learned from the context sentences to identify the correct definition of each Power Word. In the blank next to each Power Word, write the letter of its correct definition.

Power Words

_____ figment
_____ regicide
_____ dearth
_____ euphemistic
_____ construed
_____ genocide
_____ apparition
_____ plagiarism

Definitions

a. copying without giving credit
b. interpreted, understood
c. the killing of a king; the killer of a king
d. shortage, scarcity
e. killing of a racial or cultural group
f. something made up; something created in the mind but not real
g. using gentle, mild words instead of harsh words to describe something
h. ghost, phantom

Context Application

Directions: Each of the following sentences has two blanks. Use what you have learned about the Power Words to determine which Power Word best belongs in each of the blanks. Then write the appropriate Power Word in each blank. Use each Power Word only once.

1. The _____ of her dead brother which she saw one night was not real, but a _____ of her sorrowful, troubled mind.

2. _____ , killing of a racial or cultural group, and _____ , killing of a king, both contain the Latin root "cide," which means "killing" or "killer."

3. The _____ of evidence against the accused killer was _____ by the jury as a sign that the man was not guilty.

4. To say the student "borrowed" some ideas for his paper from the encyclopedia would be _____ since he actually copied whole paragraphs and was clearly guilty of _____ .

Muscle Builder Analogies

Directions: Each exercise below is an analogy, with one or two terms missing. Choose the Power Word which belongs in each blank of the analogy so that the analogy reads correctly. Write the appropriate Power Word in each blank. Note that some of the Power Words will not be used.

1. UNKIND is to KIND as HARSH is to _____

2. REAL is to IMAGINED as PERSON is to _____

3. _____ is to GROUP as _____ is to KING

Word Power II

Directions: Study each of the Power Words below. Note how each word is pronounced. Then read the context sentences to figure out what each Power Word means. In the left-hand margin next to each Power Word, try to jot down a synonym or short definition which defines that word.

Power Words

remiss	nefarious	procrastinator	omniscient
pariah	omnipotent	mercenary	ostracized

1. **remiss** | rĭ **mĭs′** |
   - Because the security staff was remiss in guarding the store, burglars were able to steal valuable merchandise.

2. **pariah** | pə **rī′** ə |
   - When he joined the motorcycle gang, Lucius became a pariah among his old, conservative friends.

3. **nefarious** | nə **fâr′** ē əs |
   - Hitler's nefarious acts of killing thousands of Jews and attacking peaceful nations were condemned worldwide.
   - She was expelled because of her nefarious activities.

4. **omnipotent** | ŏm′ **nĭp′** ə tənt |
   - The Egyptian pharaohs had absolute power and were as omnipotent as any humans have ever been.
   - Chris's confidence in her skills is so great that she feels omnipotent when she steps onto a tennis court.

5. **procrastinator** | prə **krăs′** tə nāt′ ər |
   - Every class has a few procrastinators who never do their homework on time.
   - An effective leader cannot be a procrastinator.

6. **mercenary** | **mûr′** sə nĕr′ ē |
   - Mercenary soldiers will fight for any country that pays them enough money.
   - That man is so mercenary he would sell his own mother!

7. **omniscient** | ŏm **nĭsh′** ənt |
   - God is said to be omniscient because nothing is hidden or unknown to Him.
   - Only a fool would believe he or she is omniscient.

8. **ostracized** | **ŏs′** trə sīzd |
   - Because of his rude manners, Mike was ostracized from the club.
   - Sigmund Freud was ostracized from the Vienna Medical Society due to his radical theories.

ă pat / ā pay / â care / ä father / ĕ pet / ē be / ĭ pit / ī pie / î fierce / ŏ pot / ō go / ô paw, for / oi oil / ŏŏ book /
ōō boot / ou out / ŭ cut / û fur / *th* the / th thin / hw which / zh vision / ə ago, item, pencil, atom, circus

Meaning Comprehension

Directions: Use what you have learned from the context sentences to identify the correct definition of each Power Word. In the blank next to each Power Word, write the letter of its correct definition.

Power Words

_____ remiss
_____ pariah
_____ nefarious
_____ omnipotent
_____ procrastinator
_____ mercenary
_____ omniscient
_____ ostracized

Definitions

a. one who puts off doing things because of laziness or irresponsibility
b. an outcast, a person despised or rejected by society
c. negligent in performing one's duty, careless
d. thrown out from society or some group, banished
e. all-powerful, almighty, having unlimited power
f. very wicked, vicious
g. knowing everything, knowing all
h. concerned primarily with money

Context Application

Directions: Each of the following sentences has two blanks. Use what you have learned about the Power Words to determine which Power Word best belongs in each of the blanks. Then write the appropriate Power Word in each blank. Use each Power Word only once.

1. A _____ person will engage in unlawful and even _____ acts as long as they bring him or her money.

2. A _____ is often _____ in meeting deadlines.

3. A _____ is one who is _____ by society.

4. _____, which means "all-knowing," and _____, which means "all-powerful," both contain the Latin root "omni," which means "all" or "every."

Muscle Builder Analogies

Directions: Each exercise below is an analogy, with one or two terms missing. Choose the Power Word which belongs in each blank of the analogy so that the analogy reads correctly. Write the appropriate Power Word in each blank. Note that some of the Power Words will not be used.

1. KNOWLEDGE is to _____ as POWER is to _____

2. LOVE is to ROMANTIC as MONEY is to _____

3. ENROLLEE is to ENROLLED as PARIAH is to _____

INTRODUCTION

A large proportion of reading material centers around descriptions of how things are ordered (arranged in sequence). The types of order commonly expressed in written material include chronological order, alphabetical order, and numerical order, as well as orders determined by procedure, priority, convenience, position, and scale (size, weight, etc.). The ability to reason out and comprehend descriptions of order is crucial to effective reading (and writing). In this unit, you will build your skills in comprehending written descriptions of order.

INSTRUCTIONS FOR THE EXERCISES

Each of the following exercises contains a written description of the order (sequence) of certain items of information. Read the description presented, and then use the diagram provided to illustrate the exact order described. Try the example below.

EXAMPLE:

Ed is taller than Jim but shorter than Willy. Write the names of the three men in order on the diagram.

taller

shorter

ANSWER: Here is how you should have written the three names.

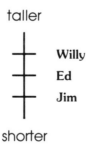

taller

Willy

Ed

Jim

shorter

According to the description, Ed is taller than Jim, so Ed comes above Jim on the scale. Also, Ed is shorter than Willy, so Ed comes below Willy. Thus, the order of the men from taller to shorter is: Willy, Ed, Jim.

Do each of the following exercises in the same manner.

EXERCISE 1

Gold is heavier than aluminum. Also, lead is heavier than gold. Write the names of the three metals in order on the diagram to the right.

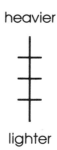

heavier

lighter

EXERCISE 2

Jim is heavier than Bill, but Jim is lighter than Bob. Write the names of the three men in order on the diagram to the right.

heavier

lighter

EXERCISE 3

Jim is heavier than Bill but lighter than Bob. Write the names of the three men on the diagram to the right.

heavier

lighter

EXERCISE 4

A. Check to see that your answers to Exercises 2 and 3 are the same.

You can conclude then that the following two statements have the same meaning:

— **Jim is heavier than Bill but lighter than Bob.**
— **Jim is heavier than Bill, but Jim is lighter than Bob.**

B. (Now try this problem.) Atlanta has a larger population than Birmingham but a smaller population than Chicago. Write the names of the three cities in order on the diagram to the right.

larger population

smaller population

EXERCISE 5

Among famous 19th-century painters, Gauguin was born before van Gogh but after Whistler. Matisse was born after van Gogh. Write the names of the four artists in order on the diagram to the right.

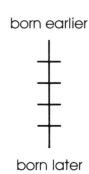

EXERCISE 6

Among famous 19th-century composers, Sullivan was born after Dvorak. Debussy was born before Stravinsky but after Sullivan. Write the names of the four composers in order on the diagram.

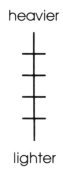

EXERCISE 7

A. June and Sally are both heavier than Arlene. Dorothy is heavier than Sally but lighter than June. Write the names of the four women in order on the diagram.

B. Sally is heavier than Arlene. Dorothy is heavier than Sally but lighter than June. Write the names of the four women in order on the diagram.

C. Check to see that your answers to parts A and B are the same. On both diagrams, June should be at the top and Arlene should be at the bottom.

What is the name of the woman who comes immediately below June on both diagrams?
_____

"STEP-BY-STEP ANALYSIS"

In solving complicated serial order problems you must carefully work through the information in a step-by-step fashion. You will often find that you must create a different rough "working-diagram" for each step of your problem solving process. As a final step, you will combine all of your rough working-diagrams into one complete, final diagram.

To illustrate this, here is how you could work out the solution to Exercise 7A, step-by-step.

STEP 1—Represent the first sentence of the problem with a working-diagram: *June and Sally are both heavier than Arlene.*

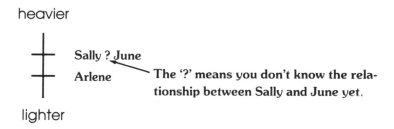

heavier

Sally ? June

Arlene   The '?' means you don't know the relationship between Sally and June yet.

lighter

STEP 2—Represent the second sentence of the problem with another working-diagram: *Dorothy is heavier than Sally but lighter than June.*

heavier

June

Dorothy

Sally

lighter

STEP 3—Combine all of the information from your two working-diagrams into one final diagram.

From STEP 2, you can see that Sally is at the bottom of the working-diagram. Then, from STEP 1, you can see that Arlene is below (lighter than) Sally. Thus, the final diagram must look like the one at the top of the next page.

heavier

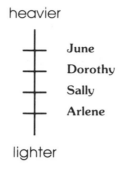

June

Dorothy

Sally

Arlene

lighter

Apply careful step-by-step analysis to solve the remaining exercises. For each exercise, use as many rough working-diagrams as you find helpful. Then combine the information from your working-diagrams into the final diagram of the solution.

EXERCISE 8

Althea and Gwen are both slower than Faye. Estella is faster than Althea but slower than Gwen. Write the names of the four women in order on the diagram.

faster

slower

EXERCISE 9

A. Statistics collected in 1981 revealed that *Woman's Day* and *TV Guide* had a larger circulation than *Time*. Also, *Reader's Digest* had a larger circulation than *Woman's Day*, but a smaller circulation than *TV Guide*. Write the four magazines in order on the diagram.

larger circulation

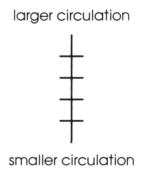

smaller circulation

B. In 1981 a survey found that *Woman's Day* had a larger circulation than *Time*. Also, *Reader's Digest* had a larger circulation than *Woman's Day*, but a smaller circulation than *TV Guide*. Write the four magazines in order on the diagram.

larger circulation

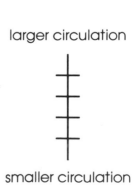

smaller circulation

C. Check to see that your answers to parts A and B are alike.

What is the magazine with the largest circulation? _____

EXERCISE 10

Prominent contributors to the invention and development of the automobile include Karl Benz (Mercedes-Benz), who was born before another contributor, Henry Ford, but after Gottlieb Daimler. Rudolf Diesel (diesel engine) was born after Karl Benz but before Henry Ford. Write the names of the four inventors in order on the diagram.

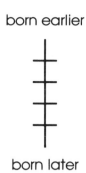

born earlier

born later

EXERCISE 11

The Amazon River, which winds for 4,000 miles through South America, is somewhat shorter than the Nile. The Mississippi River is shorter than one of its tributaries, the Missouri River. The Missouri River is shorter than the South American river mentioned earlier. Write the four rivers in order on the diagram.

(REMINDER: Work step-by-step. You may have to use several working-diagrams before you can put all of the information onto the final diagram.)

longer

shorter

EXERCISE 12

Of the presidents who preceded Lincoln, Fillmore served before Pierce but after Taylor. Buchanan served before Lincoln. And Pierce served before Buchanan. Write the names of the five presidents in order on the diagram.

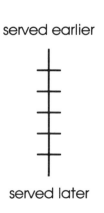

served earlier

served later

EXERCISE 13

A is greater than B. C is greater than D. E is smaller than B but greater than C. Write the five letters in order on the diagram.

(REMINDER: Make as many rough working-diagrams as you find helpful.)

greater

less

EXERCISE 14

Al is taller than Bob but shorter than Carl. Doug is taller than Ed. Frank is taller than Carl but shorter than Ed. Write the six names in order on the diagram.

taller

shorter

EXERCISE 15

Bell invented the telephone before Edison invented the electric light. Morse invented the telegraph before Otto invented the gas engine. Marconi invented the wireless before the Wright brothers flew their airplane. Furthermore, the gas engine was invented before the telephone. And the wireless was invented after the electric light.

Six inventors and their inventions are listed below. Write the inventors only in order on the diagram.

Bell—Telephone
Edison—Electric Light
Morse—Telegraph

Otto—Gas Engine
Marconi—Wireless
Wright brothers—Airplane

earlier

later

EXERCISE 16

Al is heavier than Fred. Pete is heavier than Don. Paul is heavier than Pedro. Gus is heavier than Al but lighter than Don. Harvey is heavier than Pete but lighter than Pedro. Write the eight names in order on the diagram.

(REMINDER: Make as many rough working-diagrams as you find helpful.)

EXERCISE 17

Clarence worked in Phoenix one year. The preceding year he worked in Chicago. And the year preceding that he worked in San Francisco. Show the three cities in order on the diagram.

EXERCISE 18

A. Carole is working in Miami this year. Over the preceding three years she worked first in Los Angeles, then in San Diego, and after that in New Orleans. Show the four cities in order on the diagram. (HINT: She worked in Los Angeles before San Diego.)

B. Carole first worked in Los Angeles, and in successive years in San Diego, New Orleans, and Miami. Show the four cities in order on the diagram.

C. Check to see that your answers to parts A and B are the same.

Which was the second city Carole worked in? _____

EXERCISE 19

A. Among American presidents, Madison preceded Monroe. Moreover, Madison was preceded by Jefferson. Write the names of these three presidents in order on the diagram.

earlier

later

B. Check (√) the statement which means the same as "Madison preceded Monroe."

_____ Madison came after Monroe
_____ Monroe preceded Madison
_____ Monroe was preceded by Madison
_____ Monroe was succeeded by Madison

EXERCISE 20

A. Among American presidents, Grant succeeded Johnson. Also, Grant was succeeded by Hayes. Write the names of these three presidents in order on the diagram.

earlier

later

B. Check (√) the statement which means the same as "Hayes succeeded Grant."

_____ Grant succeeded Hayes
_____ Hayes preceded Grant
_____ Grant was succeeded by Hayes
_____ Grant was preceded by Hayes

EXERCISE 21

A. In order of birth, John was preceded by Holly but succeeded by José, who, in turn, was succeeded by Darryl. Write the four names in order on the diagram.

older

younger

B. In order of birth, John was preceded by Holly. But John was succeeded by José. José was succeeded by Darryl. Write the four names in order on the diagram.

older

younger

C. Check to see that your answers to parts A and B are the same.

EXERCISE 22

A. Roberto's occupation requires that he change cities annually. In 1981 he worked in Washington, D.C. Several years earlier he had worked in Montgomery, and then successively in Salem, Miami, and Jacksonville. The year after he was in Jacksonville was the year Roberto spent in Washington, D.C., which was mentioned previously. Write the cities in order on the diagram.

earlier

later

B. In what year did Roberto work in Jacksonville? _____

C. In what year did Roberto work in Montgomery? _____

EXERCISE 23

Bob lives in San Francisco but spent two nonconsecutive Christmases in
Madrid, Spain. He spent his second Christmas in Madrid in 1978.

A. Write <u>Madrid—2nd Visit</u> next to 1978 on the diagram.

B. Was Bob's first visit to Madrid before or after 1978?

    _____ before 1978   _____ after 1978

1975 —
1976 —
1977 —
1978 —
1979 —
1980 —
1981 —

The Christmas after Bob's first visit to Madrid he spent in New York. Bob's
second visit to Madrid was the year after the Christmas in New York.

C. Write <u>New York</u> on the diagram next to the year Bob was there.

D. Write <u>Madrid—1st Visit</u> on the diagram next to the correct year.

E. What year was Bob's first Christmas in Madrid?_____

EXERCISE 24

A. Thelma spent two enjoyable summers in Atlantic City, the second one in
1980. The summer after her first visit, business kept her from leaving
Pittsburgh. So she was especially happy to make her second visit the very
next summer. Write <u>Atlantic City</u> next to the two dates Thelma was there,
and write <u>Pittsburgh</u> next to its date.

1977 —
1978 —
1979 —
1980 —
1981 —
1982 —

B. In what year did Thelma spend her first summer in Atlantic City?

_____

EXERCISE 25

There were two presidents named Adams, a father and a son. The father's name was John Adams, and the son, John Quincy Adams, was America's sixth president. The president after the father, John Adams, was Jefferson. The president after Jefferson was Madison, and after Madison came Monroe. Then came John Quincy Adams.

A. Write the names of the five presidents in their correct positions on the diagram to the right. The diagram already shows that Washington was the first president and John Polk was the eleventh.

	U.S. Presidents
first	Washington
second	
third	
fourth	
fifth	
sixth	
seventh	
eighth	
ninth	
tenth	
eleventh	Polk

B. If you can tell from the given information who the seventh president was, write his name on the diagram.

C. If you can tell from the given information who the tenth president was, write his name on the diagram.

EXERCISE 26

The Smiths visited Algeria for the second time during their 1970 summer vacation. They had liked it so greatly on their first visit that they promised themselves a return visit the very next summer. But circumstances prevented them from keeping this promise. Mrs. Smith's mother in Holland became ill in June, so Mrs. Smith rushed to her mother's side while the rest of the family stayed home. And the summer after that an emergency in Mr. Smith's business kept the entire family home, except for the children, who went to camp for a few weeks. After these delays, the return to Algeria was especially appreciated.

1966 —
1967 —
1968 —
1969 —
1970 —
1971 —
1972 —
1973 —
1974 —

A. Show the date for the two visits to Algeria, the visit to Holland, and the business emergency on the diagram.

B. What year did Mrs. Smith visit her mother in Holland?_____

EXERCISE 27

Fernando spent the summer between his senior high school year and his
freshman college year in Detroit. He liked it so much that he had hoped to
spend the very next summer there again, but he wasn't able to return until
1976. He went to summer school between his freshman and sophomore
college years, between his sophomore and junior years, and between his
junior and senior years. And for the subsequent two summers the company
he worked for sent him for special training in St. Louis. Not until the summer
after that, in 1976, was he able to revisit Detroit.

Show the dates for the two visits to Detroit, the three summer school
sessions, and the two years in St. Louis on the diagram.

1968 —
1969 —
1970 —
1971 —
1972 —
1973 —
1974 —
1975 —
1976 —
1977 —
1978 —
1979 —
1980 —
1981 —
1982 —

"RESPECTIVELY"

The word "respectively" is used in sentences as a way of stating very precisely the relationship between several items of information. "Respectively" means that items are related to each other "in the order given."
For example, compare the following two sentences.

Juan and Steve are married to Ida and Sue.

Juan and Steve are married to Ida and Sue, respectively.

The first sentence is not very precise. Reading it, we cannot be exactly sure of its meaning. Who is married to whom? Is Steve married to Ida, or to Sue? It is even possible that all four people are part of the same group marriage, as occurs in some primitive societies. As written, the sentence is ambiguous.

The second sentence is much more precise. Through the addition of the word "respectively," the sentence now clearly states that Juan and Steve are married to Ida and Sue, *in the order given*. Since Juan is the *first* man mentioned, then he is married to the *first* woman mentioned—Ida. Also, since Steve is the *second* man mentioned, then he is married to the *second* woman mentioned—Sue.

Similarly, in the sentence "On the morning of the last Sunday of the month, Lucia, Linda, and Linus were given a card, a present, and a slap in the face, respectively", we can be certain that it was *only* Linus who received the slap. Linus is the third person mentioned and "a slap in the face" is the third item mentioned. Take away the word "respectively"—"On the morning of the last Sunday of the month, Lucia, Linda, and Linus were given a card, a present, and a slap in the face—and it sounds as if all three people were *each* given a card, a present, and a slap in the face.

"Respectively" precisely spells out the relationships between items of information according to the rule: in the order given.

EXERCISE 28

Belinda's company moves her to a different city every year. Most recently she worked in Miami, and prior to that in Tampa, another of Florida's urban centers. The time Belinda spent in Florida plus some time spent in Georgia constitute her last five years of employment. While in Georgia, Belinda worked in Atlanta before she worked in Athens but after she worked in Macon. Prior to her assignment to the southern states of Georgia and Florida, Belinda worked first in California and later in Utah, in the cities of Palo Alto and Salt Lake City, respectively.

A. Write the seven cities (not states) in order on the diagram.

earlier

more recent

B. If Belinda worked in Palo Alto in 1975, what year did she work in Salt Lake City?_____

C. If Belinda worked in Palo Alto in 1975, what year did she work in Miami? _____

Word Power III

Power Words

| celibacy | surreptitiously | lecherousness | virtuoso |
| intimidated | autobiography | amphibious | predilection |

---

1. **celibacy** | sĕl′ ə bə sē |
   - Priests may take vows of celibacy to free them from the earthly responsibilities of raising and supporting a family.
   - At the age of 30, Paul decided to end his celibacy and get married.

2. **intimidated** | ĭn tĭm′ ĭ dā′ tĭd |
   - The mayor was intimidated by the financial threats of the businessman and granted him special privileges.
   - Jennifer was so intimidated by the job requirements that she did not apply for the position.

3. **surreptitiously** | sûr′ əp tĭsh′ əs lē |
   - The newspaper opposing the government was published surreptitiously so its writers would not be arrested.
   - The spy met surreptitiously with her contact to avoid exposure.

4. **autobiography** | ô tō bī ŏg′ rə fē |
   - A biography is the story of a person's life and an autobiography is a biography written by the person him or herself.
   - One type of autobiography is called memoirs.

5. **lecherousness** | lĕch′ ər əs nĕs |
   - The lecherousness of the king toward married women caused him to lose the respect and support of his noblemen.

6. **amphibious** | ăm fĭb′ ē əs |
   - A frog is an amphibious animal, adapted to live in water as well as on land.

7. **virtuoso** | vûr′ chōō ō′ sō |
   - It requires thousands of hours of practice to become a virtuoso with a musical instrument.
   - A gourmet cook must be a virtuoso with spices.

8. **predilection** | prĕd′ ə lĕk′ shən |
   - She had a predilection for math and studied it several hours a day.
   - His apartment full of sculptures indicated he had a predilection for sculpture over other art forms.

ă pat / ā pay / â care / ä father / ĕ pet / ē be / ĭ pit / ī pie / î fierce / ŏ pot / ō go / ô paw, for / oi oil / ŏŏ book /
ōō boot / ou out / ŭ cut / ü fur / th the / th thin / hw which / zh vision / ə ago, item, pencil, atom, circus

Meaning Comprehension

Directions: Use what you have learned from the context sentences to identify the correct definition of each Power Word. In the blank next to each Power Word, write the letter of its correct definition.

Power Words

_____ celibacy
_____ intimidated
_____ surreptitiously
_____ autobiography
_____ lecherousness
_____ amphibious
_____ virtuoso
_____ predilection

Definitions

a. liking, preference
b. an expert with a musical instrument; an expert in a science or art
c. tendency to be overly or inappropriately interested in sex
d. frightened, made timid
e. state of not being married or having sexual relations
f. able to live or operate in water or on land
g. secretly
h. biography of a person written by the person him/herself

Context Application

Directions: Each of the following sentences has two blanks. Use what you have learned about the Power Words to determine which Power Word best belongs in each of the blanks. Then write the appropriate Power Word in each blank. Use each Power Word only once.

1. Although her husband forbade it, Mrs. Inez continued to practice the piano _____ and in time became a _____ .

2. The words _____ , able to live in water or on land, and _____ , the self-written story of a person's life, both contain the Greek "bio," which means "life."

3. _____ , in which one avoids marriage or sexual relations often for spiritual reasons, is in a sense the opposite of _____ .

4. The football player's _____ for fighting _____ . the other team.

Muscle Builder Analogies

Directions: Each exercise below is an analogy, with one or two terms missing. Choose the Power Word which belongs in each blank of the analogy so that the analogy reads correctly. Write the appropriate Power Word in each blank. Note that some of the Power Words will not be used.

1. MOBILE is to AUTOMOBILE as BIOGRAPHY is to _____

2. OVEREATING is to DIETING as _____ is to _____

3. DISPLAYED is to HIDDEN as OPENLY is to _____

Word Power IV

Directions: Study each of the Power Words below. Note how each word is pronounced. Then read the context sentences to figure out what each Power Word means. In the left-hand margin next to each Power Word, try to jot down a synonym or short definition which defines that word.

Power Words	destitute	euphoria	alleviate	depleted
	panacea	indolent	eulogize	fiasco

1. **destitute** | **dĕs′** tĭ tōōt′ |
   - The destitute poet went to friends for food.
   - The Salvation Army helps those who are destitute.

2. **panacea** | păn′ ə **sē′** ə |
   - The phoney doctor sold bottles of a red liquid that he claimed was a panacea for all diseases.
   - An experienced educator knows that no single theory of teaching is a panacea for public education.

3. **euphoria** | yōō **fôr′** ē ə |
   - After passing the final exam, the student was in a state of euphoria.
   - The team members' euphoria over tying for first place quickly disappeared when they lost the playoff game.

4. **indolent** | **ĭn′** də lənt |
   - Extremely hot weather makes one indolent and unable to work hard.
   - An idolent student does not learn much.

5. **alleviate** | ə **lē′** vē āt′ |
   - Cold tablets alleviate the symptoms of a cold although they do not cure the cold.

6. **eulogize** | **yōō′** lə gīz′ |
   - Many friends came to eulogize the scientist in speeches of praise for her research.
   - During a funeral, the deceased person is typically eulogized.

7. **depleted** | dĭ **plē′** tĭd |
   - The treasury was depleted and there was no money to pay the employees.
   - A special hunting party was sent out when the tribe's food supply was depleted.

8. **fiasco** | fē **ăs′** kō |
   - Her attempt to pass the exam without studying was a fiasco.
   - When the leading actor forgot all his lines, the play turned into a fiasco.

ă pat / ā pay / â care / ä father / ĕ pet / ē be / ĭ pit / ī pie / î fierce / ŏ pot / ō go / ô paw, for / oi oil / ŏŏ book /
ōō boot / ou out / ŭ cut / û fur / th the / th thin / hw which / zh vision / ə ago, item, pencil, atom, circus

Meaning Comprehension

Directions: Use what you have learned from the context sentences to identify the correct definition of each Power Word. In the blank next to each Power Word, write the letter of its correct definition.

Power Words

_____ destitute
_____ panacea
_____ euphoria
_____ indolent
_____ alleviate
_____ eulogize
_____ depleted
_____ fiasco

Definitions

a. very lazy; disinclined to work
b. emptied, used up
c. complete failure
d. a cure for all ills and difficulties
e. praise, speak well or highly about someone
f. relieve, lessen, reduce
g. happy feeling, strong feeling of well-being, elation
h. poor, lacking possessions and necessities of life

Context Application

Directions: Each of the following sentences has two blanks. Use what you have learned about the Power Words to determine which Power Word best belongs in each of the blanks. Then write the appropriate Power Word in each blank. Use each Power Word only once.

1. Aspirin is not a _____ , but it does _____ fever, headache, tension, and many other common ailments.

2. The family had no income, had _____ their savings, and had become _____ .

3. The words _____ , a feeling of well-being, and _____ , speak well of someone, stem from the Greek root "eu," which means "good" or "well."

4. The employee was extremely _____ , and when his boss relied upon him to manage the project it soon turned into a _____ .

Muscle Builder Analogies

Directions: Each exercise below is an analogy, with one or two terms missing. Choose the Power Word which belongs in each blank of the analogy so that the analogy reads correctly. Write the appropriate Power Word in each blank. Note that some of the Power Words will not be used.

1. FULL is to EMPTY as WEALTHY is to _____

2. SADNESS is to FAIL as _____ is to SUCCEED

3. _____ is to FAILURE as _____ is to CURE

ADDITIONAL ASSIGNMENTS

In the following exercises you will be asked to write problems of your own. After you write each problem, ask a peer to try to solve it. As your peer works, observe whether he/she has any difficulty. Check to see if this difficulty is because the problem is not clearly written or not correct, or because the peer needs help with the skill of processing serial orders. Rewrite the problem if necessary; or teach your peer the techniques of solving these type of problems.

1. Do both parts of this exercise.

   (A) Paul and Sam are both taller than Juan. Fred is shorter than Sam but taller than Paul. Write the names of the four men in order on the diagram.

   (B) Write a similar problem using the same four men, but starting with this sentence:

   Fred and Juan are both shorter than Sam.

   _____

   _____

   _____

2. Using the names Lincoln, Fillmore, Pierce, Taylor, and Buchanan, write a problem about the order of these names in the telephone book (alphabetical order). Have your problem start with this sentence:

   Lincoln comes after Fillmore in the telephone book but before Taylor.

   _____

   _____

   _____

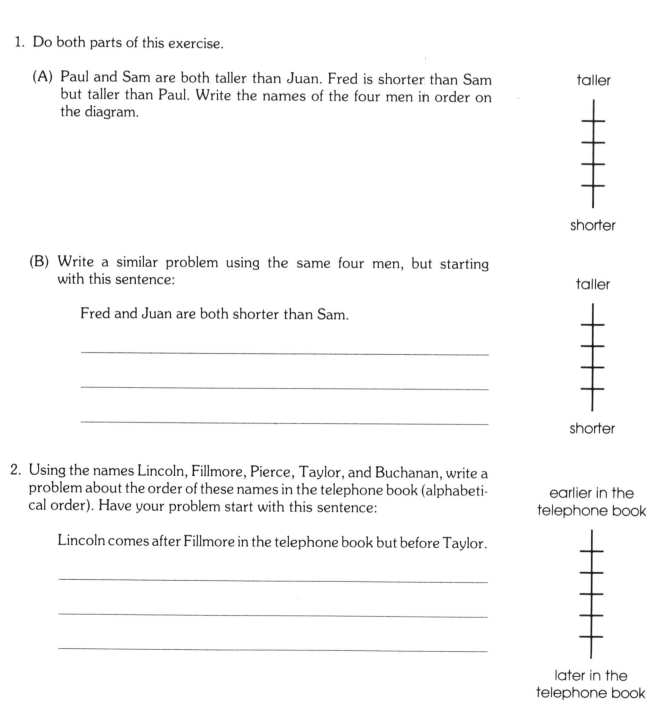

ADDITIONAL ASSIGNMENTS (continued)

3. Using the names John, Harriet, Bob, Clarence, Al, Cassandra, Brenda, and Billy, write a problem about the order of the names in length (number of letters). Let the problem start with this sentence:

   The name Billy is shorter than Clarence but longer than Bob.

   longer

   shorter

   _____

   _____

   _____

4. Write a problem like number 27, but use different dates and events. Create your own diagram to go with this problem in the space at the right.

   _____

   _____

   _____

   _____

   _____

   _____

   _____

   _____

   _____

   _____

ADDITIONAL ASSIGNMENTS (continued)

5. Using what you have learned about the meaning of "euphoria" (page 98), write a sentence on the lines below in which the meaning of "euphoria" is given by contrast (Case III).

_____

_____

6. Using what you have learned about the meaning of "genocide" (page 78), write a sentence on the lines below in which the meaning of "genocide" is stated with punctuation (Case I).

_____

_____

7. Using what you have learned about the meaning of "fortuitous" (page 66), write a sentence on the lines below in which the meaning of "fortuitous" is stated without punctuation (Case II).

_____

_____

8. Using what you have learned about the meaning of "impromptu" (page 68), write a sentence on the lines below in which the meaning of "impromptu" is inferred from the rest of the sentence (Case IV).

_____

_____

UNIT
5
READING TEXT FOR FULL COMPREHENSION I

OBJECTIVES: When you have completed this unit you should

- be able to comprehend the facts and relationships in various selections of text material;
- know the meanings of the following POWER WORDS.

POWER WORDS

replete	garrulous	sobriety	diverse
promulgated	obstinate	sporadically	genial
coalition	parsimonious	intrepid	schism
aberration	moderate	disheveled	incongruous
coerce	extol	distraught	credible
melancholic	whimsical	maudlin	frivolous
conservative	pandemonium	simile	pugnacious
resolution	stupor	interim	commence

Word Power I

Power Words	replete promulgated	coalition aberration	melancholic coerce	conservative resolution

1. **replete** | rĭ **plēt′** |
   - The Egyptian tomb was replete with ancient treasures.
   - The Thanksgiving dinner table was replete with all the traditional holiday trappings.

2. **promulgated** | **prŏm′** əl gā′ tĭd |
   - TV will promulgate the outcome of the election.
   - The white smoke rising from the Vatican chimney promulgated the election of a new Pope.

3. **coalition** | kō ə **lĭsh′** ən |
   - Countries should join together in a coalition against the common enemy—poverty.
   - The Progressives and the Liberals formed a coalition in an attempt to defeat the Democrats.

4. **aberration** | ăb ə **rā′** shən |
   - A criminal act is an aberration in social behavior.
   - An aberration in health is called an illness or disease.

5. **coerce** | kō **ûrs′** |
   - A parent may sometimes coerce obedience with threats.
   - The robber coerced him into handing over his watch.

6. **melancholic** | mĕl′ ən **kŏl′** ĭk |
   - An extremely melancholic personality can be a depressing curse.
   - A melancholic person tends to avoid contact with other people.

7. **conservative** | kən **sûr′** və tĭv |
   - Conservative advisors to the king were opposed to new laws which would give more power to Parliament.
   - Of course, the conservative senators voted against any change in the present system.

8. **resolution** | rĕs′ ə **lōō′** shən |
   - The resolution from the committee included a provision for freedom of speech.
   - Smokers Anonymous issued a resolution asking the FCC to ban cigaret ads from TV.

Meaning Comprehension

Directions: Use what you have learned from the context sentences to identify the correct definition of each Power Word. In the blank next to each Power Word, write the letter of its correct definition.

Power Words

_____ replete
_____ promulgated
_____ coalition
_____ aberration
_____ coerce
_____ melancholic
_____ conservative
_____ resolution

Definitions

a. a formal statement of opinion or intent voted by an official group; the act of analyzing or solving

b. tendency to preserve or maintain current conditions; person desiring to maintain the status quo

c. made known, declared, proclaimed

d. filled, abundantly full

e. union, combination; temporary alliance

f. something differing from the normal

g. tending to be depressed, despondent

h. force, compel

Context Application

Directions: Each of the following sentences has two blanks. Use what you have learned about the Power Words to determine which Power Word best belongs in each of the blanks. Then write the appropriate Power Word in each blank. Use each Power Word only once.

1. He had a character _____ or abnormality—his constantly pessimistic, _____ disposition.

2. The committee passed a new _____ to seek more information on political bribery and _____ it throughout the district.

3. The old government was _____ and against change, so it was frightened by the people's demands which were _____ with threats to the established social order.

4. In a country where there are many small political parties, several parties often form a _____ in order to _____ the ruling party into a desired action.

Muscle Builder Analogies

Directions: Each exercise below is an analogy, with one or two terms missing. Choose the Power Word which belongs in each blank of the analogy so that the analogy reads correctly. Write the appropriate Power Word in each blank. Note that some of the Power Words will not be used.

1. PROPOSAL is to SUGGESTION as _____ is to OPINION

2. HIGH is to LOW as EUPHORIC is to _____

3. THREE-LEAF CLOVER is to NORMALITY as FOUR-LEAF CLOVER is to _____

Word Power II

Directions: Study each of the Power Words below. Note how each word is pronounced. Then read the context sentences to figure out what each Power Word means. In the left-hand margin next to each Power Word, try to jot down a synonym or short definition which defines that word.

Power Words	garrulous	parsimonious	extol	pandemonium
	obstinate	moderate	whimsical	stupor

---

1. **garrulous** | **găr′** ə ləs |
   - For the entire day, garrulous, tiring speeches were heard in the Senate.
   - Larry is so garrulous that my ears hurt!

2. **obstinate** | **ŏb′** stə nĭt |
   - An obstinate person refuses to listen to reason.
   - One juror remained obstinate and would not change her vote.

3. **parsimonious** | pär′ sə **mō′** nē əs |
   - He had a parsimonious bent and probably still owned the first dollar he ever earned.
   - Juan lives richly, but compared to his cousin he seems parsimonious!

4. **moderate** | **mŏd′** ər ĭt |
   - The climate of the U.S. is neither too hot nor too cold for agriculture, but is moderate and supportive.
   - Before a date, it is wise to use only a moderate amount of garlic on your food.

5. **extol** | ĭk **stōl′** |
   - After hearing the math teacher, Mrs. Io, extol his daughter's ability, Mr. Wong developed an entirely new respect for his offspring.
   - That woman is so proud that she continuously extols the talents of her trained monkey.

6. **whimsical** | **hwĭm′** sĭ kəl |
   - A whimsical mind changes more often than the wind.
   - Hop Sing's whimsical nature made him very unpredictable.

7. **pandemonium** | păn′ də **mō′** nē əm |
   - When the home team scored the last touchdown, pandemonium reigned among the fans.
   - New Year's Eve is a night of great pandemonium in Times Square.

8. **stupor** | **stōo′** pər |
   - Several days of continuous drinking left the alcoholic in a stupor.

ă pat / ā pay / â care / ä father / ĕ pet / ē be / ĭ pit / ī pie / î fierce / ŏ pot / ō go / ô paw, for / oi oil / ŏŏ book /
ōō boot / ou out / ŭ cut / û fur / *th* the / th thin / hw which / zh vision / ə ago, item, pencil, atom, circus

Meaning Comprehension

Directions: Use what you have learned from the context sentences to identify the correct definition of each Power Word. In the blank next to each Power Word, write the letter of its correct definition.

Power Words	Definitions
_____ garrulous	a. state of reduced consciousness, feeling or sensibility
_____ obstinate	b. talkative, long-winded, chatty
_____ parsimonious	c. stubborn, unyielding, pigheaded
_____ moderate	d. given to sudden changes of mind, capricious
_____ extol	e. excessively thrifty, frugal, stingy
_____ whimsical	f. a wild uproar, tumult
_____ pandemonium	g. not extreme or excessive, restrained, mild
_____ stupor	h. praise, speak highly about, glorify

Context Application

Directions: Each of the following sentences has two blanks. Use what you have learned about the Power Words to determine which Power Word best belongs in each of the blanks. Then write the appropriate Power Word in each blank. Use each Power Word only once.

1. He was not _____ in his own spending, but he would continually _____ the virtues of thrift to his wife.

2. Listening to a _____ person for an extended period can put one into a zombi-like _____ .

3. If a _____ person, one who is constantly changing his mind, is also _____ about getting his way, he can be very difficult to work with.

4. People of a _____ nature tend to react mildly in all situations, even _____ .

Muscle Builder Analogies

Directions: Each exercise below is an analogy, with one or two terms missing. Choose the Power Word which belongs in each blank of the analogy so that the analogy reads correctly. Write the appropriate Power Word in each blank. Note that some of the Power Words will not be used.

1. ORDER is to COURT as _____ is to MOB

2. DISHONESTY is to CONDEMN as HONESTY is to _____

3. _____ is to EBENEZER SCROOGE as _____ is to MULES

INTRODUCTION

This unit is similar to the work you did in Unit 2. Each exercise consists of a reading passage followed by a set of questions about that passage.

The passages and questions in this unit are slightly more complex than those in Unit 2. The questions will require you to use the analytical reading skills you have developed through Units 1-4.

INSTRUCTIONS FOR THE EXERCISES

In reading and answering the exercises that follow, use the same procedures and techniques you used in Unit 2. That is, read each passage very carefully. Read for comprehension of ideas, not coverage of words. Try to understand everything the writer is saying.

Try to achieve total accuracy (100% performance) in answering the questions. Do not work so quickly or sloppily that you make silly "I wasn't thinking" mistakes. Refer back to the passage as many times as necessary to be sure you have selected the correct answer. As in Unit 2, you should be able to identify specific line numbers from the passage where the answer to certain questions is found. For other questions, you may have to pull together information from several different points in the passage. In either case, you should be able to explain aloud to yourself or to a peer the precise information and the analytical reasoning you used in arriving at your answer.

Also, you will again be asked to evaluate possible titles for the passages. If needed, refer back to Unit 2 to familiarize yourself with how this is done.

Lastly, several of the questions in this unit will ask you to identify an idea which is *implied* in the passage. *Implied* means "suggested but not specifically stated; or, conveyed indirectly." So, an idea implied in a passage is an idea that is suggested by the passage, but is not directly stated in the passage. Keep this definition in mind as you answer the questions.

PASSAGE A

¹   Dr. Daniel Hale Williams, a Negro physician,
² was raised from an unsung master of medicine to
³ a position of national renown as one of America's
⁴ greatest surgeons, by a husky, young street
⁵ fighter named James Cornish. In a brawl, Cornish
⁶ suffered a knife wound in an artery a fraction of an
⁷ inch from the heart. Heart wounds, or even
⁸ wounds in the thoracic cavity, prior to the date of
⁹ this incident in 1893, were treated with sedatives
¹⁰ and prayer, and the patient invariably died.
¹¹   "Dr. Dan," as he was often called, decided to
¹² do something no other doctor had ever done: to
¹³ open Cornish's chest and operate on the heart.
¹⁴ X-rays, sulfa drugs, blood transfusion—now ab-
¹⁵ solute necessities—were unknown medical tools
¹⁶ at the time. Calling six of his colleagues on the
¹⁷ staff of the struggling Provident Hospital in Chi-
¹⁸ cago, Dr. Dan operated. The patient lived. The
¹⁹ doctor had performed the impossible operation.

1. Below are three possible titles for this passage. In each blank, write the letter of the phrase (A, B or C) which best describes that title.

_____ Milstones in Medical History
_____ James Cornish's Knife Wound
_____ Surgery Near Heart Performed by Williams

    (A) comprehensive title
    (B) too narrow
    (C) too broad

2. The word "unsung" in the first sentence, according to the context, means

    ☐ (A) lacking a good singing voice
    ☐ (B) lacking faults
    ☐ (C) lacking fame
    ☐ (D) having fame

3. James Cornish's knife wound was

    ☐ (A) very close to his heart
    ☐ (B) directly in his heart
    ☐ (C) near a major vein
    ☐ (D) near a tooth cavity

4. Before Dr. Williams' operation

    ☐ (A) surgery for wounds in the thoracic cavity of the chest was common, but heart surgery had never been done
    ☐ (B) wounds in the thoracic cavity were not treated by surgery
    ☐ (C) wounds in the thoracic cavity were treated with sulfa drugs
    ☐ (D) wounds in the heart were treated with medical tools such as forceps and clamps

5. In performing the surgery, Dr. Williams

    ☐ (A) used medical tools such as forceps and clamps
    ☐ (B) used medical tools such as x-rays, sulfa drugs, and blood transfusion
    ☐ (C) used only sedatives and prayer
    ☐ (D) did not use medical tools such as x-rays, sulfa drugs, and blood transfusion

PASSAGE B

¹   Infectious diseases are the only ones that can
² be transmitted. They may be spread by infected
³ animals, infected people, or contaminated sub-
⁴ stances such as food and water. Infectious dis-
⁵ eases that can be transmitted to humans from
⁶ infected animals are known as zoonoses. Zoo-
⁷ noses may be transmitted by carriers, such as
⁸ insects; by the bite of an infected animal; by direct
⁹ contact with an infected animal or its excretions;
¹⁰ or by eating animal products.

1. Below are three possible titles for this passage. In each blank, write the letter of the phrase (A, B, or C) which best describes that title.

_____ Transmission of Infectious Diseases
_____ Types and Mechanisms of Diseases
_____ How Zoonoses are Transmitted

    (A) too narrow
    (B) too broad
    (C) comprehensive title

2. According to the selection, zoonoses are

    ☐ (A) insects that carry diseases
    ☐ (B) infected animals that transmit infectious diseases to humans
    ☐ (C) infectious diseases that man gets from animals
    ☐ (D) carriers that transmit infectious diseases

3. On which line(s) did you find the answer to the preceding question?

    LINE NUMBER(S): _____

4. Which of the following ideas is *not* stated in the passage, but is only implied?

    ☐ (A) Some diseases may be spread by animals.
    ☐ (B) Some diseases cannot be transmitted.
    ☐ (C) All diseases can be transmitted.
    ☐ (D) Some diseases may be transmitted by people.

5. On which line(s) is the idea that is the answer to the preceding question implied?

    LINE NUMBER(S): _____

6. The passage implies that

    ☐ (A) noninfectious diseases can be transmitted by animals
    ☐ (B) noninfectious diseases can be transmitted by sick people
    ☐ (C) noninfectious diseases cannot be transmitted by sick people

PASSAGE C

1   The dog is a domesticated wolf, and its his-
2 tory must be traced through the ancestors of this
3 carnivore. (It used to be thought that the jackal
4 had contributed to the ancestry of the dog, but on
5 morphological and behavioral grounds this is no
6 longer tenable.) The forerunners of the wolf, such
7 as *Aelurodon*, were present in North America
8 during the late Miocene and early Pliocene,
9 roughly 15 million to 10 million years ago, but they
10 are not commonly found in Europe until the Villa-
11 franchian, the earliest stage of the Pleistocene,
12 about 2 million years ago. True wolves, however,
13 appeared in Europe in the middle Pleistocene,
14 some 1 million years ago, but they are not
15 recorded from the New World until some 700,000
16 years later.

1. Below are three possible titles for this passage. In each blank, write the letter of the phrase (A, B or C) which best describes that title.

    _____ The Origin of Wolves and Dogs
    _____ North American Forerunners of the Wolf
    _____ The Origin of Domestic Pets

    (A) too broad
    (B) too narrow
    (C) comprehensive title

2. A former belief, now disproven, was that

    ☐ (A) the dog was a domesticated wolf
    ☐ (B) the dog was descended partially from the jackal
    ☐ (C) primitive dogs were present in the Miocene
    ☐ (D) none of the above

3. On which line(s) did you find the answer to the preceding question?

    LINE NUMBER(S): _____

4. Given that "New World" means North America and "Old World" means Europe, which of the following statements is correct?

☐ (A) True wolves appeared first in the Old World, while forerunners of wolves appeared first in the New World.
☐ (B) True wolves appeared first in North America, while forerunners of wolves appeared first in the Old World.
☐ (C) True wolves appeared first in the Old World, while forerunners of wolves appeared first in the New World.
☐ (D) True wolves first appeared in Europe during the Villafranchian stage.

PASSAGE D

1 In the 17th century, the early colonists in
2 New England built primarily simple frame houses,
3 whereas the earliest colonists in the tidewater
4 region of Virginia built more elaborate houses of
5 brick. The generations which followed con-
6 structed other buildings out of wood, brick, and
7 stone in the styles now termed Greek Revival,
8 Georgian, and Colonial, or other names indicat-
9 ing their origin. Most of these houses were con-
10 structed in colonies populated mainly by English
11 settlers. However, the Spanish had a heavy influ-
12 ence over the dwellings that arose in California,
13 and in the Mississippi Delta, the architecture fol-
14 lowed French styles.

1. Below are three possible titles for this passage. In each blank, write the letter of the phrase (A, B or C) which best describes that title.

_____ History of the Colonies and Early United States
_____ Architecture in the Colonies and Early United States
_____ Architecture of Early New England

(A) comprehensive title
(B) too narrow
(C) too broad

2. How many types of building material are mentioned in this selection?

☐ (A) One.
☐ (B) Two.
☐ (C) Three.
☐ (D) Four.

3. According to the passage, the French influence on architecture was greatest in

☐ (A) New England
☐ (B) Virginia
☐ (C) the Mississippi Delta
☐ (D) California

4. According to the selection, in the 1600s

☐ (A) more complex houses were built in New England than in Virginia
☐ (B) brick structures were stronger than wooden structures
☐ (C) Americans were independent people who developed their own architecture
☐ (D) more complex houses were built in Virginia than in New England

5. On which line(s) did you find the answer to the preceding question?

LINE NUMBER(S): _____

6. One can conclude from the selection that

☐ (A) Virginia was part of New England
☐ (B) Virginia was settled by New Englanders
☐ (C) the French settled in the Mississippi Delta
☐ (D) the French settled in California

7. The word "elaborate" in line 4, according to the context, means

☐ (A) extend
☐ (B) plain, simple
☐ (C) complex, sophisticated
☐ (D) made from arbors (trees)

PASSAGE E

The brilliant and courageous flight surgeon, Colonel William Randolph Lovelace II, climbed out of a bomb bay into temperatures of 50° below zero to determine what would happen to the human body when subjected to bail-out at 40,000 feet. Miraculously he lived—though not without serious injury—through the ghastly jolt of his chute opening in the thin upper atmosphere. This jump proved the lifesaving ability of the small, portable oxygen bottle for emergency bail-out which was developed in 1939 by Colonel Rudolph Fink, Dr. Manley Pessman, and Mr. Sydney Winton.

1. Below are three possible titles for this passage. In each blank, write the letter of the phrase (A, B or C) which best describes that title.

   _____ Daring Jump by Colonel Lovelace II Proves Oxygen Bottle Successful
   _____ Colonel William Lovelace II Makes Courageous Jump
   _____ History of Aeronautical Science

   (A) too broad
   (B) comprehensive title
   (C) too narrow

2. The portable oxygen bottle was developed by

   ☐ (A) Colonel William Randolph Lovelace II
   ☐ (B) Colonel Lovelace II and Colonel Fink
   ☐ (C) Fink, Pessman, and Winton
   ☐ (D) Fink, Lovelace, and Winton

3. On which line(s) did you find the answer to the preceding question?

   LINE NUMBER(S): _____

4. One result of Colonel Lovelace's jump was that

   ☐ (A) Dr. Pessman designed a stronger parachute
   ☐ (B) Colonel Fink was seriously injured
   ☐ (C) parachute jumping from 40,000 feet was outlawed
   ☐ (D) he was seriously injured

5. The writer's main purpose is to

   ☐ (A) describe the courageous jump of Colonel Lovelace II
   ☐ (B) describe Colonel Lovelace's jump and its role in developing safe bail-out procedures and equipment
   ☐ (C) present a biography of Colonel Lovelace II
   ☐ (D) describe bail-out procedures at 40,000 feet

PASSAGE F

The greatest "conductor" on the Underground Railroad—an organized network of way-stations which helped black slaves escape from the South to the free states and as far north as Canada—was an ex-slave and a woman, Harriet Ross Tubman.

In 1860, Harriet Tubman began to canvass the nation, appearing at anti-slavery meetings and speaking on behalf of women's rights. Shortly before the outbreak of the Civil War, she was forced for a time to leave for Canada, but she soon returned to the United States, serving the Union cause openly and actively as a nurse, soldier, spy, and scout. She was particularly valuable in the latter capacity, since her work on the "Railroad" had made her thoroughly familiar with much of the terrain.

1. Below are three possible titles for this passage. In each blank, write the letter of the phrase (A, B or C) which best describes that title.

   _____ Harriet Tubman's Role in the Underground Railroad
   _____ Harriet Tubman's Role in Emancipating Slaves
   _____ Contributors to the Emancipation of Slaves

   (A) too narrow
   (B) too broad
   (C) comprehensive title

2. According to the selection, Harriet Tubman

   □ (A) was the first woman "conductor" to work on a high-speed train
   □ (B) was born in Canada
   □ (C) received excellent wages for her work on the Underground Railroad
   □ (D) had been a slave at one time in her life

3. On which line(s) did you find the answer to the preceding question?

   LINE NUMBER(S): _____

4. The Underground Railroad was, according to the selection,

   □ (A) a network for capturing and returning escaped slaves
   □ (B) a train which ran underground through mountains by means of a network of tunnels
   □ (C) an organization of hiding places and routes for helping slaves escape to the free states
   □ (D) the first high-speed train route, which ran from the South to Canada

5. As used in the second paragraph, the word "canvass" (in contrast to "canvas") means

   □ (A) a strong cloth such as that employed in making tents and sails
   □ (B) travel around discussing, debating, or surveying ideas
   □ (C) a material upon which a painting or sketch can be made
   □ (D) travel around door-to-door selling products

6. According to the passage, Harriet Tubman

   □ (A) fought exclusively for Negroes' rights
   □ (B) fought exclusively for women's rights
   □ (C) fought for both Negroes' and women's rights
   □ (D) fought for the rights of Negroes, women, and endangered animals

7. Harriet Tubman was especially useful as a scout during the Civil War because

   □ (A) she was also a nurse, soldier, and spy
   □ (B) she was acquainted with the geography of the land
   □ (C) she appeared at anti-slavery meetings and therefore would not be suspected of spying
   □ (D) she was an excellent public speaker

PASSAGE G

1   In reality no one place has been the only
2 source, and no one man the true and only progen-
3 itor of rocketry and the Space Age. The dream of
4 astronautics has been long growing in many
5 minds. It began perhaps as far back as the year
6 A.D. 1500, when the legendary Wan-Hu sup-
7 posedly took off on the first rocket-powered pas-
8 senger flight. It developed thereafter through
9 many generations, pushed and propelled along
10 the way by pioneer thinkers and achievers like Sir
11 Isaac Newton, Roger Bacon, Claude and Gae-
12 tano Ruggieri, Sir William Congreve, the Ameri-
13 can William Hale, and writers like Bishop John
14 Wilkins, Daniel Defoe, Bishop Godwin, Cyrano
15 de Bergerac, and, of course, Jules Verne and H.
16 G. Wells.

1. Below are three possible titles for this passage. In each blank, write the letter of the phrase (A, B or C) which best describes that title.

   _____ Complete History and Science of Rocketry and the Space Age
   _____ Contributors to Rocketry and the Space Age
   _____ Claude and Gaetano Ruggieri

   (A) too narrow
   (B) too broad
   (C) comprehensive title

2. According to the passage,

☐ (A) Wan-Hu was the father of rocketry and the Space Age
☐ (B) one cannot pinpoint the father of rocketry and the Space Age
☐ (C) the Space Age began as far back as Ancient Greece
☐ (D) the United States is the greatest contributor to the Space Age

3. The author believes that

☐ (A) without Wan-Hu rocketry and the Space Age would definitely not have developed
☐ (B) scientists were solely responsible for the development of rocketry and the Space Age
☐ (C) nonscientists made a contribution to rocketry and the Space Age
☐ (D) none of the above

4. As used in the first sentence, the word "progenitor" means

☐ (A) progress
☐ (B) professional
☐ (C) originator
☐ (D) astronaut

5. The writer's main purpose is to

☐ (A) describe the development of rocketry in China
☐ (B) describe the contributions of science fiction writers to the development of rocketry
☐ (C) describe the development of rocketry and the Space Age as stemming from many sources
☐ (D) honor Wan-Hu's contribution to the development of the Spage Age

6. The writer describes William Hale as

☐ (A) a pioneer thinker and achiever, and an American
☐ (B) a writer and an American
☐ (C) an American astronaut

PASSAGE H

1 The marsupial carnivores are lithe and lively
2 animals. While almost all of them are capable of
3 climbing trees, they are not truly arboreal. Most
4 are quick and intelligent. They attack anything
5 alive which they can overpower. They are primar-
6 ily nocturnal and sleep in caves, trees, and holes
7 in the ground when they are not active. The Tas-
8 manian devil and the Tasmanian wolf emit
9 hoarse, coughing, growling sounds. This sound
10 repertoire does not have any greater expression
11 and tonality than that of most marsupials. The
12 mouse-like species very rarely emit sounds.

1. The best title for this selection is

☐ (A) Sounds Emitted by the Tasmanian Devil
☐ (B) Marsupial Carnivore Eating Habits
☐ (C) Characteristics of Marsupial Carnivores
☐ (D) Development of Marsupial Carnivores

2. In this passage, the phrase "truly arboreal" means

☐ (A) able to climb trees
☐ (B) adapted for living in trees
☐ (C) lithe and lively
☐ (D) quick and intelligent

3. According to the passage, the Tasmanian devil and wolf are not

☐ (A) fond of darkness
☐ (B) aggressive animals
☐ (C) active and agile animals
☐ (D) different from most marsupials vocally

4. On the basis of the passage, one can conclude

☐ (A) that marsupials have a large range in vocal expression
☐ (B) that marsupials make very pleasant, gentle sounds
☐ (C) that marsupials sleep at night and roam widely during the day
☐ (D) none of the above

PASSAGE I

1 The thing that's so hard to explain to our
2 friends is that most of us who specialize in writing
3 humor for young children *have* cracked the adult
4 field and, having cracked it, have decided defi-
5 nitely that we prefer to uncrack it. We are writing
6 for the so-called Brat Field by choice. For, despite
7 the fact this brands us as pariahs, despite the fact
8 this turns us into literary untouchables, there is
9 something we get when we write for the young
10 that we never can hope to get in writing for you
11 ancients. To be sure, in some ways you are super-
12 ior to the young. You scream less. You burp less.
13 You have fewer public tantrums. You ancients
14 are, generally speaking, slightly more refined. But
15 when it comes to trying to amuse you***! Have
16 you ever stopped to consider what has happened
17 to your sense of humor?

1. As used in this passage, the word "pariah" is

   ☐ (A) complimentary
   ☐ (B) uncomplimentary
   ☐ (C) neither complimentary nor uncompli-
        mentary
   ☐ (D) indifferent

2. The tone of the writer is

   ☐ (A) light
   ☐ (B) serious
   ☐ (C) direct
   ☐ (D) scathing

3. The writer implies that

   ☐ (A) a writer may be successful with chil-
        dren's books but unsuccessful with
        adults' books
   ☐ (B) successful writers of children's books
        can also write successfully for adults
   ☐ (C) adults have a good sense of humor
   ☐ (D) writers of children's books would write
        for adults and make more money if
        they could

4. In the selection, the author uses "ancients" to
   mean

   ☐ (A) adults
   ☐ (B) senior citizens
   ☐ (C) people over 50
   ☐ (D) ancient Greeks and Romans

5. The writer's major purpose in this selection is to

   ☐ (A) explain that adults have more refine-
        ment but less humor than children
   ☐ (B) explain why he writes for children
   ☐ (C) poke fun at children
   ☐ (D) ridicule the writers of children's books

6. In the first two sentences the author counters
   the argument that

   ☐ (A) writing children's books is more desir-
        able than writing adults' books
   ☐ (B) writing adults' books is more desirable
        than writing children's books
   ☐ (C) children's books are called the Brat
        Field
   ☐ (D) children have not developed a sense of
        humor

PASSAGE J

1 Nevada lies on the leeward side of the Sierra
2 Nevada. Storms traveling eastward from the
3 Pacific coast drop most of their rain and snow on
4 the western, or Pacific, side of the Sierra Nevada.
5 The little rain or snow that falls on the Nevada
6 side of these high mountains comes chiefly in
7 winter.

1. One may infer from the passage that

   ☐ (A) the Sierra Nevada is a high mountain
   ☐ (B) the Sierra Nevada is a mountain range
   ☐ (C) the Sierra Nevada causes much rain
        and snow in Nevada
   ☐ (D) the Sierra Nevada is dangerous to cross

2. Nevada is on the

   ☐ (A) western side of the Sierra Nevada
   ☐ (B) northern side of the Sierra Nevada
   ☐ (C) eastern side of the Sierra Nevada
   ☐ (D) all of the above

3. One may infer from the passage that

☐ (A) Nevada is a dry state
☐ (B) Nevada has much rain but little snow
☐ (C) Nevada has much rain and snow
☐ (D) Nevada is on the Pacific side of the Sierra Nevada

PASSAGE K

1   The general result of all this was that the
2 western states were confronted with an adverse
3 balance of trade. Their coined money was drained
4 away to Italy and the East. The accumulation of
5 treasure in the Italian towns gave rise to the first
6 medieval banking houses, such as the Bardi,
7 Alberti, and Frescobaldi—firms which received
8 deposits, issued notes, dealt in bills of exchange,
9 and extended credit throughout Europe, thereby
10 adding interest to their earnings in the West.
11 Loans to kings were given in exchange for conces-
12 sions within the state, or secured by royal taxes
13 due to be collected. Thus, in England, Florentine
14 bankers supplied the money for equipping the
15 early expeditions in the Hundred Years' War.

1. Below are three possible titles for this passage. In each blank, write the letter of the phrase (A, B or C) which best describes that title.

_____ Rise and Activities of Early Italian Banks
_____ The History of Banking
_____ Transactions of Early Italian Banks

    (A) comprehensive title
    (B) too broad
    (C) too narrow

2. The phrase "adverse balance of trade," as used in this selection, means

☐ (A) the scale for weighing goods for trade was not balanced well
☐ (B) unbalanced trade which causes inflation
☐ (C) more money came in than went out
☐ (D) more money went out than came in

3. The western states mentioned in this selection might include

☐ (A) France, England, and Holland
☐ (B) California, Nevada, and Texas
☐ (C) Italy and England
☐ (D) Florence, Bardi, and Alberti

4. All of the following are mentioned as activities of Italian bankers *except*

☐ (A) accepting deposits
☐ (B) collecting interest on loans
☐ (C) giving interest on loans
☐ (D) financing wars
☐ (E) none of the above

5. Italian banks are said to have collected interest by

☐ (A) receiving foreign deposits
☐ (B) extending credit (making loans) to foreigners
☐ (C) issuing notes
☐ (D) dealing in bills of exchange

PASSAGE L

NOTE: The following selection is somewhat long and complicated. To help organize your reading, first read the question and alternatives printed here below. Then read the selection and try to learn the answer to this question, as well as the other facts presented. (The question appears again with answer choices as question #5 following the selection.)

QUESTION: *According to the selection, which three characteristics listed below are absent from international law but are considered by some observers to be necessary for real law?*

    I. *voluntary compliance and the force of public opinion*
    II. *a legislative body to write laws*
    III. *an organ to enforce laws*
    IV. *a judicial body to decide all cases*

1 In comparison with other civilized systems of
2 law, international law has distinctive character-
3 istics that have led some observers to question the
4 propriety of calling it "law." There is no interna-
5 tional legislature comparable to a congress or
6 parliament that can enact, by a majority vote, new
7 rules of law binding on all states. Treaties, which
8 are sometimes called "international legislation,"
9 bind only such states as consent to be bound by
10 them. Very few treaties have been accepted by all
11 states. The development of new rules through
12 customary practice is a slow and uncertain pro-
13 cess, giving rise to many controversies. There
14 are, furthermore, no international courts with
15 jurisdiction over all states. Even the International
16 Court of Justice, a principal organ of the United
17 Nations, has no such jurisdiction. If a state sues
18 another state before the International Court of
19 Justice, or any other international tribunal, the
20 suit will fail unless it is shown that the defendant
21 state has consented to be sued. As a result, only a
22 small proportion of international disputes are
23 decided by international tribunals. Other dis-
24 putes remain unsettled or are settled by political
25 procedures in which law often plays a minor part.
26 And, finally, there is no world government to
27 enforce international law by coercive measures.
28 Although the United Nations has wide powers to
29 maintain international peace and security, the
30 enforcement of international law in situations not
31 involving peace and security is not one of its
32 functions. The observance of international law
33 thus rests largely on voluntary compliance and on
34 the force of public opinion.

1. Below are three possible titles for this passage. In each blank, write the letter of the phrase (A, B, or C) which best describes that title.

   _____ The International Court of Justice
   _____ Weaknesses of International Law
   _____ History and Characteristics of Laws

   (A) comprehensive title
   (B) too narrow
   (C) too broad

2. The word "states," according to the context of this passage, refers to

   ☐ (A) states in the United States
   ☐ (B) all U.S. states except Hawaii and Alaska
   ☐ (C) all countries of the world
   ☐ (D) countries like the U.S. and the U.S.S.R. which are divided into states

3. The selection indicates that

   ☐ (A) national laws are generally weak and unenforceable
   ☐ (B) the International Court of Justice of the United Nations creates international laws
   ☐ (C) countries are bound only by treaties they accept
   ☐ (D) The United Nations' International Court of Justice settles the majority of conflicts between countries

4. According to the selection, all of the following statements are correct *except*

   ☐ (A) a country cannot be sued in the International Court of Justice unless it agrees to be sued
   ☐ (B) the International Court of Justice cannot depend on the United Nations to enforce that court's decisions
   ☐ (C) the United Nations enforces all international law
   ☐ (D) some observers have questioned whether international law should really be called law

5. According to the selection, which three characteristics listed below are absent from international law but are considered by some observers to be necessary for real law?

   I. *voluntary compliance and the force of public opinion*
   II. *a legislative body to write laws*
   III. *an organ to enforce laws*
   IV. *a judicial body to decide all cases*

   ☐ (A) I, II, and III
   ☐ (B) I, III, and IV
   ☐ (C) II, III, and IV
   ☐ (D) I, II, and IV

Word Power III

Directions: Study each of the Power Words below. Note how each word is pronounced. Then read the context sentences to figure out what each Power Word means. In the left-hand margin next to each Power Word, try to jot down a synonym or short definition which defines that word.

Power Words	sobriety	intrepid	distraught	simile
	sporadically	disheveled	maudlin	interim

1. **sobriety** | sə **brī′** ĭ tē |
   - After the accident, the driver's sobriety was questioned.

2. **sporadically** | spô **răd′** ĭk ə lē |
   - Earthquakes occur sporadically in California, perhaps once a year.
   - I put money into my savings account sporadically, not according to a fixed schedule.

3. **intrepid** | ĭn **trĕp′** ĭd |
   - She was an intrepid hunter and boldly turned to face the charging elephant.
   - Becoming an astronaut requires an intrepid personality.

4. **disheveled** | dĭ **shĕv′** əld |
   - Her clothes were so disheveled it appeared she had slept in them.
   - When he stepped out of the wind, he took a second to comb his disheveled hair.

5. **distraught** | dĭ **strôt′** |
   - The accident left the driver shaken and distraught.
   - I'm so distraught I can't think straight!

6. **maudlin** | **môd′** lĭn |
   - The maudlin play, with people crying in every scene, did not attract a big audience.
   - At our family reunion, my mother became so maudlin she even hugged and kissed the dog!

7. **simile** | **sĭm′** ə lē |
   - "The child is as quiet as a mouse" is a simile.

8. **interim** | **ĭn′** tər ĭm |
   - We were between our Florida and California shows, so in the interim we visited friends in Massachusetts.
   - If you have quit your job and your new job does not start until next month, how will you fill the interim?

ă pat / ā pay / â care / ä father / ĕ pet / ē be / ĭ pit / ī pie / î fierce / ŏ pot / ō go / ô paw, for / oi oil / o͝o book / o͞o boot / ou out / ŭ cut / û fur / th the / th thin / hw which / zh vision / ə ago, item, pencil, atom, circus

Meaning Comprehension

Directions: Use what you have learned from the context sentences to identify the correct definition of each Power Word. In the blank next to each Power Word, write the letter of its correct definition.

Power Words

_____ sobriety
_____ sporadically
_____ intrepid
_____ disheveled
_____ distraught
_____ maudlin
_____ simile
_____ interim

Definitions

a. fearless, not trembling
b. time between
c. seriousness; mastery of oneself; opposite of drunkenness
d. mentally agitated, extremely upset, crazed
e. overly and weakly sentimental, excessively emotional
f. a figure of speech comparing two things, generally with "as" or "like"
g. disarranged, messy, rumpled, in disorder
h. occasionally, irregularly

Context Application

Directions: Each of the following sentences has two blanks. Use what you have learned about the Power Words to determine which Power Word best belongs in each of the blanks. Then write the appropriate Power Word in each blank. Use each Power Word only once.

1. When he is intoxicated he only speaks _____ , with long silences in between, and he becomes _____ , crying over how much he'll miss his friends after they pass away.

2. The _____ mother who had lost her daughter took us all out of our party mood and into an attitude of _____ and concern.

3. To show how _____ his father had been during the attack, the child used a _____ and said "He was brave as a lion."

4. In the _____ between acts of the show, the clown re-arranged her _____ costume.

Muscle Builder Analogies

Directions: Each exercise below is an analogy, with one or two terms missing. Choose the Power Word which belongs in each blank of the analogy so that the analogy reads correctly. Write the appropriate Power Word in each blank. Note that some of the Power Words will not be used.

1. COWARDLY is to FEARFUL as BRAVE is to _____

2. SOMETIMES is to ALWAYS as _____ is to REGULARLY

3. CALM is to _____ as NEAT is to _____

Word Power IV

Directions: Study each of the Power Words below. Note how each word is pronounced. Then read the context sentences to figure out what each Power Word means. In the left-hand margin next to each Power Word, try to jot down a synonym or short definition which defines that word.

Power Words	diverse	schism	credible	pugnacious
	genial	incongruous	frivolous	commence

1. **diverse** | dĭ **vûrs′** |
   - Americans are people of diverse national origin but common pride.
   - Gina's and Leah's interests are so diverse, I'd be surprised if they have anything in common.

2. **genial** | **jēn′** yəl |
   - After a cold winter, the genial sunshine of spring is a welcome change.
   - What a genial, kind person he is!

3. **schism** | **skĭz′** əm |
   - The schism between the student's goals and willingness to work caused her much frustration.
   - The argument between the two husbands created a schism between the Doe and Jones families.

4. **incongruous** | ĭn **kǒng′** grōō əs |
   - The tophat on his head was incongruous with the soiled overalls on his body.
   - Our children were puzzled by the incongruous seriousness of that clown.

5. **credible** | **krĕd′** ə bəl |
   - The story told by the suspect did not strike the detective as credible.
   - Her excuse for being late was credible, so Andy forgave her.

6. **frivolous** | **frĭv′** ə ləs |
   - His silly, frivolous remarks disrupted the meeting.
   - Let's be serious and not waste time on frivolous ideas.

7. **pugnacious** | pŭg **nā′** shəs |
   - A wild pig is a pugnacious animal that is rumored to attack men.
   - A bully is characterized by a pugnacious personality.

8. **commence** | kə **mĕns′** |
   - At the age of 35, Smithy took the necessary English courses to commence a literary career.
   - In the United States, most sporting events commence with the playing of the National Anthem.

ă pat / ā pay / â care / ä father / ĕ pet / ē be / ĭ pit / ī pie / î fierce / ŏ pot / ō go / ô paw, for / oi oil / ŏŏ book /
ōō boot / ou out / ŭ cut / ü fur / *th* the / th thin / hw which / zh vision / ə ago, item, pencil, atom, circus

Meaning Comprehension

Directions: Use what you have learned from the context sentences to identify the correct definition of each Power Word. In the blank next to each Power Word, write the letter of its correct definition.

Power Words

_____ diverse
_____ genial
_____ schism
_____ incongruous
_____ credible
_____ frivolous
_____ pugnacious
_____ commence

Definitions

a. aggressive, quarrelsome, belligerent
b. begin, start
c. friendly, warm, pleasant
d. different, unlike, distinct
e. separation, division
f. believable, plausible; reliable
g. lacking harmony, consistency or compatibility; fitting together poorly, even humorously
h. lacking seriousness; unimportant, irrelevant

Context Application

Directions: Each of the following sentences has two blanks. Use what you have learned about the Power Words to determine which Power Word best belongs in each of the blanks. Then write the appropriate Power Word in each blank. Use each Power Word only once.

1. Wanda's _____ attitude towards academic work was _____ with her hope of attending medical school.

2. Because of the great _____ between his promises and actions, the politician's former supporters no longer found him _____ .

3. A _____ traveler will often _____ friendly conversation with other passengers on a plane or ship.

4. Although the ambassadors represented the _____ needs and interests of their countries, they were not _____ people and were able to arrive at reasonable compromises.

Muscle Builder Analogies

Directions: Each exercise below is an analogy, with one or two terms missing. Choose the Power Word which belongs in each blank of the analogy so that the analogy reads correctly. Write the appropriate Power Word in each blank. Note that some of the Power Words will not be used.

1. BEGIN is to END as _____ is to TERMINATE

2. SERIOUS is to SERMON as _____ is to JOKE

3. CONSISTENT is to INCONSISTENT as CONGRUOUS is to

_____

ADDITIONAL ASSIGNMENTS

1. Pick a section from one of your textbooks, encyclopedias, or other sources which is about 100 words long. Then write two multiple-choice questions on the material. Each question should have only one correct answer and at least one incorrect alternative which a person might choose if he or she is not reading carefully.

    Let a peer read the section and answer the questions. If the peer has difficulty answering either question, check to see whether the difficulty is because the question is unclear, or because the passage is too difficult for that person. Rewrite your questions if necessary.

    (Note: The ability to ask clear questions is a crucial life skill. Spending the effort to become better at asking clear, meaningful questions will reap large benefits in later life.)

2. On the lines below, write a short summary of Passage L in your own words. In your summary, be sure to include the main idea of the passage and all of the details that are crucial to understanding the passage.

_____

_____

_____

_____

_____

_____

_____

_____

_____

_____

_____

_____

_____

_____

_____

UNIT
6

CAUSE-EFFECT, REASON-CONSEQUENCE, PREMISE-CONCLUSION

OBJECTIVES: When you have completed this unit you should

- be able to identify one or more reasons and consequences stated in a written description;
- be able to identify one or more premises and a conclusion stated in a written description;
- know the meanings of the following POWER WORDS.

POWER WORDS

solicitous	enthralled	universal	amoral
ebullient	inclination	inextricably	atrophied
inscrutable	assimilate	vehement	archaeology
anomaly	amend	excavated	aficionado
abhorrence	discern	prognosis	alacrity
dissuade	authentic	manifestation	anemic
squalid	listless	notorious	antipathy
duplicity	ensue	utopian	asymmetrical

Word Power I

Directions: Study each of the Power Words below. Note how each word is pronounced. Then read the context sentences to figure out what each Power Word means. In the left-hand margin next to each Power Word, try to jot down a synonym or short definition which defines that word.

Power Words

solicitous	inscrutable	abhorrence	squalid
ebullient	anomaly	dissuade	duplicity

---

1. **solicitous** | sə **lĭs′** ĭ təs |
   - The coach was solicitous about the players' health and advised them to eat and sleep properly.

2. **ebullient** | ĭ **bŭl′** yənt |
   - Happy, ebullient music raised their spirits.
   - The reviewer described that actor's performance as light-hearted and ebullient.

3. **inscrutable** | ĭn **skrōō′** tə bəl |
   - A good poker player keeps an inscrutable facial expression.
   - It has been said that for the Westerner the mind of the Oriental is inscrutable.

4. **anomaly** | ə **nŏm′** ə lē |
   - A two-headed animal is an anomaly of nature.
   - A horse and buggy travelling on an interstate highway would be an anomaly.

5. **abhorrence** | ăb **hôr′** əns |
   - She had a strong abhorrence for snakes and killed all she found while hiking.
   - Pedro felt he could not serve in the military because of his abhorrence of war.

6. **dissuade** | dĭ **swād′** |
   - Alvin had decided to quit, and it was impossible to dissuade him from that decision.
   - Can you be dissuaded from doing that or is your mind made up?

7. **squalid** | **skwŏl′** ĭd |
   - The neglected children's squalid clothing had not been washed for weeks.
   - It distressed me to see them living in such a squalid building.

8. **duplicity** | dōō **plĭs′** ĭ tē |
   - His duplicity became known and he was no longer trusted.
   - Hitler's duplicity became clear when, shortly after he signed a peace treaty with Poland, he invaded that country.

ă pat / ā pay / â care / ä father / ĕ pet / ē be / ĭ pit / ī pie / î fierce / ŏ pot / ō go / ô paw, for / oi oil / ŏŏ book / ōō boot / ou out / ŭ cut / û fur / *th* the / th thin / hw which / zh vision / ə ago, item, pencil, atom, circus

Meaning Comprehension

Directions: Use what you have learned from the context sentences to identify the correct definition of each Power Word. In the blank next to each Power Word, write the letter of its correct definition.

Power Words

_____ solicitous
_____ ebullient
_____ inscrutable
_____ anomaly
_____ abhorrence
_____ dissuade
_____ squalid
_____ duplicity

Definitions

a. not easily known or understood
b. hatred, loathing, scorn
c. irregularity, abnormality
d. persuade against, talk out of
e. deceptiveness, saying one thing but acting differently
f. bubbling with happiness, effervescent
g. having a dirty, shabby appearance
h. anxious and concerned

Context Application

Directions: Each of the following sentences has two blanks. Use what you have learned about the Power Words to determine which Power Word best belongs in each of the blanks. Then write the appropriate Power Word in each blank. Use each Power Word only once.

1. It is difficult to have a joyful, _____ personality when you live under poverty-stricken, _____ conditions.

2. The _____ mother was worried her son might have an accident and tried to _____ him from entering the race.

3. The boss's feelings are _____; she never exhibits affection or _____ for anything, but always maintains a calm outward appearance.

4. His _____ is an _____ in a family known for its high morals.

Muscle Builder Analogies

Directions: Each exercise below is an analogy, with one or two terms missing. Choose the Power Word which belongs in each blank of the analogy so that the analogy reads correctly. Write the appropriate Power Word in each blank. Note that some of the Power Words will not be used.

1. TRUTH is to HONESTY as DECEPTION is to _____

2. ELEGANT is to PALACE as _____ is to SLUM

3. _____ is to ELATED as _____ is to TROUBLED

Word Power II

Power Words	enthralled	assimilate	discern	listless
	inclination	amend	authentic	ensue

1. **enthralled** | ĕn **thrôld'** |
   - People are inspired and enthralled on visiting the Grand Canyon.
   - The beauty of Thelma's voice enthralls all who listen to her.

2. **inclination** | ĭn' klə **nā'** shən |
   - He had an inclination to be aggressive and this cost him many friendships.
   - My inclination is to leave rather than wait around.

3. **assimilate** | ə **sĭm'** ə lāt' |
   - American culture has been able to assimilate the customs of other countries.
   - In our fast-paced world, we must be able to assimilate changes in lifestyle without undue fuss.

4. **amend** | ə **mĕnd'** |
   - To amend the Constitution means to formally change it.
   - Can I amend my answer by changing 1490 to 1492?

5. **discern** | dĭ **sûrn'** |
   - The child was unable to discern right from wrong.
   - In aerial bombing, bombardiers must be able to discern specific targets miles before they are reached.

6. **authentic** | ŏ **thĕn'** tĭk |
   - That is an authentic art treasure, not an imitation.
   - The university's library has an authentic Gutenberg Bible.

7. **listless** | **lĭst'** lĭs |
   - Failure to get sufficient sleep left him listless and uninterested in studying.
   - Rainy days make me feel so listless that I just want to stay in bed.

8. **ensue** | ĕn **sōō'** |
   - If a person works hard, success will generally ensue.
   - We were sure a fight would ensue when one of the men removed his jacket.

Meaning Comprehension

Directions: Use what you have learned from the context sentences to identify the correct definition of each Power Word. In the blank next to each Power Word, write the letter of its correct definition.

Power Words

_____ enthralled
_____ inclination
_____ assimilate
_____ amend
_____ discern
_____ authentic
_____ listless
_____ ensue

Definitions

a. recognize, distinguish, see or separate clearly
b. take place afterward, result, follow
c. genuine not imitation; trustworthy
d. tendency to act or be a certain way; preference
e. held spellbound, enchanted, charmed
f. without energy or motivation to move or exert oneself
g. absorb, take in, digest
h. formally alter or change; correct, improve

Context Application

Directions: Each of the following sentences has two blanks. Use what you have learned about the Power Words to determine which Power Word best belongs in each of the blanks. Then write the appropriate Power Word in each blank. Use each Power Word only once.

1. If Senator Walton tries to _____ the new law, a violent quarrel will _____ .

2. Elaine was _____ by the woman's jewelry, unaware that there was not one _____ gem in the collection.

3. Her _____ to be _____ was not in harmony with her ambition to be a great athlete.

4. The professor spoke so poorly that students were unable to pinpoint or _____ his main ideas and _____ them into their own knowledge of the field.

Muscle Builder Analogies

Directions: Each exercise below is an analogy, with one or two terms missing. Choose the Power Word which belongs in each blank of the analogy so that the analogy reads correctly. Write the appropriate Power Word in each blank. Note that some of the Power Words will not be used.

1. FORGERY is to ORIGINAL as FAKE is to _____

2. INACTIVE is to ACTION as _____ is to ENERGY

3. ASSIMILATE is to INCORPORATE as _____ is to MODIFY

INTRODUCTION

A major focus of text material, research reports, business literature, etc. is the explanation of *cause-effect relationships*—the *causes* of certain occurrences, and the *effects* produced by certain actions. Failure to correctly comprehend these relationships can result in major misunderstandings or misconceptions about the subject of any written material.

In your own thinking you also use this thought pattern heavily. What *caused* the boss to make me do this project over? What would be the *effect* of studying an extra hour for the upcoming exam? A worn brake is *causing* my car brakes to squeal.

Oftentimes, a cause-effect relationship is easier to understand if it is thought of as a *reason-consequence relationship*. Due to a given *reason*, a certain *consequence* resulted. Because a brake pad is worn (*reason*), my car brakes squeal (*consequence*).

A close cousin to these relationships is the *premise-conclusion relationship*. Just as causes lead to effects, in the mind's eye *premises* lead to *conclusions*. It will rain today (*premise*), so I will need to wear my raincoat (*conclusion*).

This unit is divided into several parts which will systematically build your skills in analyzing and comprehending written descriptions of cause-effect, reason-consequence, and premise-conclusion relationships.

PART I: STATED REASON AND CONSEQUENCE

INTRODUCTION

Sentences will often present a reason and a consequence together as part of a complete thought. To comprehend the complete thought, you must mentally identify the reason and the consequence being expressed. Read this sentence:

José ate an apple because he was hungry.

When you analyze the meaning of this sentence, you can identify that there is a "reason" stated in the sentence.

REASON: José was hungry.

You can also identify a "consequence."

CONSEQUENCE: José ate an apple.

By identifying the "reason" and the "consequence," the total thought expressed in the sentence is fully comprehended.

INSTRUCTIONS FOR THE EXERCISES

Each of the following exercises presents a sentence which expresses a reason-consequence relationship. Read the sentence. Then write the "reason" and the "consequence" stated in the sentence. Write the reason and the consequence as complete sentences.

EXERCISE 1

Phil drank some water because he was thirsty.

REASON: _____

CONSEQUENCE: _____

_____

EXERCISE 2

Phil was thirsty so he drank some water.

REASON: _____

CONSEQUENCE: _____

_____

EXERCISE 3

[NOTE: Check to see that your answers to exercises 1 and 2 are the same. Thus, you can conclude that the phrasing of those two sentences expresses the same idea.]

Jetta went to the store because she needed some milk.

REASON: _____

CONSEQUENCE: _____

_____

EXERCISE 4

Jetta needed some milk so she went to the store.

REASON: _____

CONSEQUENCE: _____

_____

EXERCISE 5

(Check to see that your answers to exercises 3 and 4 are the same.)

Sally was immediately hired for she had proven her ability in her previous work.

REASON: _____

CONSEQUENCE: _____

EXERCISE 6

Sally had proven her ability in her previous work, therefore she was immediately hired.

REASON: _____

CONSEQUENCE: _____

_____

EXERCISE 7

(Check to see that your answers to exercises 5 and 6 are the same.)

People rushed to their homes when the evening rain began.

REASON: _____

CONSEQUENCE: _____

_____

EXERCISE 8

Napoleon lost at Trafalgar because Nelson was a better naval strategist.

REASON: _____

CONSEQUENCE: _____

_____

EXERCISE 9

Because salaries are increasing, inflation is on the rise.

REASON: _____

CONSEQUENCE: _____

_____

EXERCISE 10

Because inflation is on the rise, salaries are increasing.

REASON: _____

CONSEQUENCE: _____

EXERCISE 11

(Look at the sentences in exercises 9 and 10. Exercise 9 says that increasing salaries cause rising inflation; exercise 10 says that rising inflation causes increasing salaries. These might represent the opposite opinions of two economists.)

The rise in inflation is causing salaries to increase.

REASON: _____

CONSEQUENCE: _____

EXERCISE 12

(Check to see that your answers to exercises 10 and 11 are the same.)

Phineas' fine cooking stemmed from his mother's teaching.

REASON: _____

CONSEQUENCE: _____

EXERCISE 13

Paula's knowledge of computer programming got her the job at Acme Electronics.

REASON: _____

CONSEQUENCE: _____

EXERCISE 14

Pericles' ability and honesty earned him the confidence of the Athenian people.

REASON: _____

CONSEQUENCE: _____

EXERCISE 15

Pericles was re-elected to office in Athens repeatedly because he had the confidence of the people.

REASON: _____

CONSEQUENCE: _____

PART II: CHAINS OF CAUSES

INTRODUCTION

Some sentences express a sequence of cause-effect relationships. That is, the sentences have the form: A caused B and B caused C. Read the sentence below.

Jennifer worked hard all day, which made her very tired, so she went to bed early.

When you analyze what this sentence is saying, you can identify that there are <u>two</u> relationships expressed in the sentence.

Relationship 1 — **Jennifer worked hard all day, which made her very tired.**

Relationship 2 — **Jennifer was very tired, so she went to bed early.**

Using what you have learned from Part I of this unit, you can further add to your understanding of this sentence by identifying the "reason" and the "consequence" stated in each of the two relationships.

Relationship 1 { **Reason: Jennifer worked hard all day.**
Consequence: Jennifer was very tired.

Relationship 2 { **Reason: Jennifer was very tired.**
Consequence: Jennifer went to bed early.

Through this type of careful analysis, sentences expressing a sequence of cause-effect relationships can be easily comprehended.

INSTRUCTIONS FOR THE EXERCISES

Each of the exercises which follow presents a sentence which expresses two cause-effect relationships. Read the sentence carefully. Then write the "reason" and the "consequence" that make up <u>each</u> of the two relationships. Write all reasons and consequences as complete sentences.

EXERCISE 1

Tanya ran for half an hour, which made her thirsty, so she drank a quart of water.

RELATIONSHIP 1 { REASON: _____
CONSEQUENCE: _____

RELATIONSHIP 2 { REASON: _____
CONSEQUENCE: _____

EXERCISE 2

Judy used her dictionary regularly, which increased her word power, so she scored high on the Scholastic Aptitude Test (SAT).

RELATIONSHIP 1 { REASON: _____
CONSEQUENCE: _____

RELATIONSHIP 2 { REASON: _____
CONSEQUENCE: _____

EXERCISE 3

Bobbie ate a lot for dinner because she worked hard all day, and that made her very hungry.

RELATIONSHIP 1 { REASON: _____
CONSEQUENCE: _____

RELATIONSHIP 2 { REASON: _____
CONSEQUENCE: _____

EXERCISE 4

Bobbie ate a lot for dinner because she was very hungry due to working hard all day.

RELATIONSHIP 1 { REASON: _____
CONSEQUENCE: _____

RELATIONSHIP 2 { REASON: _____
CONSEQUENCE: _____

EXERCISE 5

Due to working hard all day Bobbie was very hungry, so she ate a lot for dinner.

RELATIONSHIP 1 { REASON: _____
                { CONSEQUENCE: _____

RELATIONSHIP 2 { REASON: _____
                { CONSEQUENCE: _____

EXERCISE 6

Bobbie worked hard all day, which made her very hungry, so she ate a lot for dinner.

RELATIONSHIP 1 { REASON: _____
                { CONSEQUENCE: _____

RELATIONSHIP 2 { REASON: _____
                { CONSEQUENCE: _____

EXERCISE 7

(NOTE: Check to see that your answers to exercises 3, 4, 5, and 6 are the same. These four sentences all express the same ideas.)

Bill Jonet, exhausted from playing tennis, went right to bed.

RELATIONSHIP 1 { REASON: _____
                { CONSEQUENCE: _____

RELATIONSHIP 2 { REASON: _____
                { CONSEQUENCE: _____

EXERCISE 8

Because he was exhausted from playing tennis, Bill Jonet went right to bed.

RELATIONSHIP 1 { REASON: _____
                { CONSEQUENCE: _____

RELATIONSHIP 2 { REASON: _____
                { CONSEQUENCE: _____

EXERCISE 9

(Check to see that your answers to exercises 7 and 8 are the same.)

The aged bear, hungry from three months of hibernation, devoured the sweet berries.

RELATIONSHIP 1 { REASON: _____

CONSEQUENCE: _____

RELATIONSHIP 2 { REASON: _____

CONSEQUENCE: _____

EXERCISE 10

The aged bear was hungry from three months of hibernation, therefore it devoured the sweet berries.

RELATIONSHIP 1 { REASON: _____

CONSEQUENCE: _____

RELATIONSHIP 2 { REASON: _____

CONSEQUENCE: _____

EXERCISE 11

(Check to see that your answers to exercises 9 and 10 are the same.)

The development of steam power led to better transportation between countries, and this resulted in an increased exchange of goods and ideas.

RELATIONSHIP 1 { REASON: _____

CONSEQUENCE: _____

RELATIONSHIP 2 { REASON: _____

CONSEQUENCE: _____

EXERCISE 12

Because Augustus was Caesar's son, the army was loyal to him, and this allowed him to defeat his rival Mark Anthony.

RELATIONSHIP 1 { REASON: _____
CONSEQUENCE: _____

RELATIONSHIP 2 { REASON: _____
CONSEQUENCE: _____

EXERCISE 13

Pericles was elected the leader of Athens for 30 years because his ability and honesty earned him the confidence of the people.

RELATIONSHIP 1 { REASON: _____
CONSEQUENCE: _____

RELATIONSHIP 2 { REASON: _____
CONSEQUENCE: _____

EXERCISE 14

Pericles had ability and honesty which caused people to have confidence in him, and as a result they elected him leader of Athens for 30 years.

RELATIONSHIP 1 { REASON: _____
CONSEQUENCE: _____

RELATIONSHIP 2 { REASON: _____
CONSEQUENCE: _____

EXERCISE 15

Pericles started a building program that created employment, and this made him popular in Athens.

RELATIONSHIP 1 { REASON: _____
CONSEQUENCE: _____

RELATIONSHIP 2 { REASON: _____
CONSEQUENCE: _____

PART III: TWO INDEPENDENT REASONS AND A CONSEQUENCE

INTRODUCTION

In the following sentence, two "reasons" are stated which are *independent* of each other—they each can exist as a reason without the other—and then a consequence stemming from those two reasons is stated. Read the following sentence.

Tod was hungry and the refrigerator was empty, so he went to the store for food.

Can you identify the two "reasons" and the "consequence"? Your mental analysis of this sentence might look like this:

REASON 1: Tod was hungry.
REASON 2: The refrigerator was empty.
CONSEQUENCE: Tod went to the store for food.

INSTRUCTIONS FOR THE EXERCISES

Each exercise which follows presents a sentence that contains two independent reasons and a consequence. Read the sentence carefully, and then write the two reasons and the consequence.

EXERCISE 1

Paula likes oysters and they are on sale at the supermarket, so she bought two cans of them.

REASON 1: _____

REASON 2: _____

CONSEQUENCE: _____

_____

EXERCISE 2

Fred's car wouldn't start and he wanted to get to the store, so he walked there.

REASON 1: _____

REASON 2: _____

CONSEQUENCE: _____

_____

EXERCISE 3

Patrice walked to school quickly because she had left home later than usual and she didn't want to be tardy.

REASON 1: _____

REASON 2: _____

CONSEQUENCE: _____

_____

EXERCISE 4

Linda read the textbook carefully because she wanted to score well on the upcoming test and she knew she had to understand the textbook thoroughly to do so.

REASON 1: _____

REASON 2: _____

CONSEQUENCE: _____

EXERCISE 5

Socrates' ideas were seen as threatening by the Athenian establishment, yet he insisted on saying what he thought, so he was sentenced to drink hemlock poison.

REASON 1: _____

REASON 2: _____

CONSEQUENCE: _____

EXERCISE 6

The play *Lysistrata* was amusing to the Athenians because in it women take over the government, and women in politics were unheard of in ancient Athens.

REASON 1: _____

REASON 2: _____

CONSEQUENCE: _____

EXERCISE 7

In the play *Lysistrata* women take over the government, and since women in politics were unheard of in ancient Athens, the Athenians found the play amusing.

REASON 1: _____

REASON 2: _____

CONSEQUENCE: _____

EXERCISE 8

(Check to see that your answers to exercises 6 and 7 are the same.)

After touring the Grand Canyon and the Rocky Mountains, and because their homeland had a large mountain range, the tourists found the Catskill Mountains unexciting.

REASON 1: _____

REASON 2: _____

CONSEQUENCE: _____

PART IV: STATED REASON, IMPLIED REASON, CONSEQUENCE

INTRODUCTION

If an idea is suggested but not actually stated, we say it is *implied*. Here is a sentence with a stated reason, an implied reason, and a consequence:

The refrigerator was empty, so Shelly went to a restaurant to eat.

Your mental analysis of this sentence might look like:

STATED REASON: The refrigerator was empty.
IMPLIED REASON: Shelly wanted to eat.
CONSEQUENCE: Shelly went to a restaurant.

Note that the implied reason is not directly stated in the sentence, but it is suggested by the stated reason and the consequence.

INSTRUCTIONS FOR THE EXERCISES

In the following exercise set, each exercise presents a sentence that has a stated reason, an implied reason, and a consequence. After you read each sentence, write the stated reason, the implied reason, and the consequence.

EXERCISE 1

Felix's car had broken down, so he walked to the store.

STATED REASON: _____

IMPLIED REASON: _____

CONSEQUENCE: _____

EXERCISE 2

Gwen left home later than usual, so she walked to school quickly.

STATED REASON: _____

IMPLIED REASON: _____

CONSEQUENCE: _____

EXERCISE 3

The boy stood on a chair to reach the cookies because he was short.

STATED REASON: _____

IMPLIED REASON: _____

CONSEQUENCE: _____

EXERCISE 4

Riva read the textbook carefully because she knew reading the textbook carefully was the only way to score well on the upcoming quiz.

STATED REASON: _____

IMPLIED REASON: _____

CONSEQUENCE: _____

EXERCISE 5

Six inches of snow fell, so drivers put chains on their tires.

STATED REASON: _____

IMPLIED REASON: _____

CONSEQUENCE: _____

EXERCISE 6

Mr. Wize, a candidate for political office, lost his coat at a restaurant, so he bought a new one.

STATED REASON: _____

IMPLIED REASON: _____

CONSEQUENCE: _____

_____

EXERCISE 7

Although it was almost new, Juanita's blue dress was torn, so she wore her red dress to the party.

STATED REASON: _____

IMPLIED REASON: _____

CONSEQUENCE: _____

_____

EXERCISE 8

Socrates insisted on saying what he thought, so he was sentenced by the Athenian establishment to drink hemlock poison.

STATED REASON: _____

IMPLIED REASON: _____

CONSEQUENCE: _____

_____

EXERCISE 9

Since Napoleon's navy was defeated, he decided to use his army to beat England.

STATED REASON: _____

IMPLIED REASON: _____

CONSEQUENCE: _____

EXERCISE 10

Napoleon placed his troops in ports from Spain to Russia because he felt he could beat England by cutting off her trade.

STATED REASON: _____

IMPLIED REASON: _____

CONSEQUENCE: _____

_____

EXERCISE 11

Napoleon spread his troops too thin, therefore an English army defeated him at Waterloo.

STATED REASON: _____

IMPLIED REASON: _____

CONSEQUENCE: _____

PART V: PREMISE-CONCLUSION

INTRODUCTION

Some sentences are written according to a "premise-conclusion" pattern. This premise-conclusion pattern is very similar to the "reason-consequence" pattern you are now familiar with. A "premise" is a statement of information taken to be true, and a "conclusion" is a statement that logically follows from one or more premises. Read the sentence below; it contains two premises and one conclusion.

> **We know that Juan is taller than Fred, and Fred is taller than Gene, so we can conclude that Juan is taller than Gene.**

Your mental analysis of this sentence might be:

> **PREMISE 1: Juan is taller than Fred.**
> **PREMISE 2: Fred is taller than Gene.**
> **CONCLUSION: Juan is taller than Gene.**

Note that the sentence begins with the phrase "We know that," but this phrase is not itself a logical part of the basic premises, so it does not get included in our analysis of the first and second premises.

INSTRUCTIONS FOR THE EXERCISES

In the exercises that follow, each exercise contains two premises and one conclusion. Read each sentence, and then write the two premises and the conclusion. Write all premises and conclusions as complete sentences.

Remember, write just the basic premises and the conclusion. Do not write any extra information or verbiage.

EXERCISE 1

Ramona can run faster than Pedro, and Pedro can run faster than Luis, so it follows that Ramona can run faster than Luis.

PREMISE 1: _____

PREMISE 2: _____

CONCLUSION: _____

_____

EXERCISE 2

We can conclude that Napoleon was defeated after the American Revolution if we recall that the French Revolution occurred after the American Revolution and Napoleon was defeated some years after the French Revolution.

PREMISE 1: _____

PREMISE 2: _____

CONCLUSION: _____

_____

[Here is a correct analysis of EXERCISE 2. What the sentence says is: The French Revolution occurred after the American Revolution, and Napoleon was defeated some years after the French Revolution; therefore, Napoleon was defeated after the American Revolution. Your written analysis should look like the one below.]

PREMISE 1:   __The French Revolution occurred after the American Revolution._____

PREMISE 2:   __Napoleon was defeated after the French Revolution._____

CONCLUSION: __Napoleon was defeated after the American Revolution._____

_____

EXERCISE 3

Dolores is an American citizen and all American citizens are human beings, so Dolores is a human being.

PREMISE 1: _____

PREMISE 2: _____

CONCLUSION: _____

EXERCISE 4

No animals can live without air, so it follows that beavers cannot live without air because beavers are animals.

PREMISE 1: _____

PREMISE 2: _____

CONCLUSION: _____

EXERCISE 5

We can conclude that beavers cannot live without air because no animals can live without air, and beavers are animals.

PREMISE 1: _____

PREMISE 2: _____

CONCLUSION: _____

EXERCISE 6

(Check to see that your answers to exercises 4 and 5 are the same.)

We know that Audrey went to either New York or Philadelphia, and since she didn't go to Philadelphia we can conclude that she went to New York.

PREMISE 1: _____

PREMISE 2: _____

CONCLUSION: _____

EXERCISE 7

We can infer that Cisco painted his room all red because he said he would paint it either all red or all blue, and we know he didn't have enough blue paint for the entire room.

PREMISE 1: _____

PREMISE 2: _____

CONCLUSION: _____

EXERCISE 8

Ted didn't pay for it, so Rosa must have paid for it, because we know either Ted or Rosa paid for it.

PREMISE 1: _____

PREMISE 2: _____

CONCLUSION: _____

_____

EXERCISE 9

Identifying the chauffeur as the criminal was an elementary deduction, since Dr. Watson brought evidence that the butler did not commit the crime and Sherlock Holmes knew that either the butler or the chauffeur was guilty.

PREMISE 1: _____

PREMISE 2: _____

CONCLUSION: _____

_____

EXERCISE 10

John was not at the party, so we can conclude that he is not a member of the club, since all members of the club attended the party.

PREMISE 1: _____

PREMISE 2: _____

CONCLUSION: _____

_____

EXERCISE 11

If Luther went skiing he had to borrow the family car, so we can deduce that he borrowed the family car, since he did go skiing.

PREMISE 1: _____

PREMISE 2: _____

CONCLUSION: _____

_____

EXERCISE 12

We can conclude that the criminals took the money because we know they would take it if they found it, and we can be sure they found it.

PREMISE 1: _____

PREMISE 2: _____

CONCLUSION: _____

PART VI: PREMISES AND CONCLUSIONS IN PARAGRAPHS

INTRODUCTION

The remaining exercises in this unit are in the form of paragraphs that contain two premises, a conclusion, and additional information or verbiage. You will apply what you have learned so far in this unit to analyzing these larger selections.

INSTRUCTIONS FOR THE EXERCISES

Read the following paragraphs carefully. After each paragraph, write the two premises and the conclusion contained in that paragraph. Just write the premises and the conclusion. Leave out any extraneous information.

EXERCISE 1

Simon looks like a duck when he runs, but he is still faster than Fernando. This may not say much, since Andy, who is 75 years old, is also faster than Fernando. Nevertheless, we can conclude that Simon must be faster than Lewis, because in several races Fernando has proven himself faster than Lewis.

PREMISE 1: _____

PREMISE 2: _____

CONCLUSION: _____

_____

EXERCISE 2

Simon is faster than Fernando. From this we can conclude that Simon is faster than Lewis, because Fernando is faster than Lewis.

PREMISE 1: _____

PREMISE 2: _____

CONCLUSION: _____

_____

EXERCISE 3

If you kept close track of your smoking, you would realize that you smoke three packs of cigarets each day. I have kept track and, believe me, that's how much you smoke. You must therefore acknowledge the conclusion that you are reducing your life expectancy; for no human is an exception to the finding that smoking three packs of cigarets each day reduces life expectancy.

PREMISE 1: _____

PREMISE 2: _____

CONCLUSION: _____

EXERCISE 4

You smoke three packs of cigarets each day. Therefore you are reducing your life expectancy, because smoking three packs each day reduces your life expectancy.

PREMISE 1: _____

PREMISE 2: _____

CONCLUSION: _____

EXERCISE 5

(Check to see that your answers to exercises 3 and 4 are the same.)

That man across the room is the suspect. If he is the criminal, he will try to escape when he sees us. He was often in trouble during his high school years. He sees us and is trying to escape. It is a simple deduction that he is the criminal.

PREMISE 1: _____

PREMISE 2: _____

CONCLUSION: _____

EXERCISE 6

If Plato's family was part of Athen's aristocracy, then Plato—like all other aristocratic Athenian boys—received a fine basic education. Actually, historians don't have much definite knowledge about Plato's early education. But we can deduce that he had a fine basic education for the following reason. In spite of Plato advocating a meritocracy rather than a hereditary aristocracy in his book *The Republic*, many historical facts indicate his family was aristocratic.

PREMISE 1: _____

PREMISE 2: _____

CONCLUSION: _____

Word Power III

Directions: Study each of the Power Words below. Note how each word is pronounced. Then read the context sentences to figure out what each Power Word means. In the left-hand margin next to each Power Word, try to jot down a synonym or short definition which defines that word.

Power Words

universal	vehement	prognosis	notorious
inextricably	excavated	manifestation	utopian

---

1. **universal** | yōō′ nə **vûr′** səl |
   - The need for nutrition is universal to all living organisms.
   - The United Nations works to maintain universal peace.

2. **inextricably** | ĭn **ĕk′** strĭ kə blē |
   - Some folks think their happiness is inextricably chained to their income.
   - A contract is a way of inextricably committing two parties to an agreement.

3. **vehement** | vē′ ə mənt |
   - The girl quit college against her parents' vehement objections.
   - The citizens' vehement opposition to the proposed factory prevented it from being built.

4. **excavated** | ĕks′ kə vā′ tĭd |
   - The machine excavated a large hole for a swimming pool.
   - Professor Rubino was certain that if she excavated at that site she would uncover an ancient tomb.

5. **prognosis** | prŏg **nō′** sĭs |
   - The prognosis of only one year to live shocked the patient.
   - "My prognosis for this product is that it will sell well," said the sales manager.

6. **manifestation** | măn′ ə fĕ **stā′** shən |
   - A radiant smile is a manifestation of inner happiness.
   - An important scientific discovery was that a light beam's color is a manifestation of its wavelength.

7. **notorious** | nō **tôr′** ē əs |
   - That gambler is known by all to be a notorious cheat.
   - That teacher is notorious for his harsh grading.

8. **utopian** | yōō tō′ pē ən |
   - In a utopian world there would be no poverty.

ă pat / ā pay / â care / ä father / ĕ pet / ē be / ĭ pit / ī pie / î fierce / ŏ pot / ō go / ô paw, for / oi oil / ŏŏ book /
ōō boot / ou out / ŭ cut / û fur / th the / th thin / hw which / zh vision / ə ago, item, pencil, atom, circus

Meaning Comprehension

Directions: Use what you have learned from the context sentences to identify the correct definition of each Power Word. In the blank next to each Power Word, write the letter of its correct definition.

Power Words

_____ universal
_____ inextricably
_____ vehement
_____ excavated
_____ prognosis
_____ manifestation
_____ notorious
_____ utopian

Definitions

a. in a way that cannot be untangled, freed or separated
b. everywhere; affecting everything
c. strong and emotional
d. dug a hole, dug up
e. prediction, forecast
f. outward display or expression
g. widely and unfavorably known
h. relating to an ideal society called a utopia which is perfect in laws and social conditions

Context Application

Directions: Each of the following sentences has two blanks. Use what you have learned about the Power Words to determine which Power Word best belongs in each of the blanks. Then write the appropriate Power Word in each blank. Use each Power Word only once.

1. In a _____ society, freedom from hunger and unnecessary suffering would be _____ .

2. The _____ for the patient was _____ tied to her attitude about regaining her health.

3. He is the _____ archaeologist who was publicly denounced because he illegally _____ several sacred Egyptian tombs.

4. Her _____ argument against signing the contract was a _____ of her deep concern for her son's future.

Muscle Builder Analogies

Directions: Each exercise below is an analogy, with one or two terms missing. Choose the Power Word which belongs in each blank of the analogy so that the analogy reads correctly. Write the appropriate Power Word in each blank. Note that some of the Power Words will not be used.

1. ABRAHAM LINCOLN is to FAMOUS as BONNIE AND CLYDE is to _____

2. MACROCOSMIC is to MICROCOSMIC as _____ is to LOCAL

3. FACT is to TRUTH as _____ is to OPINION

Word Power IV

Directions: Study each of the Power Words below. Note how each word is pronounced. Then read the context sentences to figure out what each Power Word means. In the left-hand margin next to each Power Word, try to jot down a synonym or short definition which defines that word.

Power Words	amoral	archaeology	alacrity	antipathy
	atrophied	aficionado	anemic	asymmetrical

1. **amoral** | ā **môr′** əl |
   - The criminal was amoral and felt no responsibility to be honest.
   - One can never trust an amoral person.

2. **atrophied** | **āt′** rə fēd |
   - The plant received insufficient water so it atrophied and died.
   - Tara had been confined to bed for so long that her muscles had atrophied.

3. **archaeology** | är′ kē **ŏl′** ə jē |
   - Archaeology reveals how people lived thousands of years ago.

4. **aficionado** | ə fish′ ə **nä′** dō |
   - Marcie is a classical music aficionado and owns hundreds of records.
   - The size and variety of Sean's collection reveals he is a gun aficionado.

5. **alacrity** | ə **lăk′** rĭ tē |
   - The girl loved horses and accepted the invitation to ride with alacrity.
   - The new employee's alacrity impressed the store owner.

6. **anemic** | ə **nē′** mĭk |
   - An iron deficiency can make one anemic and continually tired.
   - Lou's anemic condition confined him to bed.

7. **antipathy** | ăn **tĭp′** ə thē |
   - His antipathy for alcohol kept him from ever becoming intoxicated.
   - Although Ida felt antipathy for the task, she changed the baby's diaper anyway.

8. **asymmetrical** | ā′ sĭ **mĕt′** rĭ kəl |
   - Cutting the capital letters A or O down the center produces two symmetrical parts, but cutting F or L produces asymmetrical parts.

ă pat / ā pay / â care / ä father / ĕ pet / ē be / ĭ pit / ī pie / î fierce / ŏ pot / ō go / ô paw, for / oi oil / o͝o book / o͞o boot / ou out / ŭ cut / û fur / th the / th thin / hw which / zh vision / ə ago, item, pencil, atom, circus

Meaning Comprehension

Directions: Use what you have learned from the context sentences to identify the correct definition of each Power Word. In the blank next to each Power Word, write the letter of its correct definition.

Power Words

_____ amoral
_____ atrophied
_____ archaeology
_____ aficionado
_____ alacrity
_____ anemic
_____ antipathy
_____ asymmetrical

Definitions

a. lacking symmetry or balanced proportions
b. strong dislike
c. having no morals, no concern for right and wrong
d. scientific study of the material remains of past human life
e. lacking vitality, weak
f. shrunken or degenerated from lack of nourishment or use
g. eagerness, quickness and happiness in response
h. person highly enthusiastic about something, fan

Context Application

Directions: Each of the following sentences has two blanks. Use what you have learned about the Power Words to determine which Power Word best belongs in each of the blanks. Then write the appropriate Power Word in each blank. Use each Power Word only once.

1. After quitting boxing he ate poorly, his muscles atrophied and he looked _____; yet he was still a boxing _____ and watched all the matches he could on television.

2. Although he is an auto mechanic, Bob's hobby is _____; so when the museum needed a mechanic for the expedition to the Egyptian tombs, he volunteered with _____ .

3. He claimed to be _____ , yet he was a good, charitable person and had a strong _____ for dishonesty.

4. Ronnie had trimmed the hedge so it looked symmetrical, but one side had since _____ because it was always in the shade and now the hedge was clearly _____ .

Muscle Builder Analogies

Directions: Each exercise below is an analogy, with one or two terms missing. Choose the Power Word which belongs in each blank of the analogy so that the analogy reads correctly. Write the appropriate Power Word in each blank. Note that some of the Power Words will not be used.

1. STRONG is to ANEMIC as WELL-DEVELOPED is to _____

2. SCALDING is to FRIGID as _____ is to LOVE

3. _____ is to MORALS as _____ is to SYMMETRY

ADDITIONAL ASSIGNMENTS

In the following exercises you will be asked to write problems of your own. After you write each problem, ask a peer to solve it.

1. Write a problem like those in Part I of this unit.

_____

REASON: _____

CONSEQUENCE: _____

2. Write a problem like those in Part II of this unit.

_____

_____

RELATIONSHIP 1 { REASON: _____

CONSEQUENCE: _____

RELATIONSHIP 2 { REASON: _____

CONSEQUENCE: _____

3. Write a problem like those in Part III of this unit.

_____

_____

REASON 1: _____

REASON 2: _____

CONSEQUENCE: _____

4. Write a problem like those in Part IV of this unit.

_____

_____

STATED REASON: _____

IMPLIED REASON: _____

CONSEQUENCE: _____

ADDITIONAL ASSIGNMENTS (continued)

5. Write a problem like those in Part V of this unit.

_____

_____

_____

_____

PREMISE 1: _____

PREMISE 2: _____

CONCLUSION: _____

6. Write a problem like those in Part VI of this unit.

_____

_____

_____

_____

_____

_____

_____

_____

_____

_____

PREMISE 1: _____

PREMISE 2: _____

CONCLUSION: _____

UNIT
7
READING TEXT FOR FULL COMPREHENSION II

OBJECTIVES: When you have completed this unit you should

- be able to comprehend the facts and relationships in selections of text material;
- know the meanings of the following POWER WORDS.

POWER WORDS

brevity	paramount	confide	impulsively
malicious	hedonistic	irresolute	reign
era	frugal	tranquil	cope
caustic	feigns	inexplicable	exuberance
eccentric	taciturn	prudent	benign
convened	annual	solace	incessant
feasible	ambiguity	ensnare	spangled
indispensable	chauvinism	liberal	insurrection

Word Power I

| Power Words | brevity | era | eccentric | feasible |
| | malicious | caustic | convened | indispensable |

1. **brevity** | **brĕv′** ĭ tē |
   - The brevity of Farah's letters from college was a disappointment to her parents.
   - We were able to adjourn the meeting early thanks to the brevity of the final two speeches.

2. **malicious** | mə **lĭsh′** əs |
   - The mayor complained that the reporter's story was a malicious lie, intended to discredit her.
   - Because Angie's behavior is so often malicious, her parents found it hard to believe her when she said she hadn't meant to break her brother's arm.

3. **era** | **îr′** ə |
   - The TV era in leisure pursuits began around 1950.
   - Dinosaurs are creatures of an earlier era.

4. **caustic** | **kô′** stĭk |
   - The speaker's bitter feelings and caustic humor shocked the audience.
   - Joe's caustic remarks offended his boss, and Joe knew he would soon be fired.

5. **eccentric** | ĭk **sĕn′** trĭk |
   - My uncle has eccentric habits, like gargling every morning at 3 o'clock, that make him a difficult guest.
   - She stands out in my mind because I can still remember her eccentric mode of dress.

6. **convened** | kən **vēnd′** |
   - A world conference was convened today in London.
   - The court was convened at 8 o'clock and will be adjourned at 2 o'clock.

7. **feasible** | **fē′** zə bəl |
   - Small classes of only ten students are more desirable than larger classes, but unfortunately they're not feasible in an overcrowded school.
   - We were so badly outnumbered, our only feasible course of action was to retreat.

8. **indispensable** | ĭn′ dĭ **spĕn′** sə bəl |
   - An educated population is an indispensable ingredient of a democracy.
   - Paulette is indispensable to our team; she is our highest scorer.

ă pat / ā pay / â care / ä father / ĕ pet / ē be / ĭ pit / ī pie / î fierce / ŏ pot / ō go / ô paw, for / oi oil / o͝o book /
o͞o boot / ou out / ŭ cut / û fur / *th* the / th thin / hw which / zh vision / ə ago, item, pencil, atom, circus

Meaning
Comprehension

Directions: Use what you have learned from the context sentences to identify the correct definition of each Power Word. In the blank next to each Power Word, write the letter of its correct definition.

Power Words

_____ brevity
_____ malicious
_____ era
_____ caustic
_____ eccentric
_____ convened
_____ feasible
_____ indispensable

Definitions

a. having malice (harmful or evil intentions); spiteful
b. possible; suitable; likely
c. absolutely necessary or essential
d. briefness, conciseness, expression in few words
e. a period of time, generally beginning at a specific point in history
f. odd, different from the normal; off-center
g. severely critical or sarcastic; burning, corroding
h. assembled, called together for a meeting

Context
Application

Directions: Each of the following sentences has two blanks. Use what you have learned about the Power Words to determine which Power Word best belongs in each of the blanks. Then write the appropriate Power Word in each blank. Use each Power Word only once.

1. The major inventors of the _____ called the Industrial Revolution were generally not _____ , but were sensible, normal people.

2. When the chairman _____ the committee, he began the meeting by expressing his anger with a number of _____ , although not malicious, remarks.

3. Since it is not currently _____ to eliminate the _____ tendencies of some criminals, it is necessary to keep them incarcerated.

4. Because a newspaper has limited space, _____ in writing is not just desirable but _____ .

Muscle Builder
Analogies

Directions: Each exercise below is an analogy, with one or two terms missing. Choose the Power Word which belongs in each blank of the analogy so that the analogy reads correctly. Write the appropriate Power Word in each blank. Note that some of the Power Words will not be used.

1. GOOD is to EVIL as KIND is to _____

2. UNNECESSARY is to DISPENSABLE as NECESSARY is to

   _____

3. IMPOSSIBLE is to CANNOT as _____ is to CAN

Word Power II

Directions: Study each of the Power Words below. Note how each word is pronounced. Then read the context sentences to figure out what each Power Word means. In the left-hand margin next to each Power Word, try to jot down a synonym or short definition which defines that word.

Power Words	paramount	frugal	taciturn	ambiguity
	hedonistic	feigns	annual	chauvinism

1. **paramount** | **păr′** ə mount′ |
   - The paramount need of the survivors was for pure water.
   - Of paramount importance is a willingness to "get the job done."

2. **hedonistic** | **hēd′** n ĭz′ tĭk |
   - The hedonistic emperor spent enormous sums on lavish parties.
   - He could be found at the best restaurants and theaters pursuing his hedonistic lifestyle.

3. **frugal** | **froo′** gəl |
   - The cost of a two-week vacation was shocking to his frugal mind.
   - We must be frugal in the use of our natural resources so that our children may also benefit from them.

4. **feigns** | fānz |
   - Paul often feigns a limp to arouse sympathy.
   - Yolanda did not want to take the history test today so she feigned a cold in order to miss school.

5. **taciturn** | **tăs′** ĭ tûrn′ |
   - Cowboy heroes are often portrayed as tight-lipped, taciturn men.
   - Because of her taciturn nature, it is very difficult to get information from her.

6. **annual** | **ăn′** yoo əl |
   - The annual value of coal exports has increased each year since 1978.
   - To get the best bargains look for the annual year-end sales.

7. **ambiguity** | ăm′ bĭ **gyoo′** ĭ tē |
   - The ambiguity of poetry allows it to have more personal meaning, with different people sometimes giving different interpretations.
   - His tests are very difficult because of the ambiguity of his questions.

8. **chauvinism** | **shō′** və nĭz′ əm |
   - Nationalistic chauvinism may entail insensitivity to people of other nations.

ă pat / ā pay / â care / ä father / ĕ pet / ē be / ĭ pit / ī pie / î fierce / ŏ pot / ō go / ô paw, for / oi oil / oŏ book /
oō boot / ou out / ŭ cut / ü fur / th the / th thin / hw which / zh vision / ə ago, item, pencil, atom, circus

Meaning Comprehension

Directions: Use what you have learned from the context sentences to identify the correct definition of each Power Word. In the blank next to each Power Word, write the letter of its correct definition.

Power Words

_____ paramount
_____ hedonistic
_____ frugal
_____ feigns
_____ taciturn
_____ annually
_____ ambiguity
_____ chauvinistic

Definitions

a. believing pleasure is the chief good in life
b. unclearness in meaning, openness to several interpretations
c. highest, greatest, most powerful, major
d. having excessive pride and attachment to one's group (such as family, gender, or country)
e. thrifty, economical, not wasteful
f. habitually quiet
g. fakes, pretends
h. yearly

Context Application

Directions: Each of the following sentences has two blanks. Use what you have learned about the Power Words to determine which Power Word best belongs in each of the blanks. Then write the appropriate Power Word in each blank. Use each Power Word only once.

1. Dad _____ a bad back _____ , in December, so he won't be asked to help decorate the house for the holidays.

2. A _____ person might be described as one who is _____ with words.

3. Clarity and the avoidance of _____ are of _____ concern in technical writing.

4. A _____ individual loves personal pleasure, sometimes in excess, whereas a _____ individual takes excessive pride in his/her group.

Muscle Builder Analogies

Directions: Each exercise below is an analogy, with one or two terms missing. Choose the Power Word which belongs in each blank of the analogy so that the analogy reads correctly. Write the appropriate Power Word in each blank. Note that some of the Power Words will not be used.

1. ACTIVE is to INACTIVE as TALKATIVE is to _____

2. SUNDAY is to WEEKLY as JANUARY 1 is to _____

3. WASTEFUL is to _____ as EXTRAVAGANT is to ECONOMICAL

INTRODUCTION

The selections in this unit are generally longer and more difficult than those in Unit 5. To comprehend them fully they must be read very carefully and analytically.

In your pleasure reading you may enjoy skimming through books and magazines at a rapid pace. Some avid readers entertain themselves by consuming two or three novels in one weekend. Also, when you are pressed for time, you may have to skim portions of text material. But you must recognize that when you skim you will generally not be able to comprehend material as fully as when you read carefully.

In this unit your goal is to develop the ability to comprehend material fully so that you can achieve a high level of mastery of the content of the material. The following are some hints and suggestions that reading research shows can help facilitate reading pleasure and reading comprehension.

— *Don't skip words.* To comprehend material fully, especially material in the science, business, and math areas, you must read *every* word. Research shows that professors and other good readers basically read one large word, or at most two small words, at a time. Otherwise, information is lost. (Contrast this datum with the philosophy of speed reading courses, which often encourage reading several words, or even entire lines, at a time.)

— *Say the words silently as you read if you find it helpful.* Research shows that subvocalizing— saying words silently—tends to help the comprehension of difficult material. Some readers report that reading aloud improves their comprehension, although this is not true (nor practical) for everyone.

— *Stop to think and reread whenever necessary.* With difficult material, good readers will occasionally pause in their reading, or reread a section, to grasp the full meaning. But be careful. If you must reread sections frequently, or the same section many times, you are probably not concentrating well enough.

— *Concentrate on what you are reading.* Try not to let your mind wander, and don't let your mind become passive. You probably know that you can read mechanically without concentrating on meaning. For example, you may have had the experience of reading aloud to a group of people, yet at the end having little idea of the meaning of what you read—because you were concentrating on pronouncing the words clearly and on your stage presence, rather than on comprehending the material.

Follow these hints—and consciously apply your analytical reading skills—and you are sure to notice an improvement in your comprehension of written material.

INSTRUCTIONS FOR THE EXERCISES

As always, try to achieve 100% accuracy in answering the questions. Reread the passage as many times as necessary to ensure full comprehension. When you answer each question, refer back to the passage and pick it apart to be sure you choose the *best* answer. You should feel confident enough about each of your answers that you would be willing to defend it by pointing out the specific information in the passage that supports that answer and the line of reasoning you followed in reaching that answer.

Challenge yourself to achieve total accuracy!

PASSAGE A

¹ Prior to 1940, overland transportation in
² Honduras was poorly developed. In 1870, the
³ government had attempted to build a railroad
⁴ system throughout Honduras. However, primar-
⁵ ily due to bad planning and the mismanagement
⁶ of funds, only 88 miles (142 km) of track were
⁷ actually completed. Later, the banana companies
⁸ built some 650 miles (1,050 km) of track, but this
⁹ track was used mainly by those companies and
¹⁰ only infrequently by the private citizen.
¹¹ The rest of Honduras was forced to travel
¹² overland primarily by way of mule trails until, in
¹³ the late 1940s, a formal program in road building
¹⁴ was begun. As an initial step, the United States
¹⁵ helped finance the construction of the Pan Amer-
¹⁶ ican Highway along the Pacific coast of Hon-
¹⁷ duras. Then, during the 1950s, another highway
¹⁸ was built connecting the Pan American Highway
¹⁹ to Tegucigalpa. The first broad-scale effort to
²⁰ improve the road system in all parts of Honduras
²¹ came during the late 1960s and the early 1970s.
²² The total amount of road length was increased
²³ from 1,000 miles (1,600 km) in 1965 to 4,100 miles
²⁴ (6,600 km) in 1975.

1. Below are three possible titles for this passage. In
   each blank, write the letter of the phrase (A, B or
   C) which best describes that title.

   _____ Railroad Transportation in Honduras
   _____ Land Transportation in Honduras
   _____ Land, Air, and Water Transportation in
   Honduras

   (A) too broad
   (B) too narrow
   (C) comprehensive title

2. According to the passage, before 1940 overland
   transportation in Honduras was

   ☐ (A) exclusively by mule trail
   ☐ (B) primarily by mule trail, plus some railroad
   ☐ (C) by mule trail, railroad, and highway
   which the United States helped finance
   ☐ (D) by railroad, mule trail, automobile,
   boat, and airplane

3. Before 1940 the railroad was constructed primarily by

   ☐ (A) private industry
   ☐ (B) the Honduras government
   ☐ (C) the United States
   ☐ (D) none of the above

4. How much highway was constructed between
   the mid-1960s and mid-1970s?

   ☐ (A) 1,000 miles
   ☐ (B) 650 miles
   ☐ (C) 3,100 miles
   ☐ (D) 4,100 miles

PASSAGE B

¹ A man should make an honest effort to get
² the names of his wife's friends right. This is not
³ easy. The average wife who was graduated from
⁴ school at any time during the past 30 years keeps
⁵ in close touch with at least seven old classmates.
⁶ These ladies, known as "the girls," are named,
⁷ respectively: Mary, Marian, Melissa, Marjorie,
⁸ Maribel, Madeleine and Miriam; and all of them
⁹ are called Myrtle by the careless husband we are
¹⁰ talking about. Furthermore, he gets their nick-
¹¹ names wrong. This, to be sure, is understandable,
¹² since their nicknames are, respectively: Molly,
¹³ Muffy, Missy, Midge, Mabby, Maddy and Mims.
¹⁴ The careless husband, out of thoughtlessness or
¹⁵ pure cussedness, calls them all Mugs, or, when he
¹⁶ is feeling particularly brutal, Mucky.
¹⁷ All the girls are married, one of them to a Ben
¹⁸ Tompkins, and as this is the only one he can
¹⁹ remember, our hero calls all the husbands Ben, or
²⁰ Tompkins, adding to the general annoyance and
²¹ confusion.
²² Try, then, to get the names of your wife's girl
²³ friends and their husbands straight. This will pre-
²⁴ vent some of those interminable arguments that
²⁵ begin after Midge and Harry (not Mucky and Ben)
²⁶ have said a stiff good night and gone home.

1. The careless husband in this selection

   ☐ (A) thinks the nickname for all the girls is Myrtle and the real name for all the girls is Mugs
   ☐ (B) thinks the nickname for all the girls is Mugs and the real name for all the girls is Myrtle
   ☐ (C) calls all the girls Ben

2. The tone of this selection is

   ☐ (A) vituperative (verbally critical and abusive)
   ☐ (B) apprehensive (anxious, fearful)
   ☐ (C) jocose (joking)
   ☐ (D) censorious (judging, critical)

3. Which literary device is used in this selection?

   ☐ (A) rhyme (repetition in sound of word endings)
   ☐ (B) alliteration (repetition in sound of word beginnings)
   ☐ (C) iambic verse (an unstressed or short syllable followed by a stressed or long syllable)
   ☐ (D) onomatopoeia (naming something from an associated sound: bang, bow-wow)

4. A couple is said to have left when

   ☐ (A) the wife was called Myrtle by the careless husband
   ☐ (B) the husband was called the name of another husband, and the wife a name used "when he is feeling particularly brutal"
   ☐ (C) the wife was called Midge and the husband Harry
   ☐ (D) the wife was called Mugs and the husband Ben

5. What are the nicknames of Madeleine and Marian, respectively?

   ☐ (A) Molly and Muffy
   ☐ (B) Muffy and Maddy
   ☐ (C) Maddy and Muffy
   ☐ (D) Molly and Mims

PASSAGE C

1   The famous astronomer, Galileo, first to
2 make scientific use of the telescope, was born 393
3 years before man finally put a satellite in orbit.
4 Galileo lived for 78 years, but the year of his death
5 saw the birth of Isaac Newton, who discovered
6 the law of gravity and was co-creator, with Leib-
7 nitz, of the calculus. Newton lived to be 7 years
8 older than Galileo.

1. According to the selection,

   ☐ (A) Newton was 7 years older than Galileo
   ☐ (B) Newton died 7 years after Galileo died
   ☐ (C) Galileo's life was 7 years longer than Newton's life
   ☐ (D) none of the above

2. According to the selection,

   ☐ (A) Newton and Leibnitz discovered the law of gravity together
   ☐ (B) Galileo and Newton created the calculus
   ☐ (C) Leibnitz could not have created the calculus without Newton
   ☐ (D) Leibnitz and Newton created the calculus

3. On which line(s) did you find the answer to the preceding question?

   LINE NUMBER(S): _____

4. How many years before the first orbital satellite did Galileo die?

   ☐ (A) 315
   ☐ (B) 393
   ☐ (C) 78
   ☐ (D) 471

5. For how many years did Newton live?

   ☐ (A) 78
   ☐ (B) 93
   ☐ (C) 71
   ☐ (D) 85

6. Given that 1957 was the year of man's first orbital satellite, you can deduce that

☐ (A) Galileo and Newton were born in 1642 and 1564, respectively
☐ (B) Galileo and Newton were born in 1564 and 1642, respectively
☐ (C) Newton and Galileo were born in 1564 and 1642, respectively
☐ (D) Galileo and Newton were born in 1564 and 1571, respectively

PASSAGE D

1 In geologic time the Paleocene is the first
2 epoch of the Tertiary Period as it is usually sub-
3 divided. It began about 65,000,000 years ago and
4 lasted 11,000,000 or 12,000,000 years according
5 to current radiometric age data. The Eocene, the
6 second epoch of the Tertiary Period, lasted
7 15,000,000 to 17,000,000 years. In these relatively
8 short (geologically) intervals of time both marine
9 and nonmarine biotas (living things) made sub-
10 stantial evolutionary progress, in some instances
11 closely approaching the familiar modern inhabi-
12 tants of these realms. In the sea the gastropods,
13 pelecypods, and foraminifera dominated the
14 faunas, while on land the mammals, conifers, and
15 flowering plants were . . . dominant . . . .

1. Which of the following statements is correct?

☐ (A) The Eocene Epoch succeeded the Tertiary Period.
☐ (B) The Paleocene Epoch preceded the Tertiary Period.
☐ (C) The Paleocene Epoch preceded the Eocene Epoch.
☐ (D) The Tertiary Period preceded the Paleocene Epoch.

2. About how many years ago did the Paleocene Epoch end?

☐ (A) 65,000,000
☐ (B) 76,000,000
☐ (C) 54,000,000
☐ (D) 15,000,000 to 17,000,000

3. About how many years ago did the Eocene Epoch begin?

☐ (A) 54,000,000
☐ (B) 15,000,000
☐ (C) 17,000,000
☐ (D) 80,000,000
☐ (E) 50,000,000

4. About how many years ago did the Eocene Epoch end?

☐ (A) 17,000,000
☐ (B) 38,000,000
☐ (C) 92,000,000
☐ (D) 11,000,000

5. According to the passage,

☐ (A) conifers developed in the sea during the Eocene and Paleocene Epochs
☐ (B) a period is part of an epoch
☐ (C) an epoch is part of a period
☐ (D) fifteen million years is geologically a long period of time

PASSAGE E

1 Western civilization arose in the Near East
2 and spread eventually to North America and
3 other continents. For two thousand years, how-
4 ever, it has been intimately associated with
5 Europe. A mere peninsula of Asia, Europe is,
6 except for Australia, the smallest of the conti-
7 nents. Its population, even counting offshoots
8 overseas, has never been more than a minority of
9 mankind. Yet it has played a towering role in the
10 world. The extraordinary length and irregularity
11 of its coastline—a veritable lacework of bays,
12 inlets, channels, and internal seas—and a rich
13 system of riverways brought Europeans close to
14 one another and gave them access to the rest of
15 the world. Although it is situated in the same
16 latitudes as Canada, Europe has a moderate cli-
17 mate and a fairly regular rainfall. The resources of
18 the continent are sufficiently modest to exact
19 effort and forethought and sufficiently ample to
20 reward them. They have neither the luxuriance
21 that makes man lazy and improvident nor the
22 barrenness that makes him niggardly and takes
23 away his hope.

1. The main theme of this passage is that

   □ (A) Western civilization arose in the Near East
   □ (B) conditions in Europe favored the growth of Western civilization
   □ (C) the coastline of Europe is a lacework of bays, inlets, channels, and internal seas
   □ (D) luxuriance makes man lazy and improvident

2. The passage says that

   □ (A) Europe and Australia are the smallest and next smallest continents, respectively
   □ (B) Australia and Europe are the smallest and next smallest continents, respectively
   □ (C) Asia and Europe are the two smallest continents
   □ (D) Asia is older than Europe

3. Which of the following was not mentioned as one of Europe's qualities?

   □ (A) Conditions were good for shipping.
   □ (B) Resources were neither too plentiful nor too scarce.
   □ (C) Western civilization arose in the Near East.
   □ (D) The climate was not severe.

4. The selection says that

   □ (A) Europe has many of the minorities of mankind
   □ (B) European minorities were considered offshoots of the North American population
   □ (C) Europeans don't form a majority of the world's population
   □ (D) European populations grew rapidly with Western civilization

5. The passage implies that which of the following does not have a moderate climate?

   □ (A) Canada
   □ (B) Australia
   □ (C) Europe
   □ (D) Asia

6. In the next to the last sentence, the phrase "exact effort" means

   □ (A) precise effort
   □ (B) correct work
   □ (C) require work
   □ (D) accurate exertion

7. The phrase "sufficiently modest," as used in the next to the last sentence, means

   □ (A) somewhat scarce
   □ (B) feminine and shy
   □ (C) not conceited
   □ (D) pleasantly polite

8. According to the selection, what makes people niggardly (stingy)?

   □ (A) miserly parents
   □ (B) becoming rich too quickly
   □ (C) living in a state of luxuriance
   □ (D) deprivation and poverty

9. The author feels that society progresses best when

   □ (A) conditions are extremely hard so the people hope to better themselves
   □ (B) the people can, through their labor, attain a comfortable lifestyle
   □ (C) the people live in luxury
   □ (D) the government has a strong but fair leader

PASSAGE F

1 Mother used to say, too, that a soft answer
2 turneth away wrath, but I always thought Father's
3 system—a gay answer—was better. Later I dis-
4 covered the best system of all, and I don't mean
5 no answer; for you don't get anywhere in married
6 life not having an answer. You only get accused of
7 being an old sourpuss. No, the secret of a happy
8 married life without quarrels is always to have an
9 answer, but be sure it doesn't make any sense.
10 Nothing infuriates a woman as much as to be
11 cornered with Reason or—unforgivable sin—
12 fenced in with the Truth.
13 It was a Chinese traveling in this country who
14 evoked the magic formula which makes quarrel-

¹⁵ ing almost impossible for my wife and me. One
¹⁶ day, late for his train, he rushed over to the bag-
¹⁷ gage room in Grand Central Station, threw his
¹⁸ check on the counter, and demanded his bag.
¹⁹ The attendant couldn't find it. As precious min-
²⁰ utes went by, the Chinese began jumping up and
²¹ down with inarticulate rage. Finally he couldn't
²² stand it any longer. His train was going—his bag
²³ was nowhere to be found—and he pounded the
²⁴ counter with his fist and yelled: "Pretty darn sel-
²⁵ dom where my bag go. She no fly. You no more fit
²⁶ run station than godsake. That's all *I* hope!"
²⁷   Before hearing this, when anything of mine
²⁸ got mislaid around the house, which was every
²⁹ time my wife tidied up, I used to scream like a
³⁰ wounded banshee. But now I merely yell, "Pretty
³¹ darn seldom where my papers go!" In the old days
³² my wife used to come back snappily with, "If you
³³ put your papers where they belong, you'd know
³⁴ where to find them!"—which is sheer nonsense,
³⁵ as any husband knows who has ever tried it.
³⁶   I found the only answer to such an unreason-
³⁷ able remark was, "You no more fit run house than
³⁸ godsake!"—which put her in her place until she
³⁹ learned to retort, "That's all *I* hope!"—stopping
⁴⁰ all argument dead in its tracks.
⁴¹   In the silly old days I used to moan, "Why
⁴² don't you fill out your check stubs properly?
⁴³ What is this—$2.20, or $22, or $220? Why can't
⁴⁴ you keep your balance straight?" Now I just say,
⁴⁵ "Pretty darn seldom where my money go. She no
⁴⁶ fly." And I get just as far as I ever did—which was
⁴⁷ exactly nowhere.

1. The writer's tone is

   ☐ (A) irascible (hot-tempered)
   ☐ (B) sullen (gloomy, morose)
   ☐ (C) jocular (mirthful, playful)
   ☐ (D) lamenting (sorrowful)

2. The writer maintains that the best prevention against a marital altercation (noisy quarrel) is

   ☐ (A) to show understanding and willingness to compromise
   ☐ (B) levity (excessive joking)
   ☐ (C) to remain taciturn (silent)
   ☐ (D) irrationality (respond without reason or logic)

3. The writer's solution to marital disputes came

   ☐ (A) when he visited a Chinese marriage counselor
   ☐ (B) when he overheard a frustrated person's conversation
   ☐ (C) in a dream one night
   ☐ (D) when he worked as an attendant in the baggage room at Grand Central Station

4. If the writer couldn't find his umbrella today he would

   ☐ (A) yell like a banshee (spirit whose wailing warns of impending death)
   ☐ (B) yell, "Where the heck is my umbrella?"
   ☐ (C) yell, "You no more fit run umbrella than godsake!"
   ☐ (D) yell, "Pretty darn seldom where my umbrella go!"

PASSAGE G

¹   Actually, the argument over who was first in
² the race to civilization may be irrelevant. Some
³ prehistorians, abandoning the once-sacrosanct
⁴ belief in cultural "diffusion" from a single source in
⁵ favor of "independent inventions," consider it
⁶ unlikely that the cultivation of such different
⁷ crops as barley and wheat in Mesopotamia, rice in
⁸ Thailand, and maize in the Valley of Mexico two
⁹ millennia later, owed anything to each other.
¹⁰ Some archeologists, including Gorman, say that
¹¹ bronze metallurgy in the Middle East, Southeast
¹² Asia, and Peru also developed separately.
¹³   In fact, new discoveries and improved dating
¹⁴ techniques are upsetting archeological chronol-
¹⁵ ogies in many other areas of the world. The mega-
¹⁶ lithic tombs of Western Europe, once held to be
¹⁷ crude imitations of the Egyptian pyramids, now
¹⁸ appear to be 2000 years older. The ancient in-
¹⁹ habitants of Romania may have developed a writ-
²⁰ ten language before the Mesopotamians. And the
²¹ first humans to reach America probably arrived
²² 40,000 years ago or earlier, rather than 12,000
²³ years ago, as was long believed.

1. Below are three possible titles for this passage. In each blank, write the letter of the phrase (A, B or C) which best describes that title.

_____ The Origins of Civilizations
_____ The History of Mankind
_____ The Megalithic Tombs of Western Europe

    (A) comprehensive title
    (B) too narrow
    (C) too broad

2. The "improved dating" of the second paragraph refers to

    ☐ (A) computer dating methods for bringing men and women together
    ☐ (B) dating patterns of adolescents described by anthropologists
    ☐ (C) better methods of estimating ages of objects and events
    ☐ (D) none of the above

3. It was formerly believed that

    ☐ (A) the Egyptian pyramids were built 2000 years after the tombs of Western Europe
    ☐ (B) the Egyptian pyramids were older than the tombs found in Western Europe
    ☐ (C) the Egyptian pyramids were imitations of the tombs of Western Europe

4. According to the selection,

    ☐ (A) cultivation of barley and wheat in Mesopotamia led to cultivation of maize in the Valley of Mexico later
    ☐ (B) cultivation of barley and wheat in Mesopotamia and rice in Thailand led to the cultivation of maize in the Valley of Mexico
    ☐ (C) cultivation of barley and wheat in Mesopotamia may have had no connection with cultivation of maize in the Valley of Mexico
    ☐ (D) cultivation of barley and wheat in Mesopotamia may have occurred after bronze metallurgy in Peru

5. According to the article, many archeologists are now entertaining the idea that

    ☐ (A) developments of civilization originated in one place and "diffused" to others
    ☐ (B) the same cultural advances originated at different locations independently

6. The archeologist Gorman is cited as siding with

    ☐ (A) diffusion of culture
    ☐ (B) irrational development
    ☐ (C) independent invention
    ☐ (D) all of the above

7. The selection implies that

    ☐ (A) it was formerly accepted that written language originated in Mesopotamia
    ☐ (B) it was formerly accepted that written language originated in Rumania
    ☐ (C) it was formerly accepted that the first humans reached America 40 centuries ago
    ☐ (D) it was formerly accepted that "independent invention" explained the spread of civilization from Mexico to Egypt

PASSAGE H

1   While he won on the continent, Napoleon
2 lost on the ocean. On October 21, 1805, four days
3 after the French had captured an Austrian army
4 in Ulm, Admiral Lord Nelson won a decisive naval
5 victory. Commanding twenty-seven ships, he met
6 the combined French and Spanish fleets, count-
7 ing together thirty-three ships, near Cape Trafal-
8 gar off the coast of Spain. The allied fleet was
9 arrayed in the conventional single file, expecting
10 to pair off ship for ship for a broadside engage-
11 ment. Nelson avoided this familiar strategy in a
12 manuever resembling that of Napoleon at Auster-
13 litz. The emperor had aimed his stroke at the
14 center of the opposing army. Nelson divided his
15 fleet into two forces which advanced perpendicu-
16 larly on the long line of the enemy and severed it
17 into three parts. One of Nelson's squadrons iso-
18 lated the enemy ships in the rear to prevent them
19 from coming to the assistance of their sister ships.
20 The other tackled the center group ship for ship.

21 The French-Spanish fleet forfeited the advantage
22 of superior numbers and lost twenty-two ships.
23 Nelson virtually annihilated the naval power of
24 France and Spain and inaugurated a century of
25 British control of the oceans. The price Britain
26 paid for this victory was the great admiral
27 himself—Nelson was killed in the last moments of
28 the battle.

1. Nelson was an admiral in which navy?

   ☐ (A) Austrian
   ☐ (B) French
   ☐ (C) Spanish
   ☐ (D) British

2. According to the selection,

   ☐ (A) Napoleon's empire was crumbling so
       he was defeated on both land and sea
   ☐ (B) Napoleon was defeated at sea but was
       victorious on land
   ☐ (C) Napoleon's great power allowed him to
       be victorious on both land and sea
   ☐ (D) Napoleon was victorious at sea but was
       defeated on land

3. The note on which the selection ends is

   ☐ (A) bitter-sweet victory
   ☐ (B) resounding victory
   ☐ (C) uncontested victory

4. According to the passage, Napoleon lost at Trafalgar because

   ☐ (A) Napoleon's naval strategy backfired
   ☐ (B) Napoleon's naval strategy was dis-
       organized, while Nelson's strategy was
       well-organized
   ☐ (C) Nelson used a strategy similar to one
       Napoleon had used on land
   ☐ (D) Nelson had the help of the Spanish
       army

5. On line 23, the word "annihilated" must mean

   ☐ (A) restored
   ☐ (B) comprised
   ☐ (C) put together
   ☐ (D) wiped out

6. Which pair of words fits the blanks in this statement: Napoleon lost at _____ but won four
   days earlier at _____ ?

   ☐ (A) Trafalgar in the second blank and Ulm
       in the first blank
   ☐ (B) Ulm in the first blank and Trafalgar in
       the second blank
   ☐ (C) Ulm in the second blank and Trafalgar
       in the first blank

7. How many ships was Napoleon left with after
   Trafalgar?

   ☐ (A) 22
   ☐ (B) 27
   ☐ (C) 33
   ☐ (D) 11

8. Given that "partitioned" means "divided," which
   of the following statements is correct?

   ☐ (A) Napoleon partitioned his fleet to parti-
       tion Nelson's fleet.
   ☐ (B) Nelson partitioned his fleet to completely
       surround Napoleon's fleet.
   ☐ (C) Nelson won because of his larger force.
   ☐ (D) Nelson partitioned his fleet to parti-
       tion Napoleon's fleet.

PASSAGE I

1 A steel rudder and a bronze propeller on a
2 ship may produce a chemical reaction in seawater
3 that causes a small current of electrons to flow.
4 And while this combination does not make an
5 efficient battery, as *Encyclopedia Britannica*
6 explains, "a cell much like it is very useful. This is
7 the 'dry cell', invented by Georgés Leclanché
8 (1839-82) about 1865 and found in many portable
9 radio receivers, hearing aids, etc. For seawater
10 the dry cell substitutes a slush of sal ammoniac
11 (NH_4CL) and its solution in water; for iron, zinc;
12 and for bronze, carbon. The slush, being saltier
13 than seawater, is a better conductor; and zinc is
14 more reactive than iron. The greatest advantage
15 of this cell, however, is that in it the formation of
16 hydrogen bubbles is prevented by a layer of man-
17 ganese dioxide around the carbon electrode. This
18 readily gives up its oxygen atoms, which combine
19 with the newly formed hydrogen atoms (techni-
20 cally called nascent hydrogen) to form water."

1. The best title for this passage is

   ☐ (A) Innards of a Battery
   ☐ (B) Uses of Batteries
   ☐ (C) Biography of Georgés Leclanché
   ☐ (D) Theory of Electronics

2. According to the paragraph,

   ☐ (A) seawater is saltier than the slush used in a dry cell
   ☐ (B) seawater is less salty than the slush used in a dry cell
   ☐ (C) the saltiness of seawater can make your eyes sting
   ☐ (D) hydrogen bubbles make seawater salty

3. Which two substances are used in a dry cell?

   ☐ (A) iron and zinc
   ☐ (B) iron and bronze
   ☐ (C) zinc and carbon
   ☐ (D) bronze and carbon

4. One can conclude from the passage that

   ☐ (A) hydrogen bubbles prevent a layer of manganese dioxide from forming
   ☐ (B) hydrogen bubbles are needed in a battery
   ☐ (C) hydrogen bubbles are not needed in a battery
   ☐ (D) hydrogen bubbles form around the carbon electrode in a battery

5. Nascent hydrogen

   ☐ (A) combines with water to form oxygen
   ☐ (B) combines with oxygen to form manganese dioxide
   ☐ (C) is hydrogen combined with oxygen atoms
   ☐ (D) combines with oxygen which comes from manganese dioxide

6. In comparing a ship to a battery, the author matches the seawater, rudder, and propeller with the

   ☐ (A) slush, sal ammoniac, and iron, respectively
   ☐ (B) slush, zinc, and carbon electrode, respectively
   ☐ (C) slush, carbon electrode, and zinc electrode, respectively
   ☐ (D) seawater, iron, and bronze, respectively

PASSAGE J

1 The Industrial Revolution took place in Eng-
2 land in the production of textiles. An idea of the
3 massive increase made possible by the applica-
4 tion of machines to cloth-making is evidenced by
5 the amount of raw cotton England imported for
6 use in its textile industry. In 1760 it imported a little
7 over 1000 tons of raw cotton as compared to over
8 222,000 tons of cotton imported yearly by the
9 middle of the nineteenth century.
10 This great change in productivity was not
11 conceived in scientific laboratories by profes-
12 sional researchers. Practical men solving practi-
13 cal problems invented the machines. Each step
14 forward in removing an obstacle to production
15 posed new dilemmas which were, in their turn,
16 resolved. In 1733 John Kay, a spinner and
17 mechanic, patented the first of the great
18 machines for the cloth industry—the flying shut-
19 tle. This device made it possible for one person to
20 weave wide bolts of cloth by using a spring mech-
21 anism that sent the shuttle across the loom. Kay's
22 innovation upset the balance between the weav-
23 ers and spinners; one weaver required ten
24 spinners to produce enough yarn to keep up with
25 him. In 1764 James Hargreaves, a weaver and
26 carpenter, devised the spinning jenny, essentially
27 a mechanical spinning wheel, which allowed the
28 production of the spinners to equal that of the
29 weavers.

1. Below are three possible titles for this passage. In each blank, write the letter of the phrase (A, B, or C) which best describes that title.

   _____ Stimulation of the Cloth Industry by Inventions
   _____ John Kay's Invention of the Flying Shuttle
   _____ Major Inventions in England

       (A) too broad
       (B) comprehensive title
       (C) too narrow

2. Near the middle of the *eighteenth* century, England's yearly import of cotton was approximately

   ☐ (A) two hundred twenty-two thousand tons
   ☐ (B) one thousand tons
   ☐ (C) 222,000 tons
   ☐ (D) 221,000 tons

3. According to the selection, England's yearly import of cotton jumped from 1000 tons to 222,000 tons in approximately

   ☐ (A) 1 year
   ☐ (B) 10 years
   ☐ (C) 50 years
   ☐ (D) 100 years

4. The selection reports that

   ☐ (A) a weaving machine was invented by a man who was himself a weaver
   ☐ (B) a weaving machine was invented by a man who was himself a spinner
   ☐ (C) the new weaving machine was called the spinning jenny
   ☐ (D) a spinning machine was invented by a man who was himself a spinner

5. John Kay's invention

   ☐ (A) hurt the cloth industry by upsetting the balance between the weaver and the spinner
   ☐ (B) allowed weavers to be more efficient than spinners
   ☐ (C) allowed spinners to be more efficient than weavers
   ☐ (D) was conceived in a scientific laboratory

6. In England, improved cloth-making equipment was developed by

   ☐ (A) farmers who produced cotton
   ☐ (B) scientific laboratories with professional researchers
   ☐ (C) businessmen who owned cotton factories
   ☐ (D) workmen in cotton factories

7. According to the selection, increase in the importation of cotton was caused by

   ☐ (A) greater demand for cloth made from cotton
   ☐ (B) improved machinery for manufacturing cloth
   ☐ (C) better machines for transporting cotton
   ☐ (D) scientific farming which lowered the price of cotton

Word Power III

Directions: Study each of the Power Words below. Note how each word is pronounced. Then read the context sentences to figure out what each Power Word means. In the left-hand margin next to each Power Word, try to jot down a synonym or short definition which defines that word.

Power Words	confide	tranquil	prudent	ensnare
	irresolute	inexplicable	solace	liberal

1. **confide** | kən **fīd'** |
   - Confiding in someone with your secret worries can be very therapeutic.
   - My conscience is killing me; can I confide in you?

2. **irresolute** | ĭ **rĕz'** ə lōōt' |
   - The child sat irresolute, unable to decide which dessert to take.
   - Because of all the options presented, I was irresolute and put my decision off until tomorrow.

3. **tranquil** | **trăng'** kwĭl |
   - The park in early morning is a tranquil scene.
   - Although she could work with many distractions, she found that she worked best in a tranquil environment.

4. **inexplicable** | ĭn **ĕk'** splĭ kə bəl |
   - The normally tranquil teacher's emotional outburst was inexplicable.
   - An inexplicable fear came over me as I entered the room.

5. **prudent** | **prōōd'** nt |
   - A prudent person might gamble on safe bets in business, but seldom would you meet him or her at the race track.
   - Being a prudent shopper, Leroy checked the newspaper for sales before leaving home.

6. **solace** | **sŏl'** əs |
   - When she was sad, her books were her only solace.
   - In times of trouble we can take solace in a strong, close-knit family.

7. **ensnare** | ĕn **snâr'** |
   - One lie often leads to further lies which eventually ensnare you.
   - The police were hoping to ensnare him by having him repeat his story many times.

8. **liberal** | **lĭb'** ər əl |
   - A liberal politician may be as concerned about protecting freedom of speech as he or she is about protecting national security.

ă pat / ā pay / â care / ä father / ĕ pet / ē be / ĭ pit / ī pie / î fierce / ŏ pot / ō go / ô paw, for / oi oil / ŏŏ book /
ōō boot / ou out / ŭ cut / ü fur / *th* the / th thin / hw which / zh vision / ə ago, item, pencil, atom, circus

Meaning Comprehension

Directions: Use what you have learned from the context sentences to identify the correct definition of each Power Word. In the blank next to each Power Word, write the letter of its correct definition.

Power Words

_____ confide
_____ irresolute
_____ tranquil
_____ inexplicable
_____ prudent
_____ solace
_____ ensnare
_____ liberal

Definitions

a. unexplainable
b. political beliefs that favor individual liberties and support social progress
c. showing good judgment in managing one's affairs and resources, wise, sensible
d. calm, stable, steady
e. confidentially tell one's intimate secrets to someone
f. comfort for grief or anxiety, consolation
g. undecided, uncertain, indecisive, vacillating
h. catch, trap

Context Application

Directions: Each of the following sentences has two blanks. Use what you have learned about the Power Words to determine which Power Word best belongs in each of the blanks. Then write the appropriate Power Word in each blank. Use each Power Word only once.

1. An understanding person to _____ in can provide needed _____ in times of personal difficulties.

2. When General Howe became confused and _____ the colonists were able to _____ his troops within the mountain pass and a great victory ensued.

3. Since Senator Goodman prides himself in being _____ , his vote against the bill to expand human rights is _____ .

4. A _____ person who plans carefully for the future can expect to live a happy and _____ life.

Muscle Builder Analogies

Directions: Each exercise below is an analogy, with one or two terms missing. Choose the Power Word which belongs in each blank of the analogy so that the analogy reads correctly. Write the appropriate Power Word in each blank. Note that some of the Power Words will not be used.

1. LIBERAL is to CONSERVATIVE as RECKLESS is to

_____

2. MEDICINE is to ILLNESS as _____ is to UPSET

3. MERCY is to MERCILESS as REASON is to _____

Word Power IV

Directions: Study each of the Power Words below. Note how each word is pronounced. Then read the context sentences to figure out what each Power Word means. In the left-hand margin next to each Power Word, try to jot down a synonym or short definition which defines that word.

Power Words	impulsively	cope	benign	spangled
	reign	exuberance	incessant	insurrection

1. **impulsively** | ĭm **pŭl′** sĭv lē |
   * Hitler acted impulsively and against the advice of his generals when he attacked Russia in 1941.
   * When taking tests, it is best not to answer questions impulsively, but to think them through.

2. **reign** | rān |
   * The reign of this monarch is characterized as one in which everyone prospered.

3. **cope** | kōp |
   * Financial and psychological pressures, greater than the executive could cope with, led to his nervous breakdown.
   * I don't know how some teachers can cope with a classroom full of children.

4. **exuberance** | ĭg **zoo′** bər əns |
   * The young writer's exuberance blinded him to the difficulty of creating a best seller.
   * The team was cheered on by the exuberance of the spectators.

5. **benign** | bĭ **nīn′** |
   * Amico Li is so warm-hearted and benign that she can always be counted on for a favor.
   * Don't be misled by his imposing size, he is actually very benign.

6. **incessant** | ĭn **sĕs′** ənt |
   * Incessant noise kept the student from studying effectively.
   * When the pain became incessant, I knew it was time to get to a dentist.

7. **spangled** | **spăng′** gəld |
   * The American flag has a blue field spangled with stars.

8. **insurrection** | ĭn′ sə **rĕk′** shən |
   * An insurrection generally involves much bloodshed.
   * The colonists planned an insurrection because they were displeased with the Stamp Act.

ă pat / ā pay / â care / ä father / ĕ pet / ē be / ĭ pit / ī pie / î fierce / ŏ pot / ō go / ô paw, for / oi oil / ŏŏ book /
ōō boot / ou out / ŭ cut / ü fur / th the / th thin / hw which / zh vision / ə ago, item, pencil, atom, circus

Meaning Comprehension

Directions: Use what you have learned from the context sentences to identify the correct definition of each Power Word. In the blank next to each Power Word, write the letter of its correct definition.

Power Words

_____ impulsively
_____ reign
_____ cope
_____ exuberance
_____ benign
_____ incessant
_____ spangled
_____ insurrection

Definitions

a. sprinkled with bright or glittering spots
b. handle, deal with problems or difficulties
c. excessively quick, without sufficient thought
d. unrestrained enthusiasm, zeal
e. unceasing, continuous
f. rule like a king; period of being king
g. kindly, friendly; mild
h. rebellion against the government

Context Application

Directions: Each of the following sentences has two blanks. Use what you have learned about the Power Words to determine which Power Word best belongs in each of the blanks. Then write the appropriate Power Word in each blank. Use each Power Word only once.

1. King Louis XVI continued to _____ in name only after the _____ of the French masses against the throne.

2. In the girl's _____ at meeting the movie star, she mistook the cheap ring _____ with fake diamonds for an expensive piece of jewelry.

3. The woman found it difficult to _____ with her husband's _____ , never-ending criticism.

4. In medieval days, kings usually made political decisions _____ rather than thinking them out; and, with respect to other kingdoms, these decisions were more often hostile than _____ .

Muscle Builder Analogies

Directions: Each exercise below is an analogy, with one term missing. Choose the Power Word which belongs in each blank of the analogy so that the analogy reads correctly. Write the appropriate Power Word in each blank. Note that some of the Power Words will not be used.

1. SLAVE is to SERVE as KING is to _____

2. PRUDENTLY is to CAUTIOUS as _____ is to HASTY

3. FLOOD is to WATER as _____ is to EXCITEMENT

ADDITIONAL ASSIGNMENTS

1. Pick a section from one of your textbooks, encyclopedias, or other sources which is about 150 words long. Then write two multiple-choice questions on the material. Each question should have only one correct answer and at least one incorrect alternative which a person might choose if he or she is not reading carefully.

    Let a peer read the section and answer the questions. Observe your peer's work to see that you have written clear, meaningful questions and answer choices.

2. Using what you have learned about the meaning of "garrulous" (page 106), write a sentence on the lines below in which the meaning of "garrulous" is given by contrast (Case III).

    _____

    _____

3. Using what you have learned about the meaning of "disheveled" (page 118), write a sentence on the lines below in which the meaning of "disheveled" is stated with punctuation (Case I).

    _____

    _____

4. Using what you have learned about the meaning of "authentic" (page 126), write a sentence on the lines below in which the meaning of "authentic" is stated without punctuation (Case II).

    _____

    _____

5. Using what you have learned about the meaning of "reign" (page 176), write a sentence on the lines below in which the meaning of "reign" is inferred from the rest of the sentence (Case IV).

    _____

    _____

UNIT
8

GENERAL-SPECIFIC CLASSIFICATION OF WRITTEN IDEAS

OBJECTIVES: When you have completed this unit you should

- be able to group specific ideas into general classes;
- be able to analyze the relationships between classes of information;
- be able to identify the main idea and supporting details of a written selection;
- know the meanings of the following POWER WORDS.

POWER WORDS

paucity	macabre	myriad	inimical
lobotomy	irreparable	virulent	infamous
levity	prodigal	loquacious	retroactive
opulent	misoneism	xenophobia	retrospect
enervated	nomadic	imminent	pertinent
appendectomy	ludicrous	lethargy	relevant
obnoxious	prodigy	claustrophobia	redundant
jeopardy	misogamy	inundated	invective

Word Power I

Power Words	paucity	levity	enervated	obnoxious
	lobotomy	opulent	appendectomy	jeopardy

1. **paucity** | **pô′** sĭ tē |
   - The paucity of jobs left many people unemployed.
   - The family was poor so there was always a paucity of food on the table.

2. **lobotomy** | lō **bät′** ə mē |
   - The lobotomy was performed only after all other treatments failed to lessen the patient's mental disorder.

3. **levity** | **lĕv′** ĭ tē |
   - The widower's levity was clearly an attempt to hide his sorrow over losing his wife.
   - The priest was shocked by the pallbearer's levity.

4. **opulent** | **ŏp′** yə lənt |
   - Since Dana was opulent but not happy, she agreed there was more to life than wealth.
   - The United States is considered an opulent nation.

5. **enervated** | **ĕn′** ər vā′ tĭd |
   - Working all day in the hot sun left her totally enervated.
   - When enervated, it is best to stop working and rest briefly.

6. **appendectomy** | ăp′ ən **dĕk′** tə mē |
   - The appendectomy only left one small scar on the stomach.

7. **obnoxious** | əb **nŏk′** shəs |
   - Jack found his father-in-law's lewd humor obnoxious and preferred to avoid his company.
   - For some people, nothing can ruin a good meal as quickly as the obnoxious smell of cigar smoke.

8. **jeopardy** | **jĕp′** ər dē |
   - Her continual drinking put Leona in jeopardy of losing her driver's license.
   - "Handing the assignment in late will put you in jeopardy of failing the course," warned the professor.

ă pat / ā pay / â care / ä father / ĕ pet / ē be / ĭ pit / ī pie / î fierce / ŏ pot / ō go / ô paw, for / oi oil / ŏŏ book /
ōō boot / ou out / ŭ cut / û fur / th the / th thin / hw which / zh vision / ə ago, item, pencil, atom, circus

Meaning Comprehension

Directions: Use what you have learned from the context sentences to identify the correct definition of each Power Word. In the blank next to each Power Word, write the letter of its correct definition.

Power Words

_____ paucity
_____ lobotomy
_____ levity
_____ opulent
_____ enervated
_____ appendectomy
_____ obnoxious
_____ jeopardy

Definitions

a. lack of proper seriousness, excessive clowning or joking at the wrong time
b. rich, wealthy; plentiful, abundant
c. removal of the appendix by surgery
d. smallness of amount, short supply, scarcity
e. extremely unpleasant or offensive, repugnant
f. danger, peril
g. a type of brain surgery aimed at eliminating mental disorder
h. drained of energy, worn out, weakened

Context Application

Directions: Each of the following sentences has two blanks. Use what you have learned about the Power Words to determine which Power Word best belongs in each of the blanks. Then write the appropriate Power Word in each blank. Use each Power Word only once.

1. The _____ and giggling of the teenagers during the church service was considered _____ by the adults.

2. As his business expanded and he became _____, his waist line expanded too, putting him in _____ of a heart attack, stroke, and other ailments of obesity.

3. The _____ of food and severity of work left the political prisoner _____ .

4. The words _____ and _____ combine lobe (frontal lobe of brain) and appendix, respectively, with the Greek "tomy" meaning "cutting."

Muscle Builder Analogies

Directions: Each exercise below is an analogy, with one or two terms missing. Choose the Power Word which belongs in each blank of the analogy so that the analogy reads correctly. Write the appropriate Power Word in each blank. Note that some of the Power Words will not be used.

1. MANNERS is to PROPER as _____ is to IMPROPER

2. BANKRUPT is to MONEY as _____ is to ENERGY

3. _____ is to FEW as _____ is to ABUNDANCE

Word Power II

Directions: Study each of the Power Words below. Note how each word is pronounced. Then read the context sentences to figure out what each Power Word means. In the left-hand margin next to each Power Word, try to jot down a synonym or short definition which defines that word.

Power Words	macabre	prodigal	nomadic	prodigy
	irreparable	misoneism	ludicrous	misogamy

1. **macabre** | mə **kä′** brə |
   - The book *Dracula* by Bram Stoker tells a macabre story of a vampire leaving his coffin to attack victims.
   - Did the macabre bedtime story cause Lucy's nightmares?

2. **irreparable** | ĭ **rĕp′** ər ə bəl |
   - When Humpty Dumpty fell, the damage was irreparable.
   - Your eyes should be checked periodically; otherwise irreparable damage may develop before an eye disease is discovered.

3. **prodigal** | **prŏd′** ĭ gəl |
   - The prodigal son foolishly spent all the money he had inherited.
   - In the future, our children will pay for our prodigal waste of natural resources.

4. **misoneism** | mĭs′ ə **nē′** ĭz əm |
   - Misoneism may be a psychological disorder in which the patient cannot tolerate anything new or changed.

5. **nomadic** | nō **măd′** ĭk |
   - Nomadic Indian tribes had no permanent home but regularly moved to find better hunting areas.
   - His nomadic lifestyle prevented him from even considering marriage.

6. **ludicrous** | **lōō′** dĭ krəs |
   - The ludicrous novel made my sides ache from laughing!
   - My daughter still giggles when she recalls the clown's ludicrous costume.

7. **prodigy** | **prŏd′** ə jē |
   - The fourth-grade class prodigy could spell better than the teacher.
   - Mozart was a musical prodigy, performing in public at the age of five.

8. **misogamy** | mə **säg′** ə mē |
   - Carol remained unmarried not because of misogamy, but because her occupation took up all of her time.
   - A confirmed bachelor might be accused of misogamy.

ă pat / ā pay / â care / ä father / ĕ pet / ē be / ĭ pit / ī pie / î fierce / ŏ pot / ō go / ô paw, for / oi oil / ŏŏ book /
ōō boot / ou out / ŭ cut / û fur / th the / th thin / hw which / zh vision / ə ago, item, pencil, atom, circus

Meaning Comprehension

Directions: Use what you have learned from the context sentences to identify the correct definition of each Power Word. In the blank next to each Power Word, write the letter of its correct definition.

Power Words   Definitions

_____ macabre   a. hatred of anything new or changed

_____ irreparable   b. roaming from place to place, wandering

_____ prodigal   c. a person with exceptional talents

_____ misoneism   d. concerned with the horror of death, ghastly

_____ nomadic   e. cannot be repaired or made right

_____ ludicrous   f. hatred of marriage

_____ prodigy   g. reckless, wasteful; extravagant

_____ misogamy   h. obviously absurd and therefore laughable

Context Application

Directions: Each of the following sentences has two blanks. Use what you have learned about the Power Words to determine which Power Word best belongs in each of the blanks. Then write the appropriate Power Word in each blank. Use each Power Word only once.

1. Whereas a _____ individual is one who is wasteful, a _____ is an outstanding child.

2. Modern horror movies sometimes combine a _____ story with _____ scenes to provide the relief of laughter.

3. The parents moved from place to place; and this _____ life caused _____ damage to the child's social maturation, so that she never learned to keep friends.

4. Hatred of anything new, _____ , and hatred of marriage, _____ , both begin with the Greek "mis" or "miso," meaning "hate."

Muscle Builder Analogies

Directions: Each exercise below is an analogy, with one or two terms missing. Choose the Power Word which belongs in each blank of the analogy so that the analogy reads correctly. Write the appropriate Power Word in each blank. Note that some of the Power Words will not be used.

1. _____ is to UNECONOMICAL as THRIFTY is to FRUGAL

2. _____ is to AMUSING as _____ is to GRUESOME

3. _____ is to INNOVATION as _____ is to MARRIAGE

PART I: COMPARING GROUPS

INTRODUCTION

In much reading and thinking, people and objects are viewed as belonging to groups (or classes). For instance, George Washington was a member of the Washington family, a president of the U.S., a famous general, and a human being.

<u>Groups Which Include George Washington</u>

WASHINGTON FAMILY
PRESIDENTS OF THE U.S.
FAMOUS GENERALS
HUMAN BEINGS

As another example, my red car is included in these groups:

<u>Groups Which Include My Red Car</u>

RED CARS
CARS
TRANSPORTATION VEHICLES
MY POSSESSIONS

As part of comprehending what you read, you must often clarify in your mind the relationships between groups of objects or ideas. Some groups are included in other groups. For example, all "red cars" are included in the group "cars."

The group RED CARS <u>is included in</u> the group CARS.

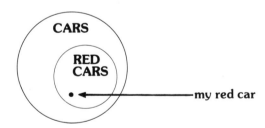

Some groups overlap. For instance, several famous generals were also U.S. Presidents—Washington, Jackson, Grant, Eisenhower.

The group FAMOUS GENERALS <u>overlaps</u> the group U.S. PRESIDENTS.

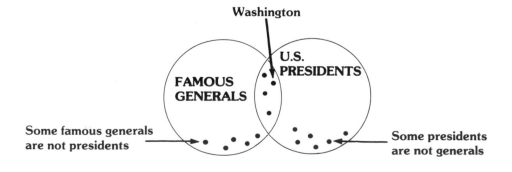

Some groups are separate from each other.

The group RED CARS <u>is separate from</u> the group BLUE CARS.

INSTRUCTIONS FOR THE EXERCISES

Each of the following exercises in Part I of this unit presents the names of two groups separated by a blank. The procedure for completing the exercises consists of two steps.

> STEP 1—Write one of the phrases below in the blank between the names of the two groups to show the relationship between those groups:

> > *includes*
> > *is included in*
> > *overlaps*
> > *is separate from.*

> STEP 2—Draw and label two circles to illustrate the relationship between the two groups.

Try now the following two examples. Remember, *first* write in the phrase which shows the relationship between the two groups (choose one of the four phrases listed in STEP 1 above). *Second*, draw and label two circles in the space below the sentence to illustrate the relationship between the two groups.

> **EXAMPLE 1:**

> The group SAILBOATS _____ the group BOATS.

ANSWER:

The group SAILBOATS ___*is included in*___ the group BOATS.

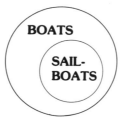

EXAMPLE 2:

The group METAL THINGS _____ the group WOODEN THINGS.

ANSWER:

The group METAL THINGS ___*is separate from*___ the group WOODEN THINGS.

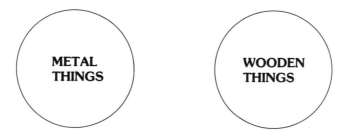

Begin now the exercises on the next page. These exercises will build your skills in comparing groups.

PART I EXERCISES

General Directions: Write one of the following phrases in the blank of each sentence, and then draw two circles to illustrate the relationship between the two groups.

includes
is included in
overlaps
is separate from

EXERCISE 1

The group AUTOMOBILES _____ the group TRANSPORTATION VEHICLES.

(Draw circles here. ⟶
Label both circles.)

EXERCISE 2

The group TRANSPORTATION VEHICLES _____ the group AIRPLANES.

EXERCISE 3

The group WOMEN _____ the group DOCTORS.

HINT: Some women are doctors.
Some women are not doctors.
Some doctors are women.
Some doctors are not women.

EXERCISE 4

The group WOODEN FURNITURE _____ the group CHAIRS.

EXERCISE 5

The group TEACHERS _____ the group MEN.

EXERCISE 6

The group LIONS _____ the group TIGERS.

EXERCISE 7

The group BIRDS _____ the group SPARROWS.

EXERCISE 8

The group BLUE CARS _____ the group CARS.

HINT: Are all blue cars included in the group CARS?

EXERCISE 9

The group HOUSES _____ the group BRICK HOUSES.

EXERCISE 10

The group WOODEN BRIDGES _____ the group BRIDGES.

EXERCISE 11

The group EDIBLE (eatable) SUBSTANCES _____ the group SEAFOOD.

EXERCISE 12

The group COLLEGE MATH COURSES _____ the group COLLEGE COURSES.

EXERCISE 13

The group TYPEWRITERS _____ the group WRITING DEVICES.

EXERCISE 14

The group LAND TRANSPORTATION FACILITIES _____ the group TRANS-PORTATION FACILITIES.

EXERCISE 15

The group SKIS _____ the group MOTOR-DRIVEN VEHICLES.

EXERCISE 16

The group POWER TOOLS _____ the group TOOLS.

EXERCISE 17

The group CONSTRUCTION MATERIALS _____ the group LUMBER MATERIALS.

EXERCISE 18

The group BLACK ANIMALS _____ the group CATS.

EXERCISE 19

The group AMERICAN LAWS _____ the group LAWS.

HINT: Are all American laws included in the group LAWS?
Are all laws included in the group AMERICAN LAWS?

EXERCISE 20

The group AMERICAN CITIZENS _____ the group WOMEN.

HINT: Are all American citizens included in the group WOMEN?
Are all women included in the group AMERICAN CITIZENS?

EXERCISE 21

The group MODERN PROBLEMS _____ the group NUCLEAR ENERGY PROBLEMS.

EXERCISE 22

The group MUSICIANS _____ the group SPORTS FANS.

EXERCISE 23

The group CARS _____ the group TRANSPORTATION VEHICLES.

EXERCISE 24

The group LUNG DISEASES _____ the group TYPES OF DISEASES.

EXERCISE 25

The group DOCTORS _____ the group GERMANS.

EXERCISE 26

The group CRIMINALS _____ the group ACCOUNTANTS.

EXERCISE 27

The group DUCKS _____ the group BIRDS.

HINT: Are all ducks included in the group BIRDS?

EXERCISE 28

The group DOGS _____ the group BROWN ANIMALS.

EXERCISE 29

The group MODERN PROBLEMS _____ the group TRANSPORTATION PROB-
LEMS OVER THE AGES.

PART II: GROUPING SPECIFICS INTO GENERAL CLASSES

INTRODUCTION

Classifying things into groups takes many forms in written material. One form is when a writer introduces a group and then describes several members of that group. For instance, a writer may say that there are many types of buildings constructed in different cultures, and then describe the Eskimo's igloo and various huts from Asia and Africa.

It is very important to be able to recognize and comprehend this form of organizing information and ideas.

INSTRUCTIONS FOR THE EXERCISES

Each exercise in the following section presents a group and two things or ideas which are included in that group. The task of the exercises is to determine which of the items listed is the group, and which two items listed are the things or ideas that are included in that group. Read the following two examples.

EXAMPLE 1—Write the letters of the three items listed in the blanks of the statement so that it shows the correct relationship between the group and the members of the group.

a. igloo
b. buildings
c. hut

_____ includes _____ and _____

ANSWER:

__b__ includes __a__ and __b__

[_buildings_ includes _igloo_ and _hut_]

EXAMPLE 2—Write the letters in the blanks to show the correct relationship.

a. reading brings enjoyment
b. reading is informative
c. reasons for reading

_____ includes _____ and _____

ANSWER: ___c___ includes ___a___ and ___b___

                              reasons for reading

                                    includes

        reading brings enjoyment and *reading is informative*

        Work carefully through the exercises beginning on the next page. These exercises will develop your skill in analyzing group-member relationships.

PART II EXERCISES

General Directions: Write the letters in the blanks to show the correct relationship between the group and the members of the group.

EXERCISE 1

    a. hate

    b. love

    c. types of emotion   _____ includes _____ and _____

EXERCISE 2

    a. transportation facilities

    b. water transportation facilities

    c. land transportation facilities   _____ includes _____ and _____

EXERCISE 3

    a. frying rice

    b. ways of cooking rice

    c. boiling rice   _____ includes _____ and _____

EXERCISE 4

    a. dogs are used for hunting

    b. dogs are used for guarding

    c. uses that man makes of dogs   _____ includes _____ and _____

EXERCISE 5

    a. the American family structure

    b. family structures

    c. the Bathonga family structure   _____ includes _____ and _____

EXERCISE 6

    a. language contributes to the formation of culture by allowing storage of knowledge

    b. language contributes to the formation of culture by allowing people to communicate and exchange ideas

    c. ways in which language contributes to the formation of culture   _____ includes _____ and _____

EXERCISE 7

    a. the symbol XXX represents poison
    b. things that symbols can represent
    c. the symbol T could represent tires   _____ includes _____ and _____

EXERCISE 8

    a. the trees are in bloom
    b. the birds are singing
    c. signs of spring   _____ includes _____ and _____

EXERCISE 9

    a. smoking marijuana increases blood pressure and heart
       rate which could precipitate a heart attack
    b. lung efficiency is reduced by marijuana
    c. effects of marijuana on body functions   _____ includes _____ and _____

EXERCISE 10

    a. sleeping around the campfire brought people together
       socially
    b. effects of using fire on social unity and human progress
    c. fire extended the day so man had time to plan for
       tomorrow   _____ includes _____ and _____

EXERCISE 11

    a. war is a social institution used by the Spaniards for con-
       quest by killing
    b. war is a social institution used by the Aztecs to obtain
       captives for religious sacrifices
    c. different forms of a social institution in different
       cultures   _____ includes _____ and _____

EXERCISE 12

    a. English-speaking people have difficulty pronouncing cer-
       tain French words
    b. difficulties adults who speak one language have in pro-
       nouncing the different sounds of another language
    c. Japanese-speaking people have trouble pronouncing
       certain English words   _____ includes _____ and _____

EXERCISE 13

a. belief that a book has weight from having held it in your hand
b. belief there is an environmental crisis because many statistics suggest it
c. beliefs based on simple (direct) or complicated experiences

_____ includes _____ and _____

EXERCISE 14

a. Europe began to produce more lumber to trade for Oriental products
b. European towns grew as people moved in to manufacture products to trade for Oriental products
c. effects of the introduction of Oriental products on Europe

_____ includes _____ and _____

EXERCISE 15

a. trumpets
b. musical instruments
c. musical instruments played by blowing

_____ includes _____ and _____

PART III: READING FOR MAIN (GENERAL) IDEAS AND SUPPORTING (SPECIFIC) DETAILS

INTRODUCTION

When you read text material, especially in the social sciences, business, and news fields, you must usually try to understand the author's general or main idea, and then the specific details he or she presents to support or explain that main idea.

Read the following paragraph carefully. Then do these three things in the blanks provided below the paragraph:

(1) Write a sentence summarizing the author's general or main idea;

(2) Write a sentence describing a specific detail the author presents to support or explain the main idea;

(3) Write another sentence describing another specific detail the author presents to support or explain the main idea.

> The family is a universal social institution. As previously mentioned, it helps to meet the need for the group's survival by providing care and protection for the young. All societies have institutionalized the family as a basic unit of social organization. The specific form of that organization and the kinds of relationships permitted to exist within it vary from one culture to the next, of course. A family structure consisting of one man, one woman, and their children, and in which all members contribute to some extent to the decision-making process is typical of American culture. A structure consisting of several related men, each with more than one wife, and their children, and in which the senior males of the senior generation made most of the decisions was, until just recently, common among the Bathonga of southern Mozambique.

MAIN IDEA: _____

_____

_____

SUPPORT I: _____

_____

_____

SUPPORT II: _____

_____

_____

Here is what you may have written for the main idea and the supporting points. Check to see that you expressed the same ideas as are written here. The exact phrasing of your sentences may differ from that below, but the ideas expressed in the sentences should be the same.

MAIN IDEA: *The family is a universal social institution, but may take different forms in different*

societies.

_____

SUPPORT I: *American culture has a family unit consisting of one man, one woman, and*

their children.

_____

SUPPORT II: *The Bathonga of southern Mozambique have a family unit consisting of several related men,*

each with more than one wife, and their children.

_____

INSTRUCTIONS FOR THE EXERCISES

Each of the following exercises contains a selection. After you read each selection, write a sentence summarizing the main idea of the selection, and two separate sentences describing two points the author presents in support of the main idea.

NOTE: As you work these exercises, you may notice that some of the ideas in the selections were introduced in Part II of this chapter. DO NOT refer back to Part II! Just read the selections carefully and write your sentences as clearly as you can. You may find yourself writing many words, phrases, and even sentences which come straight from the selection as you write your general and specific statements. This is fine. Remember, however, not to refer back to Part II.

PART III: EXERCISES

General Directions: For each exercise, read the selection carefully. Then write a sentence expressing the main idea of the selection, and two sentences describing supporting details.

EXERCISE 1

The development of language is essential to the formation of culture, because without language there could be no mature culture. Language does more than just facilitate communication. It allows us to think about the past and future as well as the present. Once our ancestors began to construct symbols, they could communicate about an object without its being present. In this manner, one person's past experiences could be communicated to another. Through symbol systems people could store such communicated experiences in their memories; this stored knowledge is the essence of culture. Language, then, facilitates the accumulation and storage of a social heritage, and the transmission of that social heritage from one generation to the next.

MAIN IDEA: _____

_____

_____

SUPPORT I: _____

_____

_____

SUPPORT II: _____

_____

_____

EXERCISE 2

One of the interesting and important things about symbols is that we can, by agreement, make anything stand for anything. For example, we could agree that A stands for pencils and B stands for pens; then we could change the agreement to let A stand for hippies and B stand for hardhats; or let A stand for China and B stand for Russia, and so forth. The point is that we are free to assign whatever meaning we choose to our symbols. In fact, we can make symbols that stand for symbols. We could, if we so desired, let K stand for all the A's in our example and let L stand for all the B's. If we wanted to, we could make another symbol, Z, stand for K and L (a symbol of symbol of symbols). As you can see, the symbolic process operates on many different levels and is quite sophisticated.

MAIN IDEA: _____

_____

_____

SUPPORT I: _____

_____

_____

SUPPORT II: _____

_____

_____

EXERCISE 3

[HINT: The main idea is contained in the second sentence.]

Sounds, as we have seen, are indispensable to language. But not all languages contain all the sounds human beings are capable of making. "The unique quality of any language is that it includes only a small set of distinct sounds derived from the potential range of sounds." A normal human infant is capable of uttering, and does in fact utter, many sounds that are not used by the adult members of his or her society. As they grow older, children learn to distinguish sounds which are appropriate to the language of their society from those which are not. They learn to make new sounds which they did not utter as infants, and to forget those which are not appropriate. There is some evidence to suggest that they even lose the ability to produce some sounds. This would explain the difficulty encountered by some English-speaking persons when they try to pronounce correctly some words from other languages, say French; or the difficulty of Japanese-speaking persons when they try to pronounce correctly the English words claw, lollipop, or dollar.

MAIN IDEA: _____

_____

_____

SUPPORT I: _____

_____

_____

SUPPORT II: _____

_____

_____

EXERCISE 4

[HINT: Only part of the main idea is found in the first sentence. The other part is found near the middle of the selection.]

Some of your beliefs, of course, are the result of direct experience. If you ask yourself why you believe this book has the quality of weight, you will answer that you have held it in your hands, and it feels like it has the quality of weight. You would probably not feel the need to explain your belief any further. Other beliefs are more complicated, and seem to rest on more than just sensory experience. If you ask yourself why you believe that we are in the midst of a serious environmental crisis, for example, you might reply by citing statistics concerning the rate of air, water, and soil pollution that, taken together, logically lead to the conclusion that we are in the midst of such a crisis. If, however, you further ask yourself why you believe those statistics are correct, you might answer that you read them in books which your teacher said were reliable sources. Then you could ask yourself why you believe what your teacher said, and so on.

MAIN IDEA: _____

_____

_____

SUPPORT I: _____

_____

_____

SUPPORT II: _____

_____

_____

EXERCISE 5

Before learning to control fire, humans probably slept in trees in order to avoid the attack of ground-dwelling predators. However, with a campfire to keep the predators away, they could sleep soundly and securely on the ground. This new physical arrangement for sleeping allowed group members to sleep closer to one another, encouraging interaction that contributed to the cohesion and solidarity of the group.

Fire was used for a number of purposes, from cooking to aiding in the hunting of animals. Probably the most important effect of learning to control fire, though, was the fact that the rhythm of life was changed. Before fire, the human daily cycle coincided with the rising and setting of the sun—roughly twelve hours of activity and twelve hours of sleep. But fire lengthened the day. It allowed the human more time to think and talk about the day's events and to prepare strategies for coping with tomorrow. The campfire afforded the opportunity to exercise the mind in a relaxed atmosphere, away from the routine daily pressures of trying to survive. "It was around such fires, too, as man stared into the flames and took comfort in the radiating warmth, that stories became myths and world views became crystallized as philosophies." Learning to control fire, then, contributed significantly to the formation of culture.

MAIN IDEA: _____

_____

_____

SUPPORT I: _____

_____

_____

SUPPORT II: _____

_____

_____

EXERCISE 6

Up to this point, we have discussed culture in terms of universals—aspects of human behavior that occur in every society. Let us now consider cultural variation. The famous anthropologist Ruth Benedict has pointed out that group life may develop in an infinite variety of directions, depending on the physical environment of the group and the imagination of its members. In fact, the spectrum of possible human arrangements for living is so broad that selection is a necessity. For instance, Benedict speaks of warfare as a social theme that may or may not be used in any given culture. The Aztecs used war to obtain captives for religious sacrifices; the Spaniards treated war as a method of conquest by killing. Partly as a result of these two different conceptions of warfare, Cortez conquered Mexico in an incredibly short time in 1519. The Aztecs' notion of war prevented them from adjusting rapidly to what the Spaniards were doing. Benedict further points out that while "it is impossible for certain peoples to conceive the possibility of a state of peace . . . it may be just as impossible for a people to conceive the possibility of a state of war." Eskimos, for example, understand the act of one man killing another, but they have no notion of organized mutual slaughter. The idea of one Eskimo tribe facing another in battle is as foreign to them as rubbing noses as an expression of affection is to us.

MAIN IDEA: _____

_____

_____

SUPPORT I: _____

_____

_____

SUPPORT II: _____

_____

_____

Word Power III

Directions: Study each of the Power Words below. Note how each word is pronounced. Then read the context sentences to figure out what each Power Word means. In the left-hand margin next to each Power Word, try to jot down a synonym or short definition which defines that word.

Power Words	myriad	loquacious	imminent	claustrophobia
	virulent	xenophobia	lethargy	inundated

1. **myriad** | **mîr′** ē əd |
   - After years of collecting stamps, Mrs. Lopez had a myriad of stamps from countries all over the world.
   - There are myriad job opportunities open to those willing to search them out.

2. **virulent** | **vĭr′** yə lənt |
   - Some snake poisons are highly virulent and cause death quickly.

3. **loquacious** | lō **kwā′** shəs |
   - A loquacious individual who talks on and on can be very boring.
   - Marc was so loquacious I could not get a word in edgewise.

4. **xenophobia** | **zĕn′** ə fō′ bē ə |
   - People who have been isolated may have xenophobia because of their limited experience and fear new things.
   - Because of her xenophobia, Vana could not walk down a busy street.

5. **imminent** | **ĭm′** ə nənt |
   - With the hurricane imminent, the last group of reporters and policemen left the area before it was too late.
   - The children were all excited because of the imminent arrival of Santa Claus.

6. **lethargy** | **lĕth′** ər jē |
   - If a library is too hot, people may develop a feeling of lethargy and have difficulty remaining alert while reading.
   - To avoid lethargy while driving, keep one window at least partly open all the time.

7. **claustrophobia** | **klô′** strə fō′ bē ə |
   - Some individuals with claustrophobia will never ride in elevators, but instead always take the stairs.
   - My mother would not ride in my small car because of her claustrophobia.

8. **inundated** | **ĭn′** ŭn dā tĭd |
   - Following her TV appearance, the doctor was inundated with mail; it took her several weeks to answer it all.
   - The company was inundated with requests for free samples.

ă pat / ā pay / â care / ä father / ĕ pet / ē be / ĭ pit / ī pie / î fierce / ŏ pot / ō go / ô paw, for / oi oil / oŏ book /
oō boot / ou out / ŭ cut / ü fur / *th* the / th thin / hw which / zh vision / ə ago, item, pencil, atom, circus

Meaning Comprehension

Directions: Use what you have learned from the context sentences to identify the correct definition of each Power Word. In the blank next to each Power Word, write the letter of its correct definition.

Power Words

_____ myriad
_____ virulent
_____ loquacious
_____ xenophobia
_____ imminent
_____ lethargy
_____ claustrophobia
_____ inundated

Definitions

a. very severe; deadly
b. fear and hatred of strangers, foreigners and foreign things
c. a large and indefinite amount, innumerable
d. flooded; overwhelmed by a large quantity
e. excessively talkative
f. about to occur, close at hand
g. laziness, sleepiness; indifference
h. fear of being in narrow or enclosed places

Context Application

Directions: Each of the following sentences has two blanks. Use what you have learned about the Power Words to determine which Power Word best belongs in each of the blanks. Then write the appropriate Power Word in each blank. Use each Power Word only once.

1. The speaker was _____ but not interesting, and yawns were heard as a state of _____ overtook people's minds.

2. During the holiday season the post office is _____ with a _____ of cards, letters, and packages.

3. Since an outbreak of a _____ disease in the storm-ravaged area was _____ , the health department advised people to leave the area.

4. _____ , fear of foreigners, and _____ , fear of small places, are both phobias, stemming from the Greek word for "fear" or "dislike."

Muscle Builder Analogies

Directions: Each exercise below is an analogy, with one term missing. Choose the Power Word which belongs in each blank of the analogy so that the analogy reads correctly. Write the appropriate Power Word in each blank. Note that some of the Power Words will not be used.

1. COUNTED is to EXACT as _____ is to INDEFINITE

2. DISINTEREST is to INTEREST as _____ is to LIVELINESS

3. MILD is to A COLD as _____ is to CANCER

Word Power IV

Directions: Study each of the Power Words below. Note how each word is pronounced. Then read the context sentences to figure out what each Power Word means. In the left-hand margin next to each Power Word, try to jot down a synonym or short definition which defines that word.

Power Words	inimical	retroactive	pertinent	redundant
	infamous	retrospect	relevant	invective

1. **inimical** | ĭ **nĭm'** ĭ kəl |
   - Countries that share a common border are sometimes inimical towards each other and fight occasional border wars.
   - The man's inimical attitude put me on guard.

2. **infamous** | **ĭn'** fə məs |
   - The infamous Jack-the-Ripper killed over a dozen people.
   - The infamous Japanese attack on Pearl Harbor occurred on December 7, 1941.

3. **retroactive** | rĕt' rō **ăk'** tĭv |
   - The decision to pay hospital bills for injured employees was retroactive, so it even applied to employees hurt before the decision was made.

4. **retrospect** | **rĕt'** rə spĕkt' |
   - The grandfather said that in retrospect he wished he had raised two more children.
   - In retrospect, now that I have looked at the completed job, I think I should have done it differently.

5. **pertinent** | **pûr'** tn ənt |
   - Phil talks a lot at meetings, but nothing he says is pertinent to the points being discussed.
   - Since we considered her remarks pertinent to the investigation, we listened very closely.

6. **relevant** | **rĕl'** ə vənt |
   - Almost everything Judy says is relevant to the issues discussed at the meetings.

7. **redundant** | rĭ **dŭn'** dənt |
   - A redundant statement is overly repetitive, like a parent saying her son is bright, smart, brainy, and intelligent.

8. **invective** | ĭn **vĕk'** tĭv |
   - A successful manager does not use invective, because insulting employees produces resentment and negative attitudes.

ă pat / ā pay / â care / ä father / ĕ pet / ē be / ĭ pit / ī pie / î fierce / ŏ pot / ō go / ô paw, for / oi oil / ŏŏ book /
ōō boot / ou out / ŭ cut / û fur / *th* the / th thin / hw which / zh vision / ə ago, item, pencil, atom, circus

Meaning Comprehension

Directions: Use what you have learned from the context sentences to identify the correct definition of each Power Word. In the blank next to each Power Word, write the letter of its correct definition.

Power Words

_____ inimical
_____ infamous
_____ retrospect
_____ pertinent
_____ relevant
_____ redundant
_____ invective
_____ retroactive

Definitions

a. related to a specific matter, relevant
b. related to a specific matter, pertinent
c. applying to a prior time, extending to conditions existing earlier
d. insulting language used to attack or abuse
e. hostile, unfriendly
f. think about past events, look back at or review the past
g. famous for being evil or vicious, having a bad reputation
h. using more words than necessary, repeating the same idea

Context Application

Directions: Each of the following sentences has two blanks. Use what you have learned about the Power Words to determine which Power Word best belongs in each of the blanks. Then write the appropriate Power Word in each blank. Use each Power Word only once.

1. Saying that Jessie was _____ , unfriendly, and hostile towards Phil would be _____ , since the words are basically synonymous.

2. "Retro" is a Latin prefix meaning "backward," so _____ means "backward acting" and _____ means "look backward."

3. The drama coach was _____ for hurting the feelings of young actors with her sharp tongue and harsh _____ .

4. The word _____ is synonymous to and would be found after the word _____ in the dictionary.

Muscle Builder Analogies

Directions: Each exercise below is an analogy, with one term missing. Choose the Power Word which belongs in each blank of the analogy so that the analogy reads correctly. Write the appropriate Power Word in each blank. Note that some of the Power Words will not be used.

1. PRAISE is to CRITICISM as COMPLIMENTS is to

_____

2. GEORGE WASHINGTON is to FAMOUS as BENEDICT ARNOLD is to _____

3. SUCCINCT is to BREVITY as _____ is to REPETITION

ADDITIONAL ASSIGNMENTS

In the following problems you will be asked to write problems of your own. After you write each problem, ask a peer to try to solve it.

1. Write four problems like the ones in Part I of this unit. Let each problem have a different answer from the four possible answers: includes, is included in, overlaps, is separate from.

    A. _____

    B. _____

    C. _____

    D. _____

ADDITIONAL ASSIGNMENTS (continued)

2. Write a problem like those in Part II of this unit.

   a. _____

   b. _____

   c. _____

   _____ includes _____ and _____

3. Find a section in one of your own books which has a main idea and at least two specific details supporting the main idea. The section you pick may have just one paragraph or it may have several paragraphs. (Note, however, that not all paragraphs have a main idea *and* specific details.)

   Write sentences summarizing the main idea and two supporting details from the material you picked on the lines below. Then have a peer do the same thing on a separate piece of paper, without seeing your answers. Compare your two interpretations of the section. Discuss any differences in your summaries.

   _____

   _____

   _____

   _____

   _____

   _____

   _____

   _____

   _____

   _____

   _____

UNIT
9

ADVANCED SERIAL ORDER

OBJECTIVES: When you have completed this unit you should

- be able to comprehend and represent with a diagram complex written descriptions of serial order;
- know the meanings of the following POWER WORDS.

POWER
WORDS

dominant	monograph	abstemious	sanctity
ostentatious	simulated	abyss	prophet
suppress	brandished	acme	ominous
ironical	prolific	adroit	inquisitive
charlatan	bellicose	admonition	implausible
disparity	clichés	acrophobia	synopsis
nepotism	disparaging	abject	candid
chaotic	disseminate	acclaim	ascribed

Word Power I

Directions: Study each of the Power Words below. Note how each word is pronounced. Then read the context sentences to figure out what each Power Word means. In the left-hand margin next to each Power Word, try to jot down a synonym or short definition which defines that word.

Power Words

dominant	suppress	charlatan	nepotism
ostentatious	ironical	disparity	chaotic

---

1. **dominant** | **dŏm′** ə nənt |
   - The dominant animal is often the largest, but the dominant human is frequently the most intelligent or cunning.

2. **ostentatious** | ŏs′ tĕn **tā′** shəs |
   - Nobody had the heart to tell Mom how ostentatious and tasteless her hat looked.
   - I found the party to be ostentatious, with an overabundance of everything.

3. **suppress** | sə **prĕs′** |
   - Teachers are taught not to suppress the curiosity of youngsters.

4. **ironical** | ī **rŏn′** ĭ kəl |
   - Social critics find it ironical that extremely high salaries go to entertainers, who produce no material products.
   - It's quite ironical; I expected everything to go wrong today, but instead it's been the best day of my life!

5. **charlatan** | **shär′** lə tən |
   - The phoney doctor was denounced as a charlatan.
   - They called her a charlatan until she was able to prove to them that her discoveries were true.

6. **disparity** | dĭ **spăr′** ĭ tē |
   - The disparity in their backgrounds did not dampen their friendship.
   - Although the two of us ran the same marketing test, there was a significant disparity in our results.

7. **nepotism** | **nĕp′** ə tĭz′ əm |
   - Favoring relatives for promotion in a company—and other forms of nepotism—can harm employee morale.

8. **chaotic** | kā **ŏt′** ĭk |
   - At midnight the party got chaotic.
   - The meeting quickly turned chaotic, with everyone talking at once.

ă pat / ā pay / â care / ä father / ĕ pet / ē be / ĭ pit / ī pie / î fierce / ŏ pot / ō go / ô paw, for / oi oil / ŏŏ book /
ōō boot / ou out / ŭ cut / û fur / *th* the / th thin / hw which / zh vision / ə ago, item, pencil, atom, circus

Meaning Comprehension

Directions: Use what you have learned from the context sentences to identify the correct definition of each Power Word. In the blank next to each Power Word, write the letter of its correct definition.

Power Words

_____ dominant
_____ ostentatious
_____ suppress
_____ ironical
_____ charlatan
_____ disparity
_____ nepotism
_____ chaotic

Definitions

a. unexpectedly opposite, sometimes comically; eventful in a way opposite to the expected
b. difference, unlikeness, inequality
c. imposter, quack, fake
d. totally mixed-up, confused, disorderly
e. favoritism shown to a relative
f. commanding, having supremacy over all others
g. showy so as to impress others
h. hold back, subdue, restrict

Context Application

Directions: Each of the following sentences has two blanks. Use what you have learned about the Power Words to determine which Power Word best belongs in each of the blanks. Then write the appropriate Power Word in each blank. Use each Power Word only once.

1. In some countries the _____ political party will _____ the communication activities (radio, TV, and print) of other parties.

2. It seems _____ that a person may wear _____ clothes, yet be shy and uncomfortable when actually made the center of attention.

3. The _____ between what the boss' son was able to do and what his job required indicated that _____ was behind his being hired.

4. She was not a true scientist but a _____ , and her research was not precise and orderly but _____ .

Muscle Builder Analogies

Directions: Each exercise below is an analogy, with one or two terms missing. Choose the Power Word which belongs in each blank of the analogy so that the analogy reads correctly. Write the appropriate Power Word in each blank. Note that some of the Power Words will not be used.

1. SHY is to BOLD as MODEST is to _____

2. BOSS is to _____ as EMPLOYEE is to SUBORDINATE

3. _____ is to EXPECTED as _____ is to ORDERLY

Word Power II

Directions: Study each of the Power Words below. Note how each word is pronounced. Then read the context sentences to figure out what each Power Word means. In the left-hand margin next to each Power Word, try to jot down a synonym or short definition which defines that word.

Power Words	monograph	brandished	bellicose	disparaging
	simulated	prolific	clichés	disseminate

1. **monograph** | **mŏn′** ə grăf′ |
   - After studying butterflies for fifteen years, he must be qualified to write a monograph on them.
   - The information you are looking for can be found in my monograph, "The Effects of Gamma Rays on the Development of Marigolds."

2. **simulated** | **sĭm′** yə lā′ tĭd |
   - The film showed a simulated auto crash, not a real one.
   - In order to test out landing procedures, they simulated a lunar landing.

3. **brandished** | **brăn′** dĭshd |
   - The policemen brandished their nightsticks as they approached the mob.

4. **prolific** | prə **lĭf′** ĭk |
   - Unfortunately, weeds are prolific plants.
   - She is our most prolific author, with twenty books published so far.

5. **bellicose** | **bĕl′** ĭ kōs′ |
   - A watchdog should have a bellicose nature.
   - When Fillipe does not like what is being presented to him, he tends to become bellicose.

6. **clichés** | klē **shāz′** |
   - When you go to some people for help, all you get are clichés like "I told you so."

7. **disparaging** | dĭ **spăr′** ə jĭng |
   - A jealous person may make disparaging, insulting remarks about those he/she envies.
   - The salesman's disparaging remarks about the cheaper-model car made me decide against buying it.

8. **disseminate** | dĭ **sĕm′** ə nāt′ |
   - The function of a textbook is to disseminate information on a topic.
   - We needed to disseminate the information as quickly as possible, so we ran ads in newspapers and on radio and TV.

ă pat / ā pay / â care / ä father / ĕ pet / ē be / ĭ pit / ī pie / î fierce / ŏ pot / ō go / ô paw, for / oi oil / ŏŏ book /
ōō boot / ou out / ŭ cut / û fur / *th* the / th thin / hw which / zh vision / ə ago, item, pencil, atom, circus

Meaning Comprehension

Directions: Use what you have learned from the context sentences to identify the correct definition of each Power Word. In the blank next to each Power Word, write the letter of its correct definition.

Power Words

_____ monograph
_____ simulated
_____ brandished
_____ prolific
_____ bellicose
_____ clichés
_____ disparaging
_____ disseminate

Definitions

a. distribute widely, spread about, broadcast
b. discrediting, belittling, slighting
c. overused expressions or ideas
d. very productive, fertile, reproduces rapidly
e. ready to fight, belligerent, combative
f. showed or waved threateningly
g. written work on a single subject
h. imitated, duplicated the appearance of; pretended

Context Application

Directions: Each of the following sentences has two blanks. Use what you have learned about the Power Words to determine which Power Word best belongs in each of the blanks. Then write the appropriate Power Word in each blank. Use each Power Word only once.

1. The museum published a _____ on the polar bear to _____ information on this endangered species.

2. Nina asked questions and _____ interest during the lecture, but afterward made negative, _____ comments about how boring it was.

3. He was a _____ writer with over 20 books to his credit, yet his ideas were always fresh and there were few _____ .

4. The knight had a _____ temperament and _____ his sword immediately upon seeing a newcomer.

Muscle Builder Analogies

Directions: Each exercise below is an analogy, with one term missing. Choose the Power Word which belongs in each blank of the analogy so that the analogy reads correctly. Write the appropriate Power Word in each blank. Note that some of the Power Words will not be used.

1. GENEROUS is to GIVE as _____ is to FIGHT

2. TRANSMIT is to ENERGY as _____ is to INFORMATION

3. BELLICOSE is to EASYGOING as _____ is to STERILE

INTRODUCTION

This unit covers the same analytical reading process as in Unit 4. But, in this unit, the exercises are more advanced and require more careful, controlled thinking. Generally, a larger number of elements must be ordered in these exercises than in Unit 4. Also, there is more superfluous information to sort through in isolating the relationships. And, as in most text and report material, a great many mental steps are needed to keep the information comprehensible.

INSTRUCTIONS FOR THE EXERCISES

Follow the same working procedure you developed in Unit 4. The key is to work patiently and carefully. Make separate working-diagrams for the different sections of an exercise if it is helpful. Read the complex parts of an exercise several times until the relationships are completely clear.

You can be sure that when you have developed the confidence and ability to work the most difficult exercises in this unit, you will be able to handle and comprehend even the most complex written descriptions of serial order that you may encounter in your text reading.

EXERCISE 1

Theodore Roosevelt was, except for McKinley, the first American president in the twentieth century. Taft followed Roosevelt and was, in turn, followed by Wilson.

Write the names of the four presidents in order on the diagram.

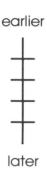

earlier

later

EXERCISE 2

Except for Australia, Europe is the smallest continent. With the exceptions of Asia and Africa, North America is the largest continent. Africa is not as large as Asia. Antarctica and South America (the latter is larger) are between North America and Europe in size.

Write the names of the seven continents in order on the diagram.

larger

smaller

EXERCISE 3

Lake Superior in the U.S. is the world's largest lake, with the exception of the Caspian Sea, which was mistakenly thought to be a sea by the ancient Romans but is considered a lake by modern geographers because it is landlocked. Skipping over Lakes Aral and Victoria, the next largest lake is also in the U.S., Lake Huron. The African Lake Victoria is larger than the Russian Lake Aral.

Write the names of the five lakes in order on the diagram.

larger

smaller

EXERCISE 4

Fred Turner, Al Black, and José Torro weighed themselves. Torro was heavier than Al but lighter than Fred.

Write the *last names* of the men in order on the diagram.

heavier

lighter

EXERCISE 5

Patti is a left-handed mechanic; Sandra, a dentist, is nicknamed Cuspid; Nadine, who has four boys, is a lawyer; and Marie is a French teacher born in Italy. The mother of the four boys is taller than the teacher but shorter than the left-handed woman. Cuspid is shorter than the lawyer but taller than the Italian.

Write the *first names* of the women in order on the diagram.

taller

shorter

EXERCISE 6

The modern English alphabet that we use has roots in the alphabets of ancient people. The Egyptian alphabet preceded both the Greek and Semitic alphabets. Moreover, the Greek alphabet succeeded the Semitic alphabet. From the Greek alphabet came the modern English alphabet.

Four alphabets are listed below. Write them in order on the diagram.

    —modern English alphabet   —Greek alphabet
    —Egyptian alphabet   —Semitic alphabet

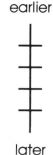

earlier

later

EXERCISE 7

In archery class, Laurie hit closer to the target than Ari but not as close as Julie. Julie hit closer than Laurie but not as close as Ramon.

The diagram shows the target at the top. Write the four names in order from closest to farthest from the target.

target

farther from target

EXERCISE 8

Indianapolis is farther than Columbus, Ohio, from the Atlantic Ocean but closer than Kansas City. Kansas City is closer than Wichita to the Atlantic Ocean but farther than St. Louis. St. Louis is farther than Indianapolis from the Atlantic Ocean.

A. The diagram shows the Atlantic Ocean at the top. Write the five cities in order from closest to farthest from the Atlantic Ocean.

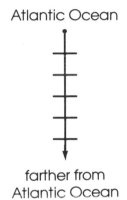

Atlantic Ocean

farther from
Atlantic Ocean

B. Which of the cities is closest to the Atlantic Ocean? _____

EXERCISE 9

The Copper Age occurred before the Early Iron Age and the Bronze Age, but it was after the New Stone Age. The Early Iron Age was after the Bronze Age, and the Old Stone Age was before the New Stone Age.

Write the five Ages in order on the diagram.

earlier

later

EXERCISE 10

America was discovered by Columbus after the Turks captured Constantinople but before Shakespeare wrote in England. However, the major colonization of the Americas occurred after Shakespeare. The beginning of the Crusades preceded the Magna Carta in England, and the Magna Carta preceded the Turkish capture of Constantinople.

Six historical events are listed below. Write them in chronological order on the diagram.

—Magna Carta
—America discovered
—Americas colonized

—Turks capture Constantinople
—Shakespeare
—beginning of Crusades

earlier

later

EXERCISE 11

Portuguese and Spanish soldiers conquered South America 300 years before Napoleon invaded Spain. Napoleon's invasion allowed South American governments to build power, and shortly thereafter Simon Bolivar freed Venezuela, Columbia, Bolivia, Ecuador, and part of Peru from Spanish rule. In the period between the Spanish conquerors and Napoleon's invasion, missionaries and ranchers established settlements in South America. Before the Portuguese and Spanish conquerors, South America was dominated first by the Maya Indians, and later by the Inca and the Aztec Indians.

Six facts on South American history are listed below. Write them in order on the diagram.

—Portuguese and Spanish conquerors
—Napoleon invades Spain
—Bolivar frees countries
—missionaries and ranchers settle
—Mayas dominate
—Incas and Aztecs dominate

earlier

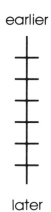

later

EXERCISE 12

Documents for Freedom

Two noteworthy documents for political freedom are the U.S. Constitution written in 1787, and the French Constitution of 1791. The U.S. Bill of Rights was written after the U.S. Constitution. By contrast, the French Declaration of the Rights of Man was written before the French Constitution, perhaps because the U.S. Bill of Rights was already in existence as a model. The U.S. Declaration of Independence preceded the U.S. Constitution, and England's Petition of Right preceded the Declaration of Independence by about 150 years. Still earlier by 400 years, England's Magna Carta planted the seeds for freedom from the tyranny of kings.

earlier

later

A. Seven documents of political freedom are listed below. Write them in chronological order on the diagram.

—U.S. Constitution
—French Constitution
—U.S. Bill of Rights
—French Declaration of the Rights of Man
—English Petition of Right
—English Magna Carta
—U.S. Declaration of Independence

B. By approximately how many years did England's Magna Carta precede the U.S. Declaration of Independence? Circle your answer.

(A) 400 years
(B) 150 years
(C) 250 years
(D) 550 years
(E) cannot be determined from the information given

EXERCISE 13

Steam Propulsion for Ships and Railroads

In 1786 the American inventor John Fitch began operating a steamship on the Delaware River, but his venture failed financially and it wasn't for several years that another American, Robert Fulton, launched the first successful steamship, the *Clermont*, running between Albany and New York. Between these two nautical milestones a Cornish inventor, Richard Trevithick, built a steam locomotive that pulled a coal train, but it was too expensive to operate and not commercially successful. The first commercially successful locomotive was built by George Stephenson before a ship called the *Royal William* crossed the ocean for the first time entirely by steam, but after the *Clermont* was already operating. Steam-propelled vehicles can be traced back to Fernand Verbiest, who built a toy cart with a steam turbine. And about 100 years later, but still before Fitch's steamship, a French inventor, Nicholas Cugnot, ran a steam locomotive on the road.

earlier

later

A. Seven steam-propelled vehicles are listed below. Write them in chronological order on the diagram.

—Fitch's steamboat
—*Clermont*
—Trevithick's locomotive
—Stephenson's locomotive
—*Royal William*
—Verbiest's cart
—Cugnot's locomotive

B. (Check the correct answer.) The *Clermont* and the *Royal William* were launched by

☐ (A) Stephenson and Fitch, respectively
☐ (B) Stephenson and Fulton, respectively
☐ (C) Fulton and Stephenson, respectively
☐ (D) none of the above

EXERCISE 14

Royal Houses (Families) of England

The House of York ruled England before the House of Tudor but after the Plantagenet family. The House of Saxe-Coburg ruled England after the House of Hanover but before the House of Windsor. The House of Stuart was preceded by the House of Tudor, was interrupted by the Commonwealth (during which England had no royal family), and was succeeded by the House of Hanover.

Write the seven royal houses (or families) in order on the diagram.

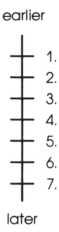

earlier

1.
2.
3.
4.
5.
6.
7.

later

EXERCISE 15

Although Van Buren preceded Harrison as President, he succeeded him in birth. Polk succeeded Tyler in both presidency and birth, but preceded Taylor in both. Van Buren preceded Tyler in both presidency and birth.

Write the names of the five Presidents in order of birth on the diagram.

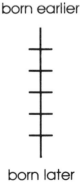

born earlier

born later

EXERCISE 16

Some Milestones in the History of Medicine

William Harvey, the Englishman who published the first description of the blood's circulation, was born between Marcell Malpighi, a Bologna professor who was younger than Harvey and extended Harvey's theory by using a microscope to show that blood passed from the arteries to the smaller veins, and Galileo, the astronomer who introduced the microscope to science. Thomas Sydenham, a London physician born between the two aforementioned pioneers of research on circulation, is sometimes called the founder of modern clinical medicine because of his precise description of diseases like malaria and smallpox, whereas Hermann Boerhaave, a Dutch physician born after the Bologna professor mentioned earlier, was considered the greatest medical professor of his day as a result of his use of the clinical method in teaching and research. Athanasius Kircher—born before Anton van Leeuwenhoek (who made a microscope that magnified 270 times and who wrote the first complete description of red blood cells and was also the first to see bacteria) but after "the greatest medical professor of his day"—theorized from his microscopic research that bacteria caused disease and decay, although this went unconfirmed for 200 years.

A. Create your own diagram in the space to the right with "born earlier" at the top and "born later" at the bottom. Write the names of the seven researchers in order by birth date on your diagram.

B. Which researcher is cited for having made a major contribution to medicine's understanding of blood cells? Circle your answer.

(A) Harvey
(B) Malpighi
(C) Kircher
(D) van Leeuwenhoek

EXERCISE 17

Epochs, Periods, and Eras

In geology the last 11,000 years are called the Recent epoch, and the Recent epoch together with the Pleistocene epoch make up the Quaternary period. Moreover, the Quaternary together with the Tertiary period make up the Cenozoic era. The Cenozoic is the only era in which periods are broken down into epochs. The other eras are only subdivided into periods. The era immediately preceding the Cenozoic is the Mesozoic, during which the Jurassic period represents the age of the dinosaurs, although these giant reptiles appeared slightly before the Jurassic and became extinct slightly later than the Jurassic in the Triassic and Cretaceous periods, respectively. In the still earlier Paleozoic era, the first sharks and reptiles appeared during the next to the last period, the Carboniferous, while in the last period of this era, the Permian, reptiles flourished. Preceding the Carboniferous period was the Devonian, and before that, from earliest to latest, the Cambrian, Ordovician, and Silurian periods.

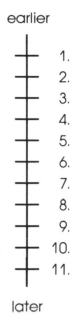

earlier

1.
2.
3.
4.
5.
6.
7.
8.
9.
10.
11.

later

A. Write the eleven periods in order on the diagram. <u>Do not</u> write eras or epochs.

B. Which is the only era that has periods divided into epochs? _____

Word Power III

Directions: Study each of the Power Words below. Note how each word is pronounced. Then read the context sentences to figure out what each Power Word means. In the left-hand margin next to each Power Word, try to jot down a synonym or short definition which defines that word.

Power Words	abstemious	acme	admonition	abject
	abyss	adroit	acrophobia	acclaim

1. **abstemious** | ăb **stē′** mē əs |
   - Fred owes his trim waist to abstemious eating habits.
   - They found themselves lost in the wilderness and had to be abstemious and ration their supplies.

2. **abyss** | ə **bĭs′** |
   - In the hiker's dream, the woman fell into an abyss and seemed to drop endlessly.

3. **acme** | **ăk′** mē |
   - Most scientists attain the acme of their productivity between the ages of 30 and 50.
   - The acme of Fran's career was being promoted to president of the company.

4. **adroit** | ə **droit′** |
   - The speaker was adroit at answering questions, and everyone was satisfied with the answers.
   - In order to survive their first year in the New World, the colonists had to be adroit in areas ranging from farming to medicine.

5. **admonition** | ăd′ mə **nĭsh′** ən |
   - The teacher's admonition to work carefully helped the student score well on the test.
   - The coach's admonition prevented us from making some foolish errors on the field.

6. **acrophobia** | ăk′ rə **fō′** bē ə |
   - Tom has extreme acrophobia and trembles whenever he drives over a high bridge.

7. **abject** | **ăb′** jĕkt′ |
   - The boxer was beaten into prideless, abject surrender.

8. **acclaim** | ə **klām′** |
   - The book was greeted with great acclaim by the critics.
   - After their winning season, the team was met at the station with much acclaim.

ă pat / ā pay / â care / ä father / ĕ pet / ē be / ĭ pit / ī pie / î fierce / ŏ pot / ō go / ô paw, for / oi oil / o͝o book /
o͞o boot / ou out / ŭ cut / û fur / *th* the / th thin / hw which / zh vision / ə ago, item, pencil, atom, circus

Meaning Comprehension

Directions: Use what you have learned from the context sentences to identify the correct definition of each Power Word. In the blank next to each Power Word, write the letter of its correct definition.

Power Words

_____ abstemious
_____ abyss
_____ acme
_____ adroit
_____ admonition
_____ acrophobia
_____ abject
_____ acclaim

Definitions

a. advice, gentle warning
b. skillful or clever at something difficult
c. miserable; contemptible, low
d. enthusiastic praise or applause
e. sparing in use of food or drink
f. highest point, peak, greatest degree
g. fear of heights
h. very deep and large hole or emptiness

Context Application

Directions: Each of the following sentences has two blanks. Use what you have learned about the Power Words to determine which Power Word best belongs in each of the blanks. Then write the appropriate Power Word in each blank. Use each Power Word only once.

1. When the miners were rescued from the _____ , the rescue team received tearful _____ from the miners' families.

2. If he had been more _____ with alcohol, he would not have sunk to the _____ condition of a street bum.

3. By heeding every _____ of his coach, the athlete had won the championship, which in retrospect was the _____ of his career.

4. Although Wilma was _____ at tumbling, she would never be a good gymnast because her _____ kept her from even trying the balance beam and uneven bars.

Muscle Builder Analogies

Directions: Each exercise below is an analogy, with one term missing. Choose the Power Word which belongs in each blank of the analogy so that the analogy reads correctly. Write the appropriate Power Word in each blank. Note that some of the Power Words will not be used.

1. ACCLAIM is to BOOING as _____ is to BOTTOM

2. WASTEFUL is to ECONOMICAL as PRODIGAL is to
_____

3. COMMAND is to ORDER as _____ is to SUGGEST

Word Power IV

Directions: Study each of the Power Words, below. Note how each word is pronounced. Then read the context sentences to figure out what each Power Word means. In the left-hand margin next to each Power Word, try to jot down a synonym or short definition which defines that word.

Power Words			
sanctity	ominous	implausible	candid
prophet	inquisitive	synopsis	ascribed

1. **sanctity** | **săngk′** tĭ tē |
   - Because they have served him faithfully for years, the mechanic regards his tools as possessing an air of sanctity.
   - After the burglary, Sandra was ill at ease because she felt the sanctity of her home had been violated.

2. **prophet** | **prŏf′** ĭt |
   - A "prophet of doom" is one who is continually pessimistic about the future.

3. **ominous** | **ŏm′** ə nəs |
   - The ominous dark clouds warned of the impending thunderstorm.

4. **inquisitive** | ĭn **kwĭz′** ĭ tĭv |
   - The inquisitive child kept her father busy with questions.
   - The mind of the scientist must be constantly inquisitive, seeking out the laws of the cosmos.

5. **implausible** | ĭm **plô′** zə bəl |
   - The criminal's explanation for her possession of the money was thin and implausible.
   - The boss found Leo's long-winded excuse for being late totally implausible and docked his pay.

6. **synopsis** | sĭ **nŏp′** sĭs |
   - When you are in a hurry, you may read a synopsis of a book instead of the entire book.
   - The teacher told us that our essays should be a synopsis of what we had learned about the Roman culture.

7. **candid** | **kăn′** dĭd |
   - The politician's candid remarks lost her many votes.
   - Since we did not want to mislead each other, we tried to be as candid as possible.

8. **ascribed** | ə **skrībd′** |
   - The writer ascribed his success to years of practice.
   - Senator Dorf's failure to get re-elected was ascribed to the mistakes he made while in office.

ă pat / ā pay / â care / ä father / ĕ pet / ē be / ĭ pit / ī pie / î fierce / ŏ pot / ō go / ô paw, for / oi oil / ŏŏ book /
ōō boot / ou out / ŭ cut / ü fur / th the / th thin / hw which / zh vision / ə ago, item, pencil, atom, circus

Meaning Comprehension

Directions: Use what you have learned from the context sentences to identify the correct definition of each Power Word. In the blank next to each Power Word, write the letter of its correct definition.

Power Words

_____ sanctity
_____ prophet
_____ ominous
_____ inquisitive
_____ implausible
_____ synopsis
_____ candid
_____ ascribed

Definitions

a. said to be caused by, attributed
b. sacredness; holiness, godliness
c. one who can foretell future events, or has divine revelations
d. condensation, brief summary or outline
e. threatening, foreshadowing evil or danger
f. direct and frank, honest, straightforward
g. not believable or acceptable
h. inclined to ask questions; eager to learn

Context Application

Directions: Each of the following sentences has two blanks. Use what you have learned about the Power Words to determine which Power Word best belongs in each of the blanks. Then write the appropriate Power Word in each blank. Use each Power Word only once.

1. An _____ individual is not satisfied with superficial or _____ answers, but probes with more questions to find the truth.

2. The _____ of the Vatican can be _____ to it being the residence of the Pope.

3. Good-naturedly, we listened as the _____ presented us with a _____ of the doom to befall Earth in the next five years.

4. "To be absolutely _____ ," the doctor said, "your persistent cough is an _____ sign of lung disease."

Muscle Builder Analogies

Directions: Each exercise below is an analogy, with one term missing. Choose the Power Word which belongs in each blank of the analogy so that the analogy reads correctly. Write the appropriate Power Word in each blank. Note that some of the Power Words will not be used.

1. HISTORIAN is to PAST as _____ is to FUTURE

2. REASONABLE is to IMPLAUSIBLE as MISLEADING is to

_____

3. _____ is to NEGATIVE as ENCOURAGING is to POSITIVE

ADDITIONAL ASSIGNMENTS

Have a peer try each of the problems you write.

1. Write a problem on the lines below about the order of seven historical events, using the phrases "except for" and "with the exception of" as they are used in exercise #2. The historical events can be birthdates of important people, dates of discoveries, etc. Use reference books as necessary. Create your own diagram for the problem in the space at the right.

_____

_____

_____

_____

_____

_____

_____

_____

2. Write a problem on the lines below about the order of seven historical events. Include the patterns "event B preceded event C but succeeded event A" and "event C succeeded event B and event D succeeded event C." Create your own diagram to the right of your problem.

_____

_____

_____

_____

_____

_____

_____

_____

ADDITIONAL ASSIGNMENTS (continued)

3. Write a problem on the lines below about the order of seven historical events and include these patterns:

   Event D occurred after event C but before event F;
   Event E occurred between event D and event F;
   Event B occurred before event C, and event A occurred before event B.

   _____

   _____

   _____

   _____

   _____

   _____

   _____

   _____

   _____

   _____

   _____

   _____

   _____

   _____

   _____

   _____

   _____

   _____

UNIT
10
WORDS: FUNNY, WISE, AND NOT

OBJECTIVES: When you have completed this unit you should

- be able to pick the word that makes a statement facetious, from two words which sound similar;
- be able to select the two proverbs out of three which are closest in meaning;
- be able to write different forms of negative and double negative statements;
- know the meanings of the following POWER WORDS.

POWER
WORDS

fratricide	hyperactive	facade	tyranny
animated	circuitous	tenacious	cease
tripod	cajole	empathize	dupe
morphology	eloquent	monarchy	assert
staid	circumlocution	emaciated	placate
spurious	hypoactive	dejected	indifference
amorphous	cherubic	tenable	phenomena
podiatrist	incomprehensible	benevolent	alien

Word Power I

Power Words	fratricide animated	tripod morphology	staid spurious	amorphous podiatrist

1. **fratricide** | **frăt′** rĭ sĭd′ |
   - Some medieval kings committed fratricide so their thrones would go to their sons rather than to their brothers.

2. **animated** | **ăn′** ə mā′ tĭd |
   - Her enthusiastic, animated movements won her the dance contest.
   - The critic wrote, "I had hoped his performance would have been more animated, but instead found it quite dull and lifeless."

3. **tripod** | **trī′** pŏd′ |
   - A camera is sometimes placed on a collapsible tripod.
   - A tripod is more stable than a single-legged structure.

4. **morphology** | môr **fŏl′** ə jē |
   - Corpses are used so medical students can study human morphology.
   - If you want to study morphology, a good textbook would be *Gray's Anatomy*.

5. **staid** | stād |
   - Her staid appearance hid the great excitement she felt inside.
   - When we entered the classroom, we saw by the professor's staid expression that we would have to get to work immediately.

6. **spurious** | **spyŏŏr′** ē əs |
   - Vanessa's answer, based on spurious logic, was wrong.
   - His lawyer warned him that his spurious accusations would get him into trouble.

7. **amorphous** | ə **môr′** fəs |
   - Through gluttony, he degenerated from a normally shaped human into a 500-pound amorphous mass.
   - From a distance it was amorphous, but as we got closer we could make out the outline of the creature's head.

8. **podiatrist** | pə **dī′** ə trĭzt |
   - For a bone disease of the foot, you should visit a podiatrist.
   - The podiatrist recommended Nadine wear specially designed shoes to correct her pigeon-toed posture.

ă pat / ā pay / â care / ä father / ĕ pet / ē be / ĭ pit / ī pie / î fierce / ŏ pot / ō go / ô paw, for / oi oil / ŏŏ book /
ōō boot / ou out / ŭ cut / û fur / *th* the / th thin / hw which / zh vision / ə ago, item, pencil, atom, circus

Meaning Comprehension

Directions: Use what you have learned from the context sentences to identify the correct definition of each Power Word. In the blank next to each Power Word, write the letter of its correct definition.

Power Words

_____ fratricide
_____ animated
_____ tripod
_____ morphology
_____ staid
_____ spurious
_____ amorphous
_____ podiatrist

Definitions

a. foot doctor, sometimes termed chiropodist
b. without definite form, shapeless
c. full of life or action, lively
d. act of killing one's brother
e. not genuine, false, counterfeit
f. serious and drab, sedate, grave
g. a structure or vessel with three legs
h. science dealing with the form and structure of living organisms

Context Application

Directions: Each of the following sentences has two blanks. Use what you have learned about the Power Words to determine which Power Word best belongs in each of the blanks. Then write the appropriate Power Word in each blank. Use each Power Word only once.

1. The word for foot doctor, _____ , and the word for a three-legged structure, _____ , both derive from the Greek "pod" which means "foot."

2. The words _____ , the branch of biology dealing with the form or structure of organisms, and _____ which means "formless," both derive from the Greek "morph" which means "form."

3. Even when informed of the _____ in her family, she showed no emotion but maintained a _____ appearance.

4. Through lively, _____ conversation she gives a _____ impression of friendliness, but she really just wants to sell insurance.

Muscle Builder Analogies

Directions: Each exercise below is an analogy, with one or two terms missing. Choose the Power Word which belongs in each blank of the analogy so that the analogy reads correctly. Write the appropriate Power Word in each blank. Note that some of the Power Words will not be used.

1. GENUINE is to AUTHENTIC as _____ is to FAKE

2. VAGUE is to CLEAR as _____ is to OUTLINED

3. SOLEMN is to _____ as SPIRITED is to _____

Word Power II

Directions: Study each of the Power Words below. Note how each word is pronounced. Then read the context sentences to figure out what each Power Word means. In the left-hand margin next to each Power Word, try to jot down a synonym or short definition which defines that word.

Power Words	hyperactive	cajole	circumlocution	cherubic
	circuitous	eloquent	hypoactive	incomprehensible

1. **hyperactive** | hī′ pûr **ăk′** tĭv |
   - A hyperactive child is continuously restless and seems never to sit still.
   - When I drink too much coffee, I become hyperactive and can't find enough to do.

2. **circuitous** | sər **kyo͞o′** ĭ təs |
   - Because he had moved several times without informing his aunt, her letter took a circuitous route in reaching him.

3. **cajole** | kə **jōl′** |
   - With enthusiastic compliments the fan was able to cajole the star into signing an autograph.
   - Harold's mind was fixed; we could not even cajole him into going with us.

4. **eloquent** | **ĕl′** ə kwənt |
   - An eloquent speaker can move people to action with his/her words.
   - Ms. Penny's attorney presented an eloquent case, but lost the lawsuit on a technicality.

5. **circumlocution** | sûr′ kəm lō **kyo͞o′** shən |
   - A person given to circumlocution seems to take forever to "get to the point" when he/she speaks.

6. **hypoactive** | hī′ pə **ăk′** tĭv |
   - A hypoactive thyroid gland, one that is underactive, makes a person feel continually sleepy or sluggish.
   - Do reptiles become hypoactive in cold weather like insects?

7. **cherubic** | chə **ro͞o′** bĭk |
   - The painter loved children and his canvasses often contained cherubic figures.
   - Even though he had been naughty, how could you scold such a cherubic child!

8. **incomprehensible** | ĭn′ kŏm prĭ **hĕn′** sə bəl |
   - The incomprehensible mystery of creation—how it all began—has puzzled man's mind for centuries.
   - Regina's grammar is so poor that I find her memos incomprehensible.

ă pat / ā pay / â care / ä father / ĕ pet / ē be / ĭ pit / ī pie / î fierce / ŏ pot / ō go / ô paw, for / oi oil / o͝o book /
o͞o boot / ou out / ŭ cut / û fur / th the / th thin / hw which / zh vision / ə ago, item, pencil, atom, circus

Meaning Comprehension

Directions: Use what you have learned from the context sentences to identify the correct definition of each Power Word. In the blank next to each Power Word, write the letter of its correct definition.

Power Words

_____ hyperactive
_____ circuitous
_____ cajole
_____ eloquent
_____ circumlocution
_____ hypoactive
_____ cherubic
_____ incomprehensible

Definitions

a. not comprehensible, not understandable
b. innocent looking and chubby like the cherubs (child angels) in religious paintings
c. overactive
d. underactive
e. roundabout, indirect in route
f. roundabout or long-winded way of speaking
g. using language fluently, expressively and persuasively
h. persuade by flattery or insincere talk, coax

Context Application

Directions: Each of the following sentences has two blanks. Use what you have learned about the Power Words to determine which Power Word best belongs in each of the blanks. Then write the appropriate Power Word in each blank. Use each Power Word only once.

1. The child's _____ appearance and flattering comments allowed her to _____ her father into buying a new bicycle.

2. The teacher's explanation was so _____ and complex that it was _____ to most students.

3. Since _____ means "overactive" and _____ means "underactive," you can see that "hyper" means "over" and "hypo" means "under."

4. Since an _____ person is one who speaks well, and _____ means "speaking in a roundabout way," one can conclude that "locu" or "loqu" refers to speech.

Muscle Builder Analogies

Directions: Each exercise below is an analogy, with one term missing. Choose the Power Word which belongs in each blank of the analogy so that the analogy reads correctly. Write the appropriate Power Word in each blank. Note that some of the Power Words will not be used.

1. IMPLAUSIBLE is to BELIEVABLE as _____ is to UNDERSTANDABLE

2. CIRCUITOUS ROUTE is to DESTINATION as _____ is to IDEA

3. HALTING is to TONGUE-TIED as FLUENT is to _____

PART I: OOOPS, MY WORD!!

INTRODUCTION

Occasionally you will see an ad or a sign with a mistake in it that makes it funny. For example, the announcement below appeared in the Tulsa, Oklahoma, *Daily World*. See if you can find the amusing misprint.

> **The author of *Forever Amber*, Kathleen Winsor, has written another book, *Star Money*, that is called a "20th-century Amber," and is supposed to outsmell the two million copies of the first book.**

Find it? Hopefully, the newspaper had intended to print "outsell," not "outsmell."

INSTRUCTIONS FOR THE EXERCISES

For each of the following exercises, choose and then write in the blank the word which makes the statement *funny*, not logical.

EXERCISE 1

Twenty-five people suffered _____ exhaustion during a long baseball game on a hot summer day.

    (A) heat
    (B) seat

EXERCISE 2

The teacher said this youngster has _____ ability in reading and writing.

    (A) distinguished (defined as: outstanding)
    (B) extinguished (defined as: squelched, killed, put out)

EXERCISE 3

I am writing the college again because you promised to send your catalog, but due to an _____ it was not sent.

    (A) oversight (defined as: error)
    (B) insight (defined as: attainment of understanding, grasp of truth)

EXERCISE 4

Sign in plumbing store: Come In And Visit Our Humble _____

    (A) Commode (toilet or wash basin)
    (B) Abode (home)

EXERCISE 5

Classes in _____ making are being offered by the college.

    (A) scandal (disgrace, action that offends propriety)
    (B) sandal (a shoe having a sole strapped to the foot)

EXERCISE 6

The school building has just been completed and is _____ to handle 500 pupils.

    (A) resigned (having accepted something as unavoidable or inevitable)
    (B) designed (constructed, planned)

EXERCISE 7

The Swedish Angel meets Killer Bronson in the wrestling _____ event tonight.

    (A) main (major, primary)
    (B) maim (mutilate, disfigure or wound seriously)

EXERCISE 8

The free health clinic will be for _____ children only.

    (A) indigent (suffering from real deprivation and extreme poverty)
    (B) indignant (filled with anger over something unjust)

EXERCISE 9

Please peruse, _____ , and have your child return his/her report card immediately.

    (A) sigh
    (B) sign

EXERCISE 10

A sailor returned to his ship after a weekend on the town. Over the bunk which held his recumbent form, his buddies hung a sign: "Temporarily Out Of _____ ."

    (A) Order
    (B) Ardor (strong emotion, passion or energy)

EXERCISE 11

The _____ built Air Force captain prepared for takeoff.

    (A) flightly
    (B) slightly

EXERCISE 12

The guest of honor was asked to stand up and give a short speech, but she smiled and _____

    (A) reclined (leaned backwards, lay down backwards)
    (B) declined (refused)

EXERCISE 13

The young lady, trying to put on airs, told her date he couldn't meet her father that evening because her father was _____ .

    (A) decomposed (decayed, rotten)
    (B) indisposed (slightly ill)

EXERCISE 14

The new mother called her doctor and asked to make an appointment for a _____ examination.

    (A) postmortem (after death)
    (B) postpartum (after childbirth)

EXERCISE 15

The braggart insisted he was stronger and smarter than anyone else. He said he was _____ and _____ .

    (A) omnipotent (having unlimited power) and omniscient (having complete knowledge and understanding)
    (B) impotent (lacking power, weak) and impertinent (rude)

EXERCISE 16

Although everyone knew the starlet to be addle-brained and shallow, she regularly protested that she was more than just a _____ face.

    (A) petty (having little importance, having narrow interests, small-minded)
    (B) pretty

EXERCISE 17

Swen's friends got so tired of hearing him retell old jokes that they nicknamed him the _____

    (A) humorist (person who makes jokes)
    (B) exhumerist (word created from "exhume," which means "remove the dead from a grave")

EXERCISE 18

The striking actors _____ themselves outside the movie studio.

    (A) deployed (spreadout or placed in battle formation)
    (B) deplored (regretted, expressed grief about)

EXERCISE 19

Guilliermo had been a pain-in-the-neck all semester, so his teacher was glad to oblige when Guilliermo asked for a letter of _____ .

   (A) commendation (praise)
   (B) condemnation (criticism)

PART II: PROVERBS (OLD SAYINGS)

INTRODUCTION

Proverbs often contain important ideas about life. But usually you must read beyond the words to understand the full meaning of the proverb. For example, the proverb "A stitch in time saves nine," is not intended to refer only to sewing. It also applies to medical problems: it suggests that if a disease is treated early rather than being neglected, there is generally a better prognosis. A proverb expresses a truth that applies to many situations, and this gives it importance.

INSTRUCTIONS FOR THE EXERCISES

Each of the following exercises contains three proverbs or old sayings. Read each saying and think carefully about its broader, more important meaning. Then *circle* the *two* sayings that are closest in meaning.

EXERCISE 1

(A) From words to deeds is a great space.
(B) A poor man's tale cannot be heard.
(C) Saying is one thing and doing is another.

EXERCISE 2

(A) A drowning man will grasp at a straw.
(B) Necessity knows no law.
(C) Sink or swim.

EXERCISE 3

HINT: A swallow is a bird.

(A) One fool makes a hundred.
(B) Once is no custom.
(C) A single swallow does not make a summer.

EXERCISE 4

(A) A stitch in time saves nine.
(B) Time preserves nothing that you can make without its help.
(C) An ounce of prevention is worth a pound of cure.

EXERCISE 5

HINT: A knave is a tricky, deceitful person.

(A) Knaves and fools divide the world.
(B) A fool hears something, but is no wiser through it.
(C) Wise men learn by other men's harms; fools, by their own.

EXERCISE 6

(A) Experience is the mother of knowledge.
(B) Trade is the mother of money.
(C) Practice makes perfect.

EXERCISE 7

(A) Whom God would ruin, he first deprives of reason.
(B) God's mill grinds slow but sure.
(C) God hath leaden feet, but iron hands.

EXERCISE 8

(A) For age and want save while you may; no morning sun lasts a whole day.
(B) A handful of trade is a handful of gold.
(C) Sow in the spring so you may reap in the fall.

EXERCISE 9

(A) Many a treasure besides Ali Baba's is unlocked with the right words.
(B) In writing try not to compress the most words into the smallest ideas.
(C) The safest words are always those which bring us most directly to facts.

EXERCISE 10

HINT: An exigency is a demanding situation, one requiring immediate attention.

(A) Exigencies create the ability to meet and conquer them.
(B) Necessity is the mother of invention.
(C) If you want a thing done well, do it yourself.

EXERCISE 11

(A) Consider the postage stamp: its usefulness consists of the ability to stick to one thing till it gets there.
(B) A clash of doctrines is not a disaster—it is an opportunity.
(C) Remember the turtle and the hare.

EXERCISE 12

(A) Accuracy of statement is one of the elements of truth; inaccuracy is a near kin to falsehood.
(B) Consistency is the hobgoblin of small minds.
(C) Precise thinking is the basis of knowledge.

EXERCISE 13

HINT: A lark is a bird; abstinence means not indulging in food, drink or other pleasure; affluent means rich.

(A) He thinks that roasted larks will fall into his mouth.
(B) Any young person with good health and a poor appetite can become affluent.
(C) Abstinence is favorable to the pocket.

EXERCISE 14

(A) Do as you may if you can't do as you would.
(B) It is always our inabilities that vex us.
(C) What can't be cured must be endured.

EXERCISE 15

(A) Penny and penny laid up will be many.
(B) Pardon your neighbor before you forget the offense.
(C) Large streams from little fountains flow.

EXERCISE 16

(A) Better an egg today than a hen tomorrow.
(B) If thou hast not a capon, feed on an onion.
(C) One "Take it" is worth more than two "Thou shalt have it."

EXERCISE 17

(A) No man can serve two masters.
(B) Haste makes waste.
(C) Good and quickly seldom meet.

EXERCISE 18

HINT: Poverty is the state of being very poor.

(A) Want is the mother of all arts.
(B) He is rich enough that wants nothing.
(C) Poverty is a hateful good.

EXERCISE 19

(A) Time is the greatest innovator.
(B) Nothing really belongs to us but time, which even he has who has nothing else.
(C) People resemble still more the time in which they live, than they resemble their fathers.

EXERCISE 20

(A) Wise men learn more from fools than fools from the wise.
(B) He gains wisdom in a happy way, who gains it by another's experience.
(C) It is easier to be wise for others than for ourselves.

EXERCISE 21

(A) Life is a jigsaw puzzle with most of the pieces missing.
(B) Life is but a day at most.
(C) One life—a little gleam of time between two eternities.

EXERCISE 22

(A) If you ask faintly you beg a denial.
(B) Asking costs more than buying.
(C) He that cannot ask cannot live.

EXERCISE 23

(A) No kind of art exists unless it grows out of the ideas of the average man.
(B) Art is the stored honey of the human soul, gathered on wings of misery and travail.
(C) To let one's self go—that is what art is always aiming at. All art is lyrical.

PART III: NEGATIVE AND DOUBLE NEGATIVE

INTRODUCTION

Compare these four sentences:

1. Positive Statement—   He is certain.
2. Negative Statement—   He is not certain.
3. Negative Statement—   He is uncertain.
4. Double Negative Statement—   He is not uncertain.

                                    |
                                this means
                                    ↓
                            He is certain.

The prefix "un" and the word "not" have the same effect. They signify negative. But if you include them both in a sentence, you may get a double negative, which signifies positive.

The double negative is sometimes used incorrectly, when a person really means to make a true negative statement. For example, a person may mean to say "He is unlucky" or "He is not lucky"—but mistakenly say "He is not unlucky." However, occasionally the double negative is used correctly to emphasize contrast. You might say: "He is not uneducated, he manages his money stupidly." This means: In spite of being educated, he still manages his money stupidly.

INSTRUCTIONS FOR THE EXERCISES

In the first set of exercises which follows, you will be asked to use prefixes like "un" instead of the word "not" to write negative statements.

In the second set of exercises, you will be asked to rewrite double negative statements as positive statements.

EXERCISE 1

Delete <u>not</u> and add the prefix <u>un</u>.

Juanita is not happy.

Juanita is _____ .

Answer: Juanita is <u>unhappy</u>.

EXERCISE 2

Delete <u>not</u> and add the prefix <u>im</u> .

The tranquilized lion is not mobile.

The tranquilized lion is _____

EXERCISE 3

Delete both <u>not's</u> and substitute <u>in</u> and <u>im</u> .

Paul is not sensitive and he is not polite.

Paul is _____ and he is _____ .

NOTE: For the remaining exercises, rewrite the double negative statement as a positive statement.

EXERCISE 4

Ivan is not ungrateful.

Ivan is _____ .

EXERCISE 5

The student's point is not illogical.

The student's point is _____ .

EXERCISE 6

Man is not immortal.

Man is _____ .

EXERCISE 7

The widow is not without money.

The widow has _____ .

EXERCISE 8

Verona is not without skill.

Verona _____ .

EXERCISE 9

The lawyer's case is not without merit.

The lawyer's case _____ .

EXERCISE 10

The ocean is vast but it is not immeasurable.

The ocean is vast but it is _____ .

EXERCISE 11

The employee's comments are not irrelevant and should be heard.

The employee's comments are _____ and should be heard.

EXERCISE 12

Her plan is not unfeasible, but carrying it out requires ingenuity.

Her plan is _____ , but carrying it out requires ingenuity.

EXERCISE 13

Their goals are not incompatible and they will try to cooperate.

Their goals are _____ and they will try to cooperate.

EXERCISE 14

That book is not incomprehensible, but requires very careful reading.

That book is _____ , but requires very careful reading.

EXERCISE 15

None of them are immortal.

They are all _____ .

EXERCISE 16

None of them are unjust.

They _____ .

Word Power III

Directions: Study each of the Power Words below. Note how each word is pronounced. Then read the context sentences to figure out what each Power Word means. In the left-hand margin next to each Power Word, try to jot down a synonym or short definition which defines that word.

Power Words	facade	empathize	emaciated	tenable
	tenacious	monarchy	dejected	benevolent

---

1. **facade** | fə **säd′** |
   - The facade of a building may be old and neglected, yet the inside bright and new.

2. **tenacious** | tə **nā′** shəs |
   - Kim was tenacious in her belief that education would help her economically, so she studied even when her friends were out partying.

3. **empathize** | **ĕm′** pə thīz |
   - It is hard to empathize with a person who has very different values from oneself.
   - Because I had had a similar experience, I was able to empathize with Jane when her grandfather died so suddenly.

4. **monarchy** | **mŏn′** ər kē |
   - In a monarchy, one person, such as a king or queen, is the supreme ruler.
   - Many revolutions have been fought so that there would be a "government by the people" instead of a monarchy.

5. **emaciated** | ĭ **mā′** shē ā′ tĭd |
   - The war left many children poorly fed and emaciated.
   - In the drought-affected areas, we saw emaciated villagers struggling to raise crops in the parched soil.

6. **dejected** | dĭ **jĕk′** tĭd |
   - The unfair test put Alicia in a dejected mood.
   - Ben was dejected when he was turned down for the job.

7. **tenable** | **tĕn′** ə bəl |
   - The student's absence excuse was not tenable, and the teacher exposed it as a lie.

8. **benevolent** | bə **nĕv′** ə lənt |
   - A do-gooder is one who is benevolent, but usually not very practical.
   - John works for a benevolent boss; she frequently gives him the afternoon off or allows him to take long lunch hours.

ă pat / ā pay / â care / ä father / ĕ pet / ē be / ĭ pit / ī pie / î fierce / ŏ pot / ō go / ô paw, for / oi oil / o͝o book /
o͞o boot / ou out / ŭ cut / û fur / th the / th thin / hw which / zh vision / ə ago, item, pencil, atom, circus

Meaning Comprehension

Directions: Use what you have learned from the context sentences to identify the correct definition of each Power Word. In the blank next to each Power Word, write the letter of its correct definition.

Power Words

_____ facade
_____ tenacious
_____ empathize
_____ monarchy
_____ emaciated
_____ dejected
_____ tenable
_____ benevolent

Definitions

a. government ruled by a sovereign such as a king, queen, or emperor
b. understand the feelings of another person
c. depressed, in low spirits
d. persistent, stubborn
e. the front or face of something
f. reasonable, capable of being defended
g. desiring or inclined to do good, kindly
h. extremely thin from malnutrition or disease

Context Application

Directions: Each of the following sentences has two blanks. Use what you have learned about the Power Words to determine which Power Word best belongs in each of the blanks. Then write the appropriate Power Word in each blank. Use each Power Word only once.

1. Well-fed people in affluent countries cannot _____ with hungry, _____ people in poor countries.

2. A king can minimize the people's desire to overthrow his _____ by being _____ , making sure the people are treated well and are provided with as good and comfortable a life as possible.

3. She put on a happy _____ to hide her _____ feelings.

4. Although the candidate's solution to the inflation problem was weak and not _____ , he was _____ and stubbornly continued to defend it.

Muscle Builder Analogies

Directions: Each exercise below is an analogy, with one or two terms missing. Choose the Power Word which belongs in each blank of the analogy so that the analogy reads correctly. Write the appropriate Power Word in each blank. Note that some of the Power Words will not be used.

1. DICTATOR is to DICTATORSHIP as SOVEREIGN is to

_____

2. HIGH is to LOW as JOYFUL is to _____

3. _____ is to FIRM as _____ is to LOGICAL

Word
Power IV

Directions: Study each of the Power Words below. Note how each word is pronounced. Then read the context sentences to figure out what each Power Word means. In the left-hand margin next to each Power Word, try to jot down a synonym or short definition which defines that word.

Power Words	tyranny cease	dupe assert	placate indifference	phenomena alien

1. **tyranny** | **tîr'** ə nē |
   - Tyranny is an oppressive form of government.
   - The masses would no longer put up with the tyranny of their monarch and staged a revolution.

2. **cease** | sēs |
   - The landlord said the loud music must cease immediately.
   - Because we did not have the proper licenses, we had to cease doing business in three foreign countries.

3. **dupe** | do͞op |
   - Some people take great pleasure in confusing and duping other people.
   - The con man tried to dupe Valentina into believing she could buy London Bridge.

4. **assert** | ə **sûrt'** |
   - He asserted his innocence of the crime.
   - As a salesperson, you must assert yourself if you want to be successful.

5. **placate** | **plā'** kāt |
   - Hoping to satisfy and placate Hitler, Britain did not interfere with his invasion of Poland.
   - One way to placate hurt feelings is with kind and gentle words.

6. **indifference** | ĭn **dĭf'** ər əns |
   - The son's indifference to sports disappointed his father.
   - Sharon found that the best way she could show her indifference was not to offer any suggestions.

7. **phenomena** | fĭ **nŏm'** ə nə |
   - The observation of much scientific phenomena requires special instruments like microscopes and stethoscopes.

8. **alien** | **ā'** lē ən |
   - Many science fiction novels concern invasion by alien creatures.
   - Having lived in the city all her life, she found the wilderness an alien environment.

ă pat / ā pay / â care / ä father / ĕ pet / ē be / ĭ pit / ī pie / î fierce / ŏ pot / ō go / ô paw, for / oi oil / o͝o book /
o͞o boot / ou out / ŭ cut / û fur / *th* the / th thin / hw which / zh vision / ə ago, item, pencil, atom, circus

Meaning Comprehension

Directions: Use what you have learned from the context sentences to identify the correct definition of each Power Word. In the blank next to each Power Word, write the letter of its correct definition.

Power Words

_____ tyranny
_____ cease
_____ dupe
_____ assert
_____ placate
_____ indifference
_____ phenomena
_____ alien

Definitions

a. appease, soothe, calm
b. say or present strongly and positively
c. stop, terminate, halt
d. foreign, belonging somewhere else, strange
e. deceive; one who is easily deceived
f. a government where absolute power is vested in a single person
g. lack of interest or preference, neutrality
h. occurrences, observed events

Context Application

Directions: Each of the following sentences has two blanks. Use what you have learned about the Power Words to determine which Power Word best belongs in each of the blanks. Then write the appropriate Power Word in each blank. Use each Power Word only once.

1. Although John loved the horse and wanted to buy it, he pretended _____ to _____ the owner into selling it cheaper.

2. After witnessing the strange and unexplainable _____, the journalist was ready to _____ that the house was haunted.

3. Sometimes a parent will go to extreme lengths to _____ a child so it will _____ crying.

4. While Napoleon's embattled army encountered _____ troops in foreign lands, the emperor expanded his power and established a _____ at home.

Muscle Builder Analogies

Directions: Each exercise below is an analogy, with one term missing. Choose the Power Word which belongs in each blank of the analogy so that the analogy reads correctly. Write the appropriate Power Word in each blank. Note that some of the Power Words will not be used.

1. DUPE is to FOOL as _____ is to PACIFY

2. _____ is to CONCERN as CEASE is to START

3. FAMILIAR is to ALIEN as _____ is to DENY

ADDITIONAL ASSIGNMENTS

Have a peer try to answer each of the problems that you write.

1. Write a problem like those in Part I.

   _____

   _____

   a. _____

   b. _____

2. Write a problem like those in Part II. (You may find a book on proverbs, parables, or sayings from the library helpful.)

   a. _____

   b. _____

   c. _____

3. Write a problem like #3 in Part III.

   _____

   _____

   _____

4. Write a problem like #7-9 in Part III.

   _____

   _____

5. Write a problem like #10-12 in Part III.

   _____

   _____

6. Write a problem like #16 in Part III.

   _____

   _____

UNIT
11

READING TEXT FOR FULL COMPREHENSION III

OBJECTIVES: When you have completed this unit you should

- be able to comprehend the facts and relationships in various selections of text material;
- know the meanings of the following POWER WORDS.

POWER WORDS

etymology	inane	conversely	censorship
impunity	intractable	insatiable	subjected
aphorism	penal	idiosyncrasy	biased
postmortem	purports	profuse	detestable
illiterate	edict	prolonging	haughty
quixotic	docile	cumbersome	prevailing
adage	concede	inarticulate	audacity
postscript	diminutive	trespass	futile

Word Power I

Directions: Study each of the Power Words below. Note how each word is pronounced. Then read the context sentences to figure out what each Power Word means. In the left-hand margin next to each Power Word, try to jot down a synonym or short definition which defines that word.

Power Words

| etymology | aphorism | illiterate | adage |
| impunity | postmortem | quixotic | postscript |

---

1. **etymology** | ĕt ə **mŏl′** ə jē |
   - Most dictionaries give a short etymology for each word, showing its origin and history.

2. **impunity** | ĭm **pyōo′** nĭ tē |
   - Farah smoked for years with seeming impunity until one day she was diagnosed to have terminal lung cancer.
   - Diplomats in this country can do whatever they want with impunity because they are granted diplomatic immunity.

3. **aphorism** | ăf′ ə rĭz′ əm |
   - "An apple a day keeps the doctor away; an onion a day keeps everyone away," is a humorous twist on a common aphorism.
   - Aphorisms allow us to get right to the point without using too many words.

4. **postmortem** | pōst **môr′** təm |
   - A postmortem examination showed the death resulted from heart failure.

5. **illiterate** | ĭ **lĭt′** ər ĭt |
   - It is becoming increasingly difficult for an illiterate person to earn a good salary.
   - Although Susan's grandmother was illiterate, she was very bright and rose to become the best salesperson in the company.

6. **quixotic** | kwĭk **sŏt′** ĭk |
   - Some feel that true socialism (distributing wealth equally) is quixotic—wonderful but impossible.

7. **adage** | ăd′ ĭj |
   - "A stitch in time saves nine," is a popular adage.

8. **postscript** | pōst′ skrĭpt′ |
   - The P.S. that you use to add an extra idea to a letter stands for postscript.
   - At the end of his book, Dr. Thompson added a postscript which indicated further research was in progress.

ă pat / ā pay / â care / ä father / ĕ pet / ē be / ĭ pit / ī pie / î fierce / ŏ pot / ō go / ô paw, for / oi oil / ŏŏ book /
ōō boot / ou out / ŭ cut / û fur / *th* the / th thin / hw which / zh vision / ə ago, item, pencil, atom, circus

Meaning Comprehension

Directions: Use what you have learned from the context sentences to identify the correct definition of each Power Word. In the blank next to each Power Word, write the letter of its correct definition.

Power Words

_____ etymology
_____ impunity
_____ aphorism
_____ postmortem
_____ illiterate
_____ quixotic
_____ adage
_____ postscript

Definitions

a. a short saying considered wise and true, adage

b. a short saying considered wise and true

c. freedom from punishment or negative consequences

d. idealistic and impractical

e. occurring after death; occurring after an event

f. report of the origin and history of a word

g. having little education; unable to read and write

h. a message added after the end of a piece of writing

Context Application

Directions: Each of the following sentences has two blanks. Use what you have learned about the Power Words to determine which Power Word best belongs in each of the blanks. Then write the appropriate Power Word in each blank. Use each Power Word only once.

1. David thought he could neglect his schoolwork with _____, but he was left _____ and unable to get a good job.

2. The _____ of the word _____ reveals that it stems from the book *Don Quixote*, about an idealist who wanted to correct injustice.

3. Although the latter is a little longer than the former, the words _____ and _____ have basically the same meaning, as reflected by the fact that *Webster's Third New International Dictionary* presents the former as a synonym for the latter.

4. _____ and _____ combine the Latin prefix "post" (after) with "script" (write) and "mort" (death), respectively.

Muscle Builder Analogies

Directions: Each exercise below is an analogy, with one or two terms missing. Choose the Power Word which belongs in each blank of the analogy so that the analogy reads correctly. Write the appropriate Power Word in each blank. Note that some of the Power Words will not be used.

1. EDUCATED is to LITERATE as IGNORANT is to

_____

2. PREFACE is to BEGINNING as _____ is to END

3. CIRCUMLOCUTION is to ROUNDABOUT as _____ is to SUCCINCT

Word Power II

Directions: Study each of the Power Words below. Note how each word is pronounced. Then read the context sentences to figure out what each Power Word means. In the left-hand margin next to each Power Word, try to jot down a synonym or short definition which defines that word.

Power Words	inane	penal	edict	concede
	intractable	purports	docile	diminutive

1. **inane** | ĭ **nān** |
   - Kareem's inane term papers are a reflection of his shallow mind.
   - We found that none of Betty's inane arguments were based on fact.

2. **intractable** | ĭn **trăk′** tə bəl |
   - An intractable child who is constantly disobedient is a pest.

3. **penal** | **pē′** nəl |
   - A penal institution should provide rehabilitation, not just punishment.
   - The judge was unsure of the precise regulations, so she recessed court to check the penal code.

4. **purports** | pər **pôrtz′** |
   - The letter to the newspaper purports to express public opinion, but this is doubtful.
   - Are you sure he knows everything he purports to know?

5. **edict** | **ē′** dĭkt′ |
   - The emperor's edict demanding more taxes was resented by the populace.
   - Due to the impending hurricane, an edict was issued to evacuate the area immediately.

6. **docile** | **dŏs′** əl |
   - Phil is a docile husband who caters to his wife's every demand.
   - Docile children are much easier to instruct than disobedient children.

7. **concede** | kən **sēd′** |
   - The personnel manager conceded that his decision to hire that employee had been unwise.
   - After pushing herself to her limit, Mara was forced to concede that she could not finish the race.

8. **diminutive** | dĭ **mĭn′** yə tĭv |
   - Napoleon was not tall, but his diminutive stature did not prevent him from becoming great and powerful.
   - The diminutive furniture in Noreen's doll house was of such precise detail that the tiny phonograph actually had a miniscule needle.

ă pat / ā pay / â care / ä father / ĕ pet / ē be / ĭ pit / ī pie / î fierce / ŏ pot / ō go / ô paw, for / oi oil / o͝o book /
o͞o boot / ou out / ŭ cut / û fur / th the / th thin / hw which / zh vision / ə ago, item, pencil, atom, circus

Meaning Comprehension

Directions: Use what you have learned from the context sentences to identify the correct definition of each Power Word. In the blank next to each Power Word, write the letter of its correct definition.

Power Words	Definitions
_____ inane	a. small, tiny
_____ intractable	b. hard to control or manage, stubborn
_____ penal	c. lacking sense or meaning, silly, empty
_____ purports	d. unwillingly admit or acknowledge; give in
_____ edict	e. relating to penalty or punishment
_____ docile	f. a notice or decree issued by an authority
_____ concede	g. claims, suggests, implies
_____ diminutive	h. easy to manage, obedient, tractable

Context Application

Directions: Each of the following sentences has two blanks. Use what you have learned about the Power Words to determine which Power Word best belongs in each of the blanks. Then write the appropriate Power Word in each blank. Use each Power Word only once.

1. Violation of the government _____ proclaiming a six o'clock curfew is a _____ offense.

2. Mr. Kanine _____ to have a _____ dog, but I've never seen it obey any of his commands.

3. The freshman refused to _____ that he had lost the debate even though, I believe, he himself knew his arguments were _____ .

4. Through his special powers, the _____ elf was capable of putting even the most _____ creatures under his control.

Muscle Builder Analogies

Directions: Each exercise below is an analogy, with one or two terms missing. Choose the Power Word which belongs in each blank of the analogy so that the analogy reads correctly. Write the appropriate Power Word in each blank. Note that some of the Power Words will not be used.

1. UNMANAGEABLE is to TRACTABLE as _____ is to _____

2. _____ is to RESIST as GRANT is to DENY

3. DIMINUTIVE is to GIGANTIC as _____ is to PROFOUND

INTRODUCTION

This unit provides one last opportunity to practice analytically reading text material, professional publications, and business literature for full comprehension. The selections in this unit are quite complex, but if you take your time and carefully apply the analytical reading skills you have been developing you should be able to achieve 100% accuracy—full comprehension.

The issue of reading rate (speed) is an important one to many professionals and students. For various reasons, readers have a tendency to try to "plow through" reading material as quickly as possible. Unfortunately, rapid-speed reading typically results in decreased comprehension, thereby defeating the goal of the reading. The remainder of this Introduction will discuss some of the issues related to reading rate most commonly voiced by students and professionals.

How fast should you read? A study of 48 University of Michigan professors found they read an average of 303 words per minute in a controlled reading situation. As they attempted to read more quickly, they began to lose information. Moving faster forced them to begin skimming ideas rather than processing them fully. Even electronic computers take time to process information. Research indicates that the human brain is a wonderful but very slow computer.

A rate of 300 words per minute would allow you to read about 50-60 pages an hour. But many professors and professionals report that when engaged in serious study they often cover no more than 10-15 pages an hour. This is because they take time to analyze and think about what they are reading, ask themselves questions, and reread difficult sections of the material. Some professors and professionals—especially those involved in the humanities and social sciences—report that they may first skim or preview a reading selection to get an overall view of what is covered. Then they go back and read more carefully for full comprehension. By contrast, many professionals involved in mathematic and scientific or technical fields report that they do not preview a selection. They just start at the beginning and try to thoroughly understand the facts and relationships as they progress through the material. In either case, the end result is that these professors and professionals carefully read the material analytically for full comprehension; they do not hurry their reading.

People are often surprised by these findings; by how slowly professors and other professionals report they read when engaged in serious study. These people may have outside jobs or interests that drive them to seek a way (or an excuse) to read more quickly in order to save time. Unfortunately, humans are limited. They cannot breathe under water or fly unaided through the air. At one point, Bell Laboratories experimented with speeding up speech so telephone equipment would not be tied up for such long periods during telephone conversations. But they found that people had difficulty following ideas. Speeded-up speech was too fast for the brain to follow with comprehension. A good public speaker talks at about 125 words per minute. If he/she steps this up to 225 words per minute, listeners can still understand and follow the individual words, but they cannot keep track of the ideas. The mind cannot handle verbal input that quickly.

Professionals, professors, and students have learned that serious study is time-consuming. There is a rule-of-thumb that students should expect to spend two hours of study for every hour in class. Highly successful students report they spend even more time. Professionals follow a similar rule-of-thumb: for every hour spent on the job making decisions, planning strategies, and attending meetings, they expect to spend at least two hours reading journals, reports, and correspondence.

Reading is a crucial skill affecting school and on-the-job success. It must not be rushed. As you read the following selections and answer the questions, make total accuracy your primary concern, not speed.

SPECIAL NOTE TO STUDENTS—Students are often concerned that if they read carefully to ensure full comprehension, this will slow them down so much that they will labor inordinately long over reading assignments or, more fearfully, they will not read with the speed needed to score well on tests such as the Scholastic Aptitude Test (SAT), the Graduate Record Exam (GRE), or the Civil Service Exams. It is a common misconception that you must answer as many questions as possible on such tests to score well. According to the bulletin for the GRE, there are 80 questions on the verbal portion of the exam. These questions include exercises similar to those in this book: reading comprehension, sentence completion, definition identification, and verbal analogy. To achieve a score of 500 on the verbal section of the GRE, you need to answer only 35 questions correctly out of the 80. Furthermore, to achieve a score of 600—about the 85th percentile—you only need to answer 49 of the 80 questions correctly. Clearly, if you take your time to read carefully for full comprehension, you have a better chance to get the questions correct, even if you don't finish all the questions. Tests such as these are won by the strongest readers, not the quickest.

Read all of your material carefully and your performance on tests will benefit in several ways. First, you will become well educated and acquire a large store of information. Studies by reading researchers show that a person's background knowledge is a major contributor to his/her ability to score well on reading tests.

Second, by reading text carefully, you will become familiar with the different styles and forms that writers use in presenting information. Sometimes a writer uses a general-specific organization. Or he/she may present a geometrical description, arguments and counter-arguments, causes and effects, or the time arrangement of events. Furthermore, sentences can take various forms: compound, complex, having adverbial clauses, etc. As you become familiar with these forms, you will find it easier to decipher and comprehend a writer's message, and read with sufficient speed (225-300 words a minute) to score well on standardized tests.

Finally, reading carefully will help expand your vocabulary. As you know, it is difficult to answer reading comprehension questions when you do not know the meanings of many words in a passage. Studies show that most students taking developmental reading courses need to add 1500-2500 words to their vocabularies in order to attain high scores on standardized reading tests and exams such as the SAT and GRE. Obviously, this takes time and can only be accomplished by reading carefully to pick up the meanings of new words from context clues, and by frequently using the dictionary.

PASSAGE A

¹ Many inventions and improvements fur-
² thered the growth of English industry. Coal gas
³ for illumination, pioneered by William Murdock
⁴ (1754-1839), a Scottish engineer, not only lit the
⁵ streets of England's cities but also provided light
⁶ so that the factories could operate at night. About
⁷ 1816 Sir Humphry Davy (1778-1829), a distin-
⁸ guished chemist, developed his safety lamp. This
⁹ device, in which an oil flame burned behind a
¹⁰ metal screen, reduced the hazard of explosions
¹¹ from gas in coal mines. In 1825 a Scottish inven-
¹² tor, Thomas Drummond (1797-1840), introduced
¹³ incandescent lighting by putting a piece of lime in
¹⁴ the gas flame. His brilliant "limelight," widely used
¹⁵ in theaters, still survives as a synonym for promi-
¹⁶ nence in all walks of life. Meanwhile, in the 1780s
¹⁷ in Lancashire, Thomas Bell revolutionized the
¹⁸ printing of calico by substituting a roller for hand-
¹⁹ operated plates. His revolving press ultimately
²⁰ did the work of 100 men. About the same time
²¹ James Watt introduced the discovery of the
²² French chemist, Count Berthollet (1748-1822),
²³ that chlorine would bleach cloth. The use of chlo-
²⁴ rine reduced the bleaching time from months to
²⁵ hours. In sum, inventions multiplied and English
²⁶ industry moved forward quickly.

1. Below are three possible titles for this passage. In each blank, write the letter of the phrase (A, B or C) which best describes that title.

   _____ History's Most Important Inventions
   _____ Inventions That Stimulated British Industry
   _____ Etymology of "Limelight"

   (A) too narrow
   (B) too broad
   (C) comprehensive title

2. The inventor who, according to the selection, extended the working day is

   ☐ (A) Sir Humphry Davy
   ☐ (B) Thomas Drummond
   ☐ (C) William Murdock
   ☐ (D) Thomas Bell

3. Sir Humphry Davy is credited with

   ☐ (A) providing light so factories could operate at night
   ☐ (B) improving mine safety
   ☐ (C) introducing incandescent lighting
   ☐ (D) using chlorine to reduce bleaching time

4. The machine that is mentioned as doing the work of 100 men

   ☐ (A) was a press for squeezing juice from food
   ☐ (B) included hand-operated plates
   ☐ (C) was for printing patterns on a type of cloth called calico
   ☐ (D) was a rotating press for printing newspaper

5. On which line(s) did you find the answer to the preceding question?

   LINE NUMBER(S): _____

6. The word "incandescent," according to the context, means

   ☐ (A) vacuum-packed in a can
   ☐ (B) extremely bright
   ☐ (C) electric
   ☐ (D) oil-fueled

7. According to the passage, all of the following statements are correct except

   ☐ (A) incandescent lighting was often used in theaters
   ☐ (B) Thomas Drummond was Scottish
   ☐ (C) James Watt contributed to the growth of English industry
   ☐ (D) James Watt discovered that chlorine would bleach cloth

PASSAGE B

¹ In 1763, James Watt, who was a skilled
² instrument maker at the University of Glasgow,
³ was called on to repair the Newcomen engine on
⁴ display at the university. Hoping to find a way of
⁵ avoiding its waste of coal, Watt began a sys-
⁶ tematic study of steam. Two years later, on a
⁷ Sunday afternoon walk, he hit upon the essential

⁸ idea of making a good steam engine—to draw off
⁹ the steam from the cylinder into a separate con-
¹⁰ densing chamber outside. Then, Watt said to
¹¹ himself, the cylinder could be kept hot, and there
¹² would be no waste of steam in reheating it before
¹³ each stroke, as in the Newcomen engine.
¹⁴   For the next thirty-five years Watt worked to
¹⁵ make his steam engine practical. He applied all
¹⁶ that science had learned about heat, vacuum, and
¹⁷ the pressure of gases. He devised a way for steam
¹⁸ to drive the piston back and forth in precise
¹⁹ strokes. He found a way to make the back-and-
²⁰ forth motion of the piston turn a wheel so that his
²¹ steam engine could be used to turn the spindles of
²² cloth factories. When Watt retired in 1800, his
²³ engine was in general use.
²⁴   Watt had made a practical success of turn-
²⁵ ing heat into power—that was the revolutionary
²⁶ meaning of his invention. To be sure, steam
²⁷ pushed the piston, but the steam was created by
²⁸ the heat released from burning fuel, usually coal.
²⁹ The use of fire was the oldest invention of man,
³⁰ older even than stone implements. Watt had
³¹ turned this ancient friend of man, fire, into a new
³² source of power.

1. Watt's criticism of the Newcomen engine was
   that

   ☐ (A) it burned coal
   ☐ (B) it utilized steam
   ☐ (C) it was inefficient
   ☐ (D) it was too slow

2. On which line(s) did you find the answer to the
   preceding question?

   LINE NUMBER(S): _____

3. Watt improved on the Newcomen engine by
   designing an engine that

   ☐ (A) made more efficient use of steam
   ☐ (B) made more efficient use of gasoline
   ☐ (C) burned each piece of coal twice
   ☐ (D) used oil as the primary fuel

4. The selection implies that

   ☐ (A) Watt had carefully planned getting a
         chance to repair the Newcomen engine
   ☐ (B) Watt's eventual creation of a good
         steam engine stemmed from an un-
         planned, fortuitous (lucky) event
   ☐ (C) Watt studied calculus at the University
         of Glasgow
   ☐ (D) Watt owned a cloth factory

5. Watt's work

   ☐ (A) was not appreciated until after his
         death
   ☐ (B) was not appreciated until steam en-
         gines were used in steamships
   ☐ (C) caused a revolt among cloth workers
   ☐ (D) was put into commercial use in his life-
         time

6. According to the selection, the revolutionary
   significance of Watt's work was in

   ☐ (A) inventing an engine which could use
         coal or wood
   ☐ (B) discovering what is now called "man's
         oldest invention"
   ☐ (C) creating a practical method of using
         man's oldest invention to produce a
         new source of power
   ☐ (D) inventing a practical means so his
         engine could turn spindles in cloth
         factories

7. According to the article, how many years passed
   from the time Watt first worked on the Newcomen engine to the time he retired?

   ☐ (A) 37
   ☐ (B) 33
   ☐ (C) 2
   ☐ (D) 35

8. In the context of this passage, the word "stroke"
   means

   ☐ (A) rub gently
   ☐ (B) a movement of a piece from one end of
         its travel to another
   ☐ (C) a mark made on a surface

PASSAGE C

¹ Steel was a critical factor in the development ² of inland transportation, for bridges and vehicles ³ alike. It was also useful in reinforced concrete, ⁴ invented in 1867. Steel, iron with a low carbon ⁵ content, is vastly superior to iron because of its ⁶ greater flexibility and strength. In 1856 Henry ⁷ Bessemer (1813-98), an English inventor, devel- ⁸ oped the first efficient process for making steel, ⁹ by blowing air through molten iron and in that ¹⁰ way burning out the carbon. Bessemer used ¹¹ phosphorus-free iron from Sweden, but in 1878 ¹² another Englishman, Sidney Gilchrist Thomas ¹³ (1850-85), invented a process to remove the ¹⁴ phosphorus, which ruins steel, so that it was pos- ¹⁵ sible to use native British ores. Because of the ¹⁶ work of these men and others, the price of British ¹⁷ steel fell 50 percent in the years 1856-70, and the ¹⁸ volume of production increased sixfold. In the ¹⁹ years 1880-1900, world steel production rose ²⁰ from four to 28 million tons. Steel quickly ²¹ replaced iron for railway tracks, and it had, of ²² course, a thousand other uses. Technicians soon ²³ learned to make steel alloys with substances such ²⁴ as wolfram (tungsten), manganese, and chrome ²⁵ to obtain qualities, among them strength and ²⁶ hardness, not present in the original metal. These ²⁷ technological advances required unprecedented ²⁸ concentrations of capital.

1. The best title for this selection is

   ☐ (A) Inland Transportation on Bridges by Vehicles
   ☐ (B) Development and Use of Steel
   ☐ (C) The Growth of Steel in the Twentieth Century

2. Henry Bessemer invented a process to

   ☐ (A) remove air from iron to make steel
   ☐ (B) remove ore from iron to make steel
   ☐ (C) remove phosphorus from iron to make steel
   ☐ (D) remove carbon from iron to make steel

3. In which year(s) was four million tons of steel produced?

   ☐ (A) 1900
   ☐ (B) 1856
   ☐ (C) 1880-1900
   ☐ (D) 1880

4. For every ton of steel produced in England in 1856,

   ☐ (A) world production rose from four to 28 million tons
   ☐ (B) six tons were produced in 1870
   ☐ (C) twenty-eight million tons were produced in 1900
   ☐ (D) 50 percent was produced in the years 1856-70

5. According to the last sentence in the selection,

   ☐ (A) steel production depended upon financial investments
   ☐ (B) steel was concentrated for use in only the buildings in the capital of England
   ☐ (C) Henry Bessemer became wealthy by inventing the first efficient process for making steel
   ☐ (D) Thomas became wealthier than Bessemer because he had a better process

6. Which statement is supported by the selection?

   ☐ (A) Bessemer improved on Thomas' process.
   ☐ (B) Thomas improved on Bessemer's process.
   ☐ (C) Bessemer used phosphorus-free iron because it was from Sweden.
   ☐ (D) Phosphorus-free iron ruins steel.

7. The phrase "native British ores" refers to

   ☐ (A) ores that are free from carbon
   ☐ (B) ores from England that are phosphorus-free
   ☐ (C) ores that are not imported
   ☐ (D) ores from Sweden that are phosphorus-free

8. As used in this passage, "alloy" is

 ☐ (A) a form of a metal made by adding other substances to the original
 ☐ (B) a pure substance
 ☐ (C) a narrow passageway between buildings
 ☐ (D) an unchanged form of an original metal

PASSAGE D

1   When he was a young chemistry professor,
2 Pasteur taught in the heart of one of France's
3 wine-producing districts. One day the father of a
4 student came to Pasteur for help in keeping his
5 wine from turning sour. Pasteur put some of the
6 unspoiled and some of the spoiled liquid under
7 the microscope. In the unspoiled liquid he found
8 swarming yeast plants. In the spoiled liquid he
9 found no yeast plants at all, but he did discover
10 tiny specks which he called "dancing rods." Pas-
11 teur then discovered that these "dancing rods" or
12 *bacteria*, as we know them, lengthened out and
13 broke in two. Because they were growing in
14 number, Pasteur knew the bacteria were alive.
15 Bacteria were spoiling the wine.
16   But where did the bacteria come from?
17 Scientists had known of their existence, but it was
18 assumed they came out of nothing, that they were
19 created by "spontaneous generation." Tireless
20 experimenting enabled Pasteur to convince the
21 scientific world that bacteria could be carried by
22 the air, on the hands, or in many other ways.
23 Moreover, he found that bacteria can live and
24 reproduce only in a certain temperature. There-
25 fore, the wine producer could keep his wine from
26 spoiling by regulating the temperature in a way
27 which would kill the bacteria. This method of
28 killing harmful bacteria is now commonly used
29 with milk and is called pasteurization, in honor of
30 Pasteur, who discovered it.

1. Before Pasteur's research

 ☐ (A) no one else knew of bacteria
 ☐ (B) the presence, but not the precise origin, of bacteria was known
 ☐ (C) bacteria were called "dancing rods"

2. The passage suggests that the bacteria Pasteur saw were shaped like

 ☐ (A) little squares
 ☐ (B) little tubes or poles
 ☐ (C) little dancing people

3. The first two sentences suggest that Pasteur's research on bacteria arose

 ☐ (A) from an unplanned, fortuitous (lucky, chance) incident
 ☐ (B) from his dislike of spoiled wine
 ☐ (C) from the yeast plants in unspoiled wine
 ☐ (D) from his work in pasteurizing milk

4. Which modern device is based upon a principle discovered by Pasteur?

 ☐ (A) furnace for heating homes
 ☐ (B) refrigerator
 ☐ (C) indoor plumbing
 ☐ (D) home air conditioner

5. The phrase "spontaneous generation," according to the context, means

 ☐ (A) living organisms like bacteria living in wine or milk
 ☐ (B) living organisms appearing in a place with no apparent cause
 ☐ (C) living organisms like bacteria lengthening and splitting to reproduce
 ☐ (D) the opposite of "spontaneous reaction"

6. It can be inferred from the selection that before Pasteur, scientists believed

 ☐ (A) in spontaneous generation because they didn't understand how bacteria could move from one place to another
 ☐ (B) bacteria moved by air, on the hands, or other ways
 ☐ (C) in spontaneous generation because they didn't know as much chemistry as Pasteur
 ☐ (D) bacteria lengthened and split to reproduce

7. According to the selection, spoiled wine contains

 ☐ (A) only yeast plants
 ☐ (B) yeast plants and bacteria
 ☐ (C) no bacteria
 ☐ (D) bacteria and no yeast plants

PASSAGE E

¹   When the Roman legions withdrew from Bri-
² tain to Italy at the beginning of the fifth century,
³ they left the Romanized Celtic natives at the
⁴ mercy of the Anglo-Saxon invaders. These Ger-
⁵ manic tribes devastated Britain so thoroughly
⁶ that little remained of Roman civilization other
⁷ than a splendid system of roads. Proof of the
⁸ force with which the invaders struck is the fact
⁹ that almost no traces of the Celtic language
¹⁰ remain in modern English. Not only did the Anglo-
¹¹ Saxons push most of the Celts out of Britain, but
¹² they also fought among themselves. At one time
¹³ there were more than a dozen little tribal king-
¹⁴ doms, all jealous and hostile, on the island.

1. The Anglo-Saxons were

    ☐ (A) Romanized Celts
    ☐ (B) Roman legions from Italy
    ☐ (C) Germanic tribes
    ☐ (D) native Celts

2. The people dominating early England, from ear-
    lier to later, were

    ☐ (A) Romans, Anglo-Saxons, Celts
    ☐ (B) Anglo-Saxons, Romans, Celts
    ☐ (C) Anglo-Saxons, Celts, Romans
    ☐ (D) Celts, Romans, Anglo-Saxons

3. We may infer that

    ☐ (A) the Romans were greatly influenced by
          the Celts
    ☐ (B) the Romans were greatly influenced by
          the Anglo-Saxons
    ☐ (C) the Celts were greatly influenced by the
          Romans
    ☐ (D) the Romans were greatly influenced by
          the Germanic tribes

4. Which group can we infer was aggressive and
    destructive?

    ☐ (A) Anglo-Saxons
    ☐ (B) Celts
    ☐ (C) Romanized Celts
    ☐ (D) Romans

5. Which group can we infer was aggressive but
    constructive?

    ☐ (A) Anglo-Saxons
    ☐ (B) Celts
    ☐ (C) Romanized Celts
    ☐ (D) Romans

6. This paragraph mainly concerns

    ☐ (A) Britain before the Romans left
    ☐ (B) Britain under Roman occupation
    ☐ (C) Britain after the Romans left
    ☐ (D) Rome after the Anglo-Saxons invaded

7. According to the selection,

    ☐ (A) the Celts were native to Britain and
          the influence of their language can be
          seen in the contemporary English
          language
    ☐ (B) the Celts were native to Britain but
          their language had almost no influ-
          ence on English because the Celts
          withdrew to Italy
    ☐ (C) the Celts were native to Britain but
          their language had almost no influence
          on English because it was suppressed
          by the Anglo-Saxons
    ☐ (D) the Celts were native to Britain but
          their language had almost no influence
          on English because it was suppressed
          by the Romans

8. The Romanized Celts were

    ☐ (A) Roman people whose culture was in-
          fluenced by the Celts
    ☐ (B) Celtic people whose culture was in-
          fluenced by the Romans
    ☐ (C) a sub-group of Celts who had a par-
          ticularly romantic history
    ☐ (D) a special type of clothing worn by the
          Romans in Britain

PASSAGE F

1   Harvey had studied under Galileo and
2 shared his master's belief that the physical uni-
3 verse can only be understood by carefully observ-
4 ing things as they are. In an attempt to find out
5 how blood flows through the body, Harvey bound
6 a man's arm tightly above the elbow. He found
7 that the arteries above the bandage—nearer the
8 heart—swelled with blood but that the arteries
9 below the bandage emptied. Thus it seemed that
10 the heart was not taking in blood and warming it,
11 but was pumping blood out through the arteries.
12 By careful measurement Harvey showed how
13 much blood flowed in and out of the heart in a
14 short time. He concluded that the heart pumped
15 blood out through one set of tubes, the arteries,
16 and received it back through another set of tubes,
17 the veins. This was Harvey's famous hypothesis
18 of the circulation of the blood, which was soon
19 established as a law by the further experiments of
20 himself and other men. It opened the way to
21 better medicine and surgery.
22   Harvey's experiments stimulated many
23 minds during the following century to draw up
24 elaborate theories about how the body worked.
25 Such theorizings only annoyed John Hunter, a
26 rough-and-ready Britisher with a flair for facts. "I
27 think your solution is just," he wrote a fellow
28 doctor, "but why think? Why not try the
29 experiment?"

1. Below are three possible titles for this passage. In each blank, write the letter of the phrase (A, B or C) which best describes that title.

   _____ Harvey While Galileo's Student
   _____ Discovery of Basic Circulation Principles
   _____ How the Human Body Works

   (A) too broad
   (B) too narrow
   (C) comprehensive title

2. The physical universe does *not* include

   ☐ (A) plastic
   ☐ (B) ideas
   ☐ (C) blood
   ☐ (D) arteries

3. Harvey believed new knowledge was gained from

   ☐ (A) the teachings of a master like Galileo
   ☐ (B) empirical data (observed facts)
   ☐ (C) philosophical speculation (theorizing through logic with little observation)
   ☐ (D) intuitive insights (instantaneous knowledge in the mind)

4. It can be inferred that prior to Harvey's work it was believed that

   ☐ (A) blood entering the heart was cooler than blood leaving the heart
   ☐ (B) Harvey disagreed with Galileo
   ☐ (C) John Hunter was a charlatan
   ☐ (D) the heart pumped blood out through the arteries

5. According to this passage, which statement is accurate?

   ☐ (A) Blood leaves the heart through the arteries and veins.
   ☐ (B) Blood enters the heart through the arteries and veins.
   ☐ (C) Blood enters the heart through the veins and leaves through the arteries.
   ☐ (D) Blood enters the heart through the arteries and leaves through the veins.

6. On which line(s) did you find the answer to the preceding question?

LINE NUMBER(S): _____

7. Which conclusion is most probably correct?

   ☐ (A) John Hunter was annoyed by Harvey's work.
   ☐ (B) John Hunter admired Harvey's work.
   ☐ (C) Harvey admired John Hunter's work.
   ☐ (D) Harvey was annoyed by John Hunter's work.

PASSAGE G

1 A main activity of organisms is *nutrition*, a
2 process that provides the raw materials for main-
3 tenance of life. All living matter depends unceas-
4 ingly on such raw materials, for the very act of
5 living continuously uses up two basic commodi-
6 ties, energy and matter. In this respect a living
7 organism is like a mechanical engine or indeed
8 like any other action-performing system in the
9 universe. Energy is needed to power the system,
10 to make the parts operate, to keep activity
11 going—in short, to maintain function. And matter
12 is needed to replace parts, to repair breakdowns,
13 to continue the system intact and able to function
14 —in short, to maintain structure. Therefore, by
15 its very nature as an action-performing unit, a
16 "living" organism can remain alive only if it con-
17 tinuously uses up energy and matter. Both must
18 be replenished from the outside through
19 nutrition.
20 The external raw materials used in this func-
21 tion are *nutrients*. One general class of nutrients
22 includes water, salts, and other materials obtain-
23 able directly from the physical environment of the
24 earth. Another class comprises *foods*, which are
25 available within the biological environment.
26 Foods are obtained in two major ways. One
27 group of organisms manufactures its foods from
28 the raw materials present in the physical world—
29 the soil, water, and air in which such organisms
30 live. In most of these cases sunlight is used as an
31 energy source in this food-manufacturing pro-
32 cess, which is called *photosynthesis*. Such orga-
33 nisms include plants, algae, and others that con-
34 tain the green pigment *chlorophyll*, an essential
35 component in photosynthesis.
36 The second group of organisms is unable to
37 manufacture its own foods and must therefore
38 depend on already existing supplies of them. In
39 this category are animals, fungi, most bacteria,
40 and generally all those organisms that must make
41 use of ready-made foods available in other orga-
42 nisms, living or dead. Eating by animals is one
43 familiar method of obtaining preexisting foods.
44 Evidently, food-making photosynthetic types
45 could survive in a strictly physical, nonbiological
46 environment, but those that cannot make their
47 own food require a biological as well as a physical
48 environment.

1. The term "nutrients," according to the context, means

   ☐ (A) a process that provides the raw ma-
   terials for maintenance of life
   ☐ (B) the materials needed to maintain the
   structure of an organism
   ☐ (C) the materials needed to maintain the
   function of an organism
   ☐ (D) Both (A) and (B)
   ☐ (E) Both (B) and (C)

2. Chlorophyll is

   ☐ (A) used by animals in creating their own
   food
   ☐ (B) used by plants in creating food
   ☐ (C) used to prevent sunlight from burning
   plants and algae
   ☐ (D) a product of photosynthesis

3. A living organism is said to be like a mechanical engine because

   ☐ (A) both use energy for power
   ☐ (B) both use material for repair
   ☐ (C) both perform action
   ☐ (D) Both (A) and (B), but not (C)
   ☐ (E) Both (A) and (C), but not (B)
   ☐ (F) Choices (A), (B) and (C) are all correct

4. The group of organisms which manufactures its food includes

   ☐ (A) most bacteria
   ☐ (B) humans
   ☐ (C) rose bushes
   ☐ (D) sharks

5. On which line(s) did you find the answer to the preceding question?

   LINE NUMBER(S): _____

6. In contrast to organisms that can produce their own food, organisms that cannot, require

   ☐ (A) a biological environment
   ☐ (B) a physical environment
   ☐ (C) Both (A) and (B)
   ☐ (D) Neither (A) nor (B)

7. On which line(s) did you find the answer to the preceding question?

LINE NUMBER(S): _____

8. Photosynthesis is found among organisms that

☐ (A) require only a physical environment
☐ (B) require only a biological environment
☐ (C) require both a physical and a biological environment
☐ (D) eat their food

9. Animals eating is an example of

☐ (A) obtaining food from the physical environment
☐ (B) obtaining food from the biological environment
☐ (C) food-making photosynthesis
☐ (D) obtaining preexisting food through photosynthesis

PASSAGE H

1   At Alexandria, Antioch, and other terminals
2 of these three routes the trading towns of France
3 and Spain and particularly of Italy established
4 business headquarters called *fondachi*. These
5 consisted of warehouses, market places, offices,
6 churches, dwellings, and baths. The traders
7 bought from native princes the privileges of self-
8 government and protected trade. Their business
9 was to obtain the incoming oriental wares and to
10 reship them to their home cities, such as Pisa,
11 Genoa, or Venice in Italy.
12   These cities in the late Middle Ages came to
13 resemble trading corporations, in which the mer-
14 chants controlled the government for their own
15 advantage. All Venetian traders were required to
16 send to Venice the wares they purchased in the
17 East. These were to be stored in warehouses and
18 exported only on government license. After 1300,
19 fleets of vessels with galley convoys were fitted
20 out and dispatched for trade with Western
21 Europe. The "Flanders fleet" usually made a
22 yearly voyage to Spain, Portugal, France, Britain,
23 and Flanders. The expense was borne and the
24 profit made by the Venetian merchants. Oriental
25 goods were also carried to northern Europe by

26 German traders who traveled by the Danube and
27 the Rhine, or to towns brought into new impor-
28 tance, like Augsburg and Nuremburg, and over
29 the Alpine passes to Venice. The great distribut-
30 ing agency in northwestern Europe was the Han-
31 seatic League—an association of German towns
32 which included Lübeck, Hamburg, and Bremen.
33 These towns had banded together to secure out-
34 side commercial privileges for their traders. The
35 Hanseatic merchants bought their oriental wares
36 in Italy, Antwerp and other towns, and at fairs in
37 Western Europe. Then they supplied the markets
38 of England, Russia, Poland, Scandinavia, and
39 Germany. They also set up trading agencies
40 abroad, with special privileges and protection. In
41 London, the Hanse merchants were called East-
42 erlings, and their walled settlement on the
43 Thames was known as the Steelyard. The word
44 *sterling* survives as a tribute to the quality of the
45 silver money current among the Easterlings.

1. According to the selection,

☐ (A) Alexandria, Antioch, and other terminals established trading towns in France, Spain, and particularly Italy
☐ (B) Alexandria, Antioch, and other terminals housed business headquarters of France, Spain, and Italy

2. It can be inferred from the passage that

☐ (A) "sterling" is a term still in use today
☐ (B) "sterling" is an archaic term referring to the silver money current among the Easterlings
☐ (C) "sterling" is a term describing the Thames

3. Italian cities like Venice were controlled by

☐ (A) kings and other noblemen
☐ (B) commercial interests
☐ (C) mayors and governors selected by the people

4. In this period, large business interests centered in all of the following *except*

   ☐ (A) German towns forming the Hanseatic League
   ☐ (B) Italian towns like Genoa and Venice
   ☐ (C) London along the Thames
   ☐ (D) New York City

5. The Hanseatic League was formed

   ☐ (A) to give German businessmen advantages in other towns
   ☐ (B) because Hanse merchants were called Easterlings in London
   ☐ (C) to give traders from Venice and Pisa an advantage in German towns

6. Three rivers mentioned in this selection are the

   ☐ (A) Pisa, Genoa, and Venice Rivers
   ☐ (B) Danube, Rhine, and Thames Rivers
   ☐ (C) Nuremburg, Hamburg, and Bremen Rivers

7. The "Flanders fleet" was financed by

   ☐ (A) merchants of Flanders, Britain, France, Portugal, and Spain
   ☐ (B) Italian merchants
   ☐ (C) the Hanseatic League
   ☐ (D) Oriental merchants

8. On which line(s) did you find the answer to the preceding question?

   LINE NUMBER(S): _____

9. The word "sterling," according to the passage, originated in

   ☐ (A) the activities of the Hanseatic League
   ☐ (B) the quality of silver imported from Oriental centers
   ☐ (C) silver money guaranteed against "stealing"

PASSAGE I

¹   Under Pepin's son, Charlemagne (Charles
² the Great), who ruled from 768 to 814, the Frank-
³ ish state and the Carolingian House reached
⁴ the summit of their power. Einhard, in his famous
⁵ biography of Charlemagne, pictured his king as a
⁶ natural leader of men—tall, physically strong, and
⁷ a great horseman who was always in the van of
⁸ the hunt. Although he was preeminently a suc-
⁹ cessful warrior-king, leading his armies on yearly
¹⁰ campaigns, Charlemagne also sought to provide
¹¹ an effective administration for his realm. In addi-
¹² tion, he had great respect for learning and was
¹³ proud of the fact that he could read Latin.
¹⁴   Taking advantage of fueds among the Mus-
¹⁵ lims in Spain, Charlemagne sought to extend
¹⁶ Christendom southward into that land. In 778 he
¹⁷ crossed the Pyrenees with indifferent success. As
¹⁸ the Frankish army headed back north, it aroused
¹⁹ the antagonism of the Christian Basques, who
²⁰ attacked its rear guard. In the melee the Frankish
²¹ leader, a gallant count named Roland, was killed.
²² The memory of his heroism was later enshrined in
²³ the great medieval epic, the *Chanson de Roland*
²⁴ *(Song of Roland)*. On later expeditions the
²⁵ Franks drove the Muslims back to the Ebro River
²⁶ and established a frontier area known as the
²⁷ Spanish March, or Mark, centered around Bar-
²⁸ celona. French immigrants moved into the area,
²⁹ later called Catalonia, giving it a character distin-
³⁰ guishable from the rest of Spain.

1. Charlemagne was

   ☐ (A) the father of Pepin
   ☐ (B) the father of Charles the Great
   ☐ (C) the son of Charles the Great
   ☐ (D) the son of Pepin

2. We may infer from the selection that Charlemagne's family was known as

   ☐ (A) the Carolingian House
   ☐ (B) the Frankish state
   ☐ (C) the family of Charles the Great
   ☐ (D) Pepin's House

3. Einhard was

   ☐ (A) a king
   ☐ (B) a natural leader
   ☐ (C) a great horseman
   ☐ (D) a writer

4. The word "van," according to the context of the second sentence, means

□ (A) a type of truck
□ (B) forefront—short for "vanguard" which means the front of an army or action
□ (C) a covered wagon—short for "caravan"
□ (D) rear

5. In crossing the Pyrenees Mountains, Charlemagne went

□ (A) south
□ (B) north
□ (C) east
□ (D) west

6. Charlemagne's campaign in 778

□ (A) was highly successful and drove the Muslims back to the Ebro River
□ (B) resulted in the death of Count Roland, but was otherwise highly successful
□ (C) was not highly victorious and included a tragedy that inspired a noteworthy example of early European literature
□ (D) resulted in the conquest of the Christian Basques

7. Catalonia was

□ (A) part of Spain, but occupied by the French
□ (B) part of France, but occupied by the Spanish
□ (C) north of the Pyrenees
□ (D) a famous singer of the *Song of Roland*

8. The word "epic" in the sentence referring to the *Song of Roland* means

□ (A) a gravestone for a dead hero
□ (B) a war
□ (C) a funeral
□ (D) a story recounting the deeds of a hero

9. The word "medieval" in the sentence referring to the *Song of Roland* means

□ (A) of the Middle Ages
□ (B) of the Muslims
□ (C) very evil
□ (D) medically evil

PASSAGE J

1   The middle class, too, found much that was
2 irrational and indefensible in the institutions of the
3 day. Perhaps the most important factor in middle-
4 class discontent was the government-controlled
5 economy of mercantilism. Convinced that capi-
6 talism had outgrown the need for state assistance
7 with its accompanying controls, the bourgeoisie
8 were ready for a system of free enterprise. As
9 early as the seventeenth century English mer-
10 chants had denounced the hoarding of bullion,
11 advocating instead that "the exportation of our
12 moneys in trade of merchandise is a means to
13 increase our treasure." This growing concern for
14 freedom of trade led the middle class to support
15 the physiocrats, eighteenth-century economic
16 thinkers who, as their name indicates, shared
17 with *philosophes* the viewpoint that all human
18 activity—economic, social, and political—was
19 subject to natural laws similar to those governing
20 the physical universe.

1. According to the selection, the middle class was

□ (A) happy with the social order
□ (B) discontent with the government's economic policy, but satisfied with other parts of the social order
□ (C) discontent with the government's economic policy and with other elements of the social order
□ (D) pleased with the government's economic policy

2. From the passage it can be inferred that

□ (A) capitalism was basically benefited by government assistance throughout English history
□ (B) government intervention was always indefensible for English capitalism
□ (C) government intervention was formerly defensible for English capitalism

3. The physiocrats took the position that

   ☐ (A) principles governing the physical world were like the already known principles governing human events
   ☐ (B) principles governing human events were like the already known principles governing the physical world
   ☐ (C) one set of principles governed economics and sociology, while a different set governed physics and chemistry

4. On which line(s) did you find the answer to the preceding question?

   LINE NUMBER(S): _____

5. The philosophes

   ☐ (A) were eighteenth-century economic thinkers
   ☐ (B) had similar ideas as physiocrats
   ☐ (C) disagreed with physiocrats
   ☐ (D) were a viewpoint of the physiocrats

6. The word "bourgeoisie" in the third sentence means

   ☐ (A) businessmen
   ☐ (B) economists
   ☐ (C) physiocrats
   ☐ (D) philosophes

7. According to the selection, English merchants

   ☐ (A) believed the country should hoard bullion (gold)
   ☐ (B) believed it was best to accumulate large amounts of gold to increase England's treasury
   ☐ (C) believed the country should spend gold to buy products from other nations
   ☐ (D) wanted to be paid in bullion (gold) for their merchandise because gold was worth more than money

8. From the passage we may infer that the government

   ☐ (A) preferred merchandise to money because inflation decreased the value of money
   ☐ (B) preferred to keep money rather than purchase foreign merchandise
   ☐ (C) believed that spending money wisely to buy merchandise "is a means to increase our treasure"
   ☐ (D) found much that was irrational and indefensible in the institutions of the day

PASSAGE K

1 The question at once arises as to how people
2 living in the Central American jungle could
3 become civilized in the first place. The southern
4 part of the region was the least advanced, though
5 it has the best climate and the most fertile soil. It
6 was in the central area that the Maya reached his
7 peak of greatness. Yet this area has an enormous
8 rainfall, dense jungles that become savannahs
9 filled with stubborn grasses when cleared, and an
10 enervating climate. Its only manifest advantage is
11 an abundance of the limestone that went into the
12 great buildings. From the fourth to the tenth cen-
13 turies after Christ, the Maya gloried in their Clas-
14 sic period, sometimes called the Old Empire, cen-
15 tered on this unpromising region. Between the
16 tenth and the thirteenth centuries they flourished
17 farther north, in the Mexican peninsula of Yuca-
18 tan, during a less brilliant phase variously known
19 as the post-Classic, Mexican, or New Empire
20 period. This region also has defects; it is hot, dry,
21 and not particularly fertile. Instead of rivers and
22 lakes there are great natural wells, or cenotes,
23 where the limestone has cracked and permitted
24 an opening to the underground drainage system.
25 Nothing about either Maya area suggests the
26 Nile, Tigris-Euphrates, Ganges, or other famous
27 river valleys of ancient cultural splendor. They do
28 not even resemble the cool, rich uplands of Mex-
29 ico and Peru, where later Indian societies reached
30 a high stage. The growth of the Maya civilization
31 in such an unpromising setting may well support
32 Arnold Toynbee's famous theory that a people
33 confronted with a challenge powerful enough to
34 inspire them but not harsh enough to discourage
35 them can respond with a disciplined, protracted

36 effort that will civilize them. The challenge cer-
37 tainly existed in Central America. Difficulties of
38 terrain stimulated a people who wished to grow
39 corn or maize into making an organized, intelli-
40 gently directed, and ultimately successful effort
41 over a long period. Success in turn gave them the
42 confidence necessary for progress in many other
43 directions. The Maya must also have produced
44 that utterly unpredictable essential for civiliza-
45 tion: a supply of geniuses.

1. As used in the fourth sentence, the word "savannah" means

   ☐ (A) a dense jungle
   ☐ (B) a girl's name
   ☐ (C) a region with few trees but heavy grasses
   ☐ (D) places with a climate similar to that of Savannah, Georgia

2. The word "enervating," according to the context of the fourth sentence, means

   ☐ (A) energy-boosting
   ☐ (B) energy-draining
   ☐ (C) nerve-wracking
   ☐ (D) stimulating

3. Which of the following statements is contradicted by the selection?

   ☐ (A) The Maya Indian civilization was the most brilliant of ancient cultures.
   ☐ (B) An area with superb climate and agricultural potential was the seat of the Maya's greatest cultural progress.
   ☐ (C) The Nile and Tigris-Euphrates areas are physically different from the Maya area.
   ☐ (D) The Nile and Tigris-Euphrates areas were seats of culturally advanced societies.

4. The Classic Maya period extended over approximately the years

   ☐ (A) 4-10
   ☐ (B) 300-900
   ☐ (C) 1000-1300
   ☐ (D) 300-1300

5. The Classic and post-Classic Maya periods combined encompassed the years approximately

   ☐ (A) 300-1000
   ☐ (B) 400-1000
   ☐ (C) 1000-1300
   ☐ (D) 300-1200

6. According to the selection, the Classic and post-Classic Maya periods may illustrate the principle that

   ☐ (A) civilization develops when the environment is extremely harsh
   ☐ (B) civilization develops when the environment is harsh enough to require hard work, but benign enough to reward it
   ☐ (C) civilization develops when the environment is so luxurious that people have ample time for reflection and artistic pursuits
   ☐ (D) civilization cannot develop when the environment is even moderately harsh

7. In the second sentence from the end, the writer suggests Maya culture sprang from organized efforts in

   ☐ (A) breeding livestock
   ☐ (B) political revolt
   ☐ (C) manufacturing
   ☐ (D) agriculture

Word Power III

Directions: Study each of the Power Words below. Note how each word is pronounced. Then read the context sentences to figure out what each Power Word means. In the left-hand margin next to each Power Word, try to jot down a synonym or short definition which defines that word.

Power Words	conversely	idiosyncrasy	prolonging	inarticulate
	insatiable	profuse	cumbersome	trespass

1. **conversely** | kŏn′ vûrs′ lē |
   - All dogs *are* animals, but the converse, all animals are dogs, is not true.
   - On most forms and applications, one's name must be written conversely from the usual; that is, last name first.

2. **insatiable** | ĭn **sā′** shə bəl |
   - In her insatiable desire for knowledge she read several entire history textbooks!
   - He was difficult to work for because his desire for perfection was insatiable.

3. **idiosyncrasy** | ĭd′ ē ō **sĭng′** krə sē |
   - John's one idiosyncrasy is arising every morning at six and taking a cold shower.

4. **profuse** | prə **fyo͞os′** |
   - The crown was profusely decorated with expensive gems.
   - After receiving the small gift, they were surprisingly profuse in their thanks.

5. **prolonging** | prə **lông′** ĭng |
   - Many people have sought a magical substance for prolonging life indefinitely.
   - Can't we find a way of prolonging our vacation a few more days?

6. **cumbersome** | **kŭm′** bər səm |
   - A large package may be cumbersome even if it is not extremely heavy.
   - The queen constantly complained about the cumbersome garments she was forced to wear at royal ceremonies.

7. **inarticulate** | ĭn′ är **tĭk′** yə lĭt |
   - An articulate person pronounces words clearly and speaks well; whereas an inarticulate person mumbles and stammers.

8. **trespass** | **trĕs′** pəs |
   - The Great Dane would allow no other dog to trespass in his yard; his size alone kept most dogs from the yard.

ă pat / ā pay / â care / ä father / ĕ pet / ē be / ĭ pit / ī pie / î fierce / ŏ pot / ō go / ô paw, for / oi oil / o͝o book /
o͞o boot / ou out / ŭ cut / û fur / *th* the / th thin / hw which / zh vision / ə ago, item, pencil, atom, circus

Meaning Comprehension

Directions: Use what you have learned from the context sentences to identify the correct definition of each Power Word. In the blank next to each Power Word, write the letter of its correct definition.

Power Words

_____ conversely
_____ insatiable
_____ idiosyncrasy
_____ profuse
_____ prolonging
_____ cumbersome
_____ inarticulate
_____ trespass

Definitions

a. awkward, inconvenient, difficult to handle
b. unable to speak clearly, having indistinct speech
c. oppositely, reversed in order or relation
d. unable to be satisfied, continually wanting more
e. a peculiar habit or behavior
f. lengthening, extending
g. overly plentiful, greatly abundant, generous
h. invade private property or rights; make an error

Context Application

Directions: Each of the following sentences has two blanks. Use what you have learned about the Power Words to determine which Power Word best belongs in each of the blanks. Then write the appropriate Power Word in each blank. Use each Power Word only once.

1. Crows have an _____ appetite for seeds and will _____ on any farmer's property to get them.

2. Many useful things are _____ and, _____, many cumbersome things are useful.

3. Gini's one annoying _____ is bouncing the tennis ball exactly thirty times before each serve, thereby _____ our matches by at least twenty minutes.

4. Because Leo's ideas were so _____ and he had so much to say, he would sometimes speak too quickly and become almost _____ .

Muscle Builder Analogies

Directions: Each exercise below is an analogy, with one or two terms missing. Choose the Power Word which belongs in each blank of the analogy so that the analogy reads correctly. Write the appropriate Power Word in each blank. Note that some of the Power Words will not be used.

1. SATISFIABLE is to SATIABLE as UNSATISFIABLE is to _____

2. MISERLY is to STINGY as _____ is to EXCESSIVE

3. _____ is to CLUMSY as _____ is to STRETCHING

Word Power IV

Directions: Study each of the Power Words below. Note how each word is pronounced. Then read the context sentences to figure out what each Power Word means. In the left-hand margin next to each Power Word, try to jot down a synonym or short definition which defines that word.

Power Words	censorship	biased	haughty	audacity
	subjected	detestable	prevailing	futile

1. **censorship** | **sĕn′** sər shĭp′ |
   - Many feel that some censorship of newspapers is necessary to keep smut or atrocities from offending people.
   - Where censorship is widespread, an uninformed public will be found.

2. **subjected** | səb **jĕk′** tĭd |
   - The suspect was subjected to lengthy interrogation.
   - At her insistence we were subjected to the most boring evening I've had in a long time.

3. **biased** | **bī′** əst |
   - A friend of the author wrote a biased review of the book.

4. **detestable** | dĭ **tĕs′** tə bəl |
   - Driving while intoxicated, because of its risk to innocent persons, is detestable.
   - Many people feel that experiments which result in harm to animals are detestable.

5. **haughty** | **hô′** tē |
   - The haughty senior refused to talk to the freshman.
   - Ann's haughty attitude gave us the impression that she thought she was better than everyone else.

6. **prevailing** | prĭ **vāl′** ĭng |
   - The prevailing opinion in Congress favored the adoption of the new law.
   - Because the prevailing attitude was negative, we decided to take no action.

7. **audacity** | ô **dăs′** ĭ tē |
   - The teenager's audacity offended the adults.
   - The thief had the audacity to stage the robbery in broad daylight.

8. **futile** | **fyo͞ot′** l |
   - He loved to spend money, so his wife's efforts to save proved futile.
   - We were so far behind schedule that it seemed futile to try to meet the boss' deadline.

ă pat / ā pay / â care / ä father / ĕ pet / ē be / ĭ pit / ī pie / î fierce / ŏ pot / ō go / ô paw, for / oi oil / o͝o book /
o͞o boot / ou out / ŭ cut / ü fur / *th* the / th thin / hw which / zh vision / ə ago, item, pencil, atom, circus

Meaning Comprehension

Directions: Use what you have learned from the context sentences to identify the correct definition of each Power Word. In the blank next to each Power Word, write the letter of its correct definition.

Power Words

_____ censorship
_____ subjected
_____ biased
_____ detestable
_____ haughty
_____ prevailing
_____ audacity
_____ futile

Definitions

a. very bad, deserving condemnation, despicable

b. one-sided, slanted, prejudiced

c. the act of removing material from or preventing publication of

d. boldness and disrespectfulness; insolence

e. fruitless, useless, ineffective

f. dominant, strongest, most common

g. excessively proud and vain, arrogant

h. made to endure or submit, made subject

Context Application

Directions: Each of the following sentences has two blanks. Use what you have learned about the Power Words to determine which Power Word best belongs in each of the blanks. Then write the appropriate Power Word in each blank. Use each Power Word only once.

1. _____ of the news could give people a _____ perception of the world.

2. Because of the child's cruel, _____ behavior, she was _____ to a severe tongue-lashing and spanking.

3. A _____ person may be too proud to do a favor, yet have the _____ to ask for one.

4. The attempt to reach the drowning man was _____ because the _____ current continually pulled him farther and farther out to sea.

Muscle Builder Analogies

Directions: Each exercise below is an analogy, with one term missing. Choose the Power Word which belongs in each blank of the analogy so that the analogy reads correctly. Write the appropriate Power Word in each blank. Note that some of the Power Words will not be used.

1. HONOR is to PRAISEWORTHY as DISHONOR is to

   _____

2. USELESS is to WORTHWHILE as _____ is to FRUITFUL

3. HAUGHTINESS is to MODESTY as _____ is to RESPECTFULNESS

ADDITIONAL ASSIGNMENTS

1. Pick a section from one of your textbooks, encyclopedias, or other sources which is about 150 words long. Then write two multiple-choice questions on the material. Each question should have only one correct answer and at least one incorrect alternative which a person might choose if he or she is not reading carefully.

   Let a peer read the section and answer the questions. Observe your peer's work to see that you have written clear, meaningful questions and answer choices.

2. Using what you have learned about the meaning of "enervated" (page 180), write a sentence on the lines below in which the meaning of "enervated" is given by contrast (Case III).

   _____

   _____

3. Using what you have learned about the meaning of "adroit" (page 228), write a sentence on the lines below in which the meaning of "adroit" is stated with punctuation (Case I).

   _____

   _____

4. Using what you have learned about the meaning of "pertinent" (page 208), write a sentence on the lines below in which the meaning of "pertinent" is stated without punctuation (Case II).

   _____

   _____

5. Using what you have learned about the meaning of "quixotic" (page 256), write a sentence on the lines below in which the meaning of "quixotic" is inferred from the rest of the sentence (Case IV).

   _____

   _____